PERFORMANCE MANAGEMENT

PERFORMANCE MANAGEMENT

**Getting Results From
Your Performance Planning
and Appraisal System**

Roger J. Plachy

with

Sandra J. Plachy

amacom

American Management Association

This book is available at a special
discount when ordered in bulk quantities.
For information, contact Special Sales Department,
AMACOM, a division of American Management Association,
135 West 50th Street, New York, NY 10020.

Library of Congress Cataloging-in-Publication Data

Plachy, Roger.
    Performance management.

    Includes index.
    1. Performance standards.   I. Plachy, Sandra J.
II. Title.
HF5549.5.P35P55   1988   658.3'125   88-47713
ISBN 0-8144-7705-4

Printing number

10 9 8 7 6 5 4 3 2 1

For John,
who exercised
his options

Contents

Preface

Why Read This Book?

- Does your performance-management program turn off employees instead of turning them on to improved work performance?
- Do managers in your organization resist completing appraisal forms and avoid discussing performance problems with employees?
- Are employees disgruntled because their contributions are not recognized?
- Do managers and employees lack confidence in the forms and procedures of the performance-management program?
- Is there a misunderstanding between managers and employees about what constitutes important job performance?
- Do you think that improved employee job performance would benefit your organization?
- Do you want to help employees apply untapped talents to job requirements and develop their potential for more significant contributions?

If your answer is yes to any of those questions, this book can help.

Gainsharing and other forms of group reward tied to group performance are offered as the solution. It is no surprise that proponents of Japanese-style management, espousing employee loyalty, advocate abandoning individual pay for performance in favor of group rewards.

Advocates of Japanese-style management misunderstand the notions of loyalty and cooperation offered as a solution to the ills of American enterprise. The Japanese are every bit as fiercely independent as Americans. Their collective will stems from premises that differ fundamentally from ours. While the Japanese have reminded us about certain concepts of organization teamwork, teamwork is not the only concept in which they believe. It is appropriate to remind ourselves that the Japanese also have many talented employees who make significant individual contributions to their organizations.

Teams are great, not only because the individual members cooperate with each other, but first and foremost because the team has talented individual members. The high performance of individuals typically makes the team great. The manager of the team is responsible not only to bring out the best in the individuals, but also the collective best of all individuals together. The arguments for group versus individual rewards insult the talent of the individual members, relegating them to selfish participants. In simple language, individuals are very capable of understanding and adhering to the rules of the team when team participation is made a performance standard.

Organizations have neither demanded good performance nor paid for it. Consumers—employees from other organizations—are fed up with poor performance. Pressure is building in our society to emphasize good performance and quit playing around with faddish management solutions. The solutions to our technological problems have far outstripped the solutions to our human problems. The 1990s are the time to do it right, the time to get ready for the next century.

How You Can Use This Book

In this book, abstract concepts are translated into workable solutions in a causal, person-to-person writing style. Ready-to-use models are included, along with instructions on how to tailor them to the unique requirements of your organization.

The chapters take up fundamentals as well as details of designing, auditing, and installing a performance-management program. Questions are included to help you analyze your situation, and examples bring many of the considerations into tangible form.

Note that Chapters 3 (which deals with job analysis), 4 (which discusses job descriptions), and 10 (which explains program installation) are drawn with some modifications from my previous book *Building A Fair Pay Program* (AMACOM, 1986). The same issues are addressed in this book because they are key aspects of developing a performance-management program.

You will address two concerns while reading the book:

1. *Strategic policy*, which states the philosophical beliefs of your organization and establishes the general direction of the program
2. *Tactical procedures*, which determine the manner in which the program will be implemented

You will receive the most help from this book by reading it three times. On your first reading, scan the chapters briefly to obtain an overall understanding of the issues. Do not try to deal with any details. At the end of each chapter, you will find a section titled "Strategic Planning"; make notes to yourself regarding the strategic policy issues you will have to decide. You may also want to make a few notes about tactical procedures as they begin to occur to you.

Examine your initial thoughts about each chapter and decide on an integrated posture for the entire program. Although each chapter deals with a different issue, all the elements of the program must be harmonized if the total program is to be effective.

On your second reading, think through the practical aspects of implementing the program. Questions in most chapters will help you formulate a detailed, tactical plan of action. Use the Master Project Planner in Chapter 1 to organize your planning.

Finally, read the book a third time and make sure that your complete plan hangs together. Then, work through the details of the program and take the steps necessary to bring your program to a successful conclusion.

List of
Figures
and Tables

List of Figures

List of Tables

Acknowledgments

Ernest R. Tompkins, Ed.D., Director of Training for the City of Winston-Salem, North Carolina, is a human resources professional who not only believes in concepts of adult learning but applies them practically every day. He contributed his knowledge, experience, and writing to this book; especially in Chapter 2, regarding the evolution and importance of organization and job purpose statements, and in Chapter 8, where his notions of adult education are embedded.

Ruth H. Korb, Director of Personnel for Shands Hospital at the University of Florida, Gainesville, Florida, is a skilled communicator who gave her clear thinking and orderly expression to the development of the performance-criteria profile. With her beliefs in doctrines of fairness and responsibility, she eagerly participated in helping forge a model that fosters clear, objective communication and human growth.

"It is not so much the other man's words as his silences which we have to learn in order to understand him. It is not so much our sounds which give meaning, but it is through the pauses that we will make ourselves understood."

—Illich

PERFORMANCE MANAGEMENT

Chapter 1

Essentials of Managing Performance

1.1 What Is Performance Management?

Performance management is communication: A manager and an employee arrive together at an understanding of what work is to be accomplished, how it will be accomplished, how work is progressing toward desired results, and finally, after effort is expended to accomplish the work, whether the performance has achieved the agreed-upon plan. The process recycles when the manager and employee begin planning what work is to be accomplished for the next performance period.

"Performance management" is an umbrella term that includes performance *planning*, performance *review*, and performance *appraisal*. Major work plans and appraisals are generally made annually. Performance review occurs whenever a manager and an employee confirm, adjust, or correct their understanding of work performance during routine work contacts.

A familiar term, "performance appraisal" suggests a system of measurement. If we believe that appraising means measuring, then we will try to improve our appraisal of performance by measuring more precisely. However, human performance, except in such terms as things produced per hour, cannot be measured precisely. On the other hand, an excuse that some jobs cannot be described objectively is either ill-informed or cowardly. Although some job performance cannot be "counted" in numeric terms, whether or not performance achieves expectations can be assessed.

The old term "performance appraisal" also ignores the importance of the manager and the employee agreeing on work plans. Without agreement up front, an employee can psychologically disown accountability for the performance later on. The manager may autocratically demand performance, but the employee can simply quit and leave the manager without any actual authority.

Performance-management programs are more effective when they are built on a solid communication structure. A communication structure is not the same thing as a conversational technique. No amount of training to conduct conversations can overcome structural communication faults embedded in the performance-management system. When job descriptions and performance criteria are poorly written, rapport between managers and employees is in jeopardy. Unfortunately, many "how to talk to employees" training programs overlook this subtle point.

1.1.1 Focusing Job Descriptions and Criteria on Performance

The two principal ingredients for managing job performance are:

1. *Telling an employee what performance must be accomplished*—providing a job description that identifies several job results required, along with the job duties that produce the results required.
2. *Telling an employee how well the work must be performed*—stating performance criteria for each job result, using the same objective language found in the job descriptions, rather than subjective, generic language that reads the same for all jobs.

Here is a brief example of the model that will be presented in this book:

JOB TITLE: PERSONNEL ASSISTANT

JOB RESULTS [*only one shown here*]:
Job Result: Helps new employees learn about the organization, including its rules and benefits, by conducting orientations.
RELATED PERFORMANCE CRITERIA:
Performance Standard [*what management wants to have happen*]: Employees understand their fringe benefits, organization rules and regulations, and other pertinent data.
Problem [*the effect when what management wants is not accomplished*]: The organization does not receive credit for benefit dollars spent; employees become confused and angry over misunderstood eligibilities; rules violations occur, and employees must be disciplined.
Improvement [*what an employee needs to learn/do in order to accomplish the results desired by management*]: Needs to study current benefit programs, rules

and regulations, and other pertinent data, including changes as they occur; needs to practice platform presentation skills.

Performance Option [what an employee does when he or she gives management more than it desires]: Evaluates, analyzes, and updates orientation program, using employee feedback (questionnaires, interviews) to improve employee understanding, acceptance, and involvement.

The four statements of the performance-criteria profile constitute four different outcomes of the same job result. The manager matches the employee's performance with the profile. Does the outcome of the employee's performance match the *Performance Standard*? Did the performance cause the *Problem* described? If the employee's performance did not match the Performance Standard but did not cause a serious Problem for the organization, what does the employee need to learn or do in order to *Improve* performance and bring it up to standard?

Figure 1-1. The performance management process.

Phase I

1. *Employment interview*
   Manager and candidate meet.
2. *Job qualifications*
   Manager accepts candidate's qualifications.
3. *Job description*
   Manager reviews what must be accomplished on the job.
4. *Performance criteria*
   Manager describes how well the work must be performed.
5. *Employment contract*
   Manager and candidate agree on job results and performance criteria.

Phase II

6. *Job training*
   Manager prepares employee to perform job responsibilities.
7. *Performance planning*
   Manager and employee meet to agree on a performance plan to accomplish work.
8. *Work*
   Manager and employee work together to accomplish job results and specific objectives.

Phase III

9. *Performance review*
   Manager and employee meet as required to adjust performance plan to new requirements.
10. *Performance management*
    Manager and employee meet periodically for a major review of past performance and to plan performance for the next work cycle.

Or does the employee's performance exceed expectations, as described in the *Performance Option*? On the Performance-Management-Conference Form (see Chapter 5, section 5.3, Figure 5-3), the employee's performance is marked as described in one of these four categories.

The intent of planning, reviewing, and appraising performance management is to establish and maintain dialog between managers and employees in order to obtain required results (see Figure 1-1). Dialog—an exchange of information, perceptions, and opinions between two people—is what is usually missing when performance management is ineffective. Managers and employees alike are too quick to judge before they have all the facts. The promise of a better performance-management program rests on two people talking productively so that they can achieve results that are beneficial to both of them.

Figure 1-2. Elements of a well-integrated performance-management and pay program.

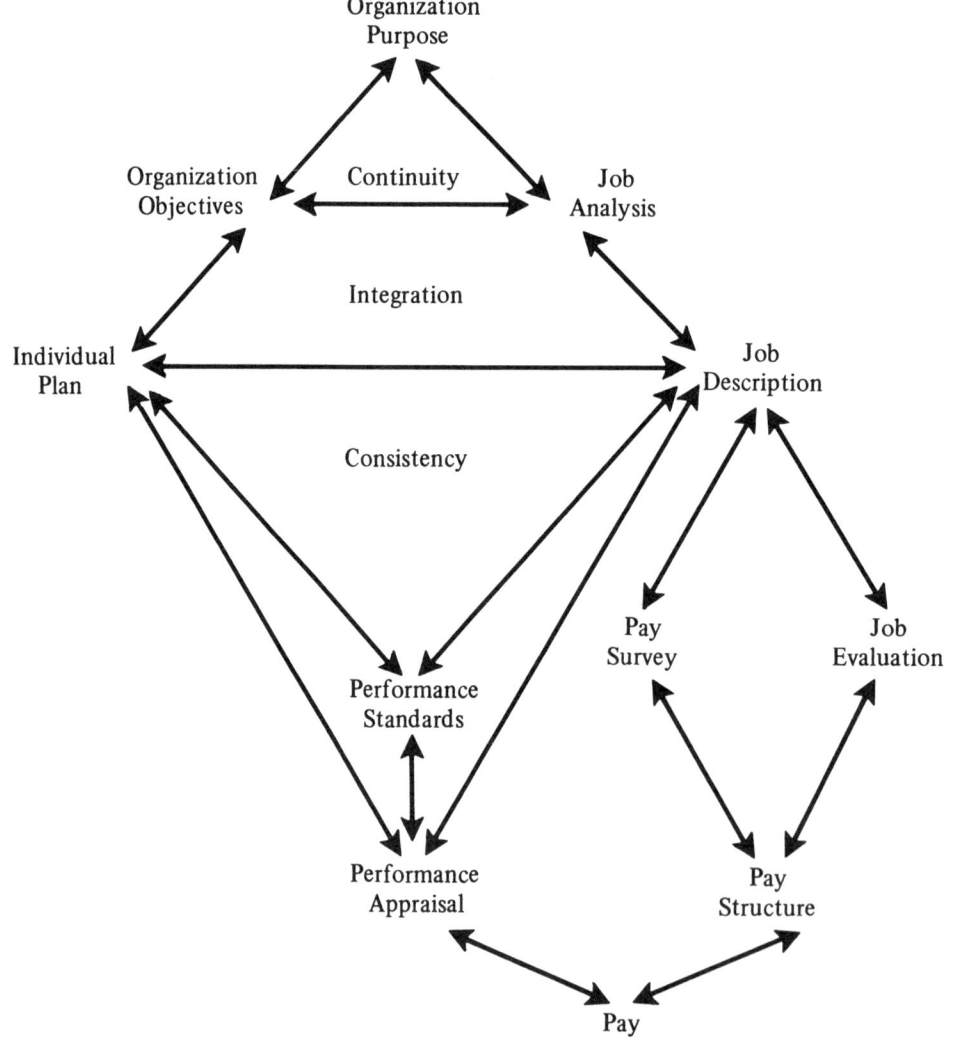

Don't look to a performance-management program to solve all your management problems. If your managers are ineffective now, a new performance-management program will not make them effective. However, teaching managers to understand how employee performance might be planned and controlled is a smart beginning (see Figure 1-2). It is more helpful, by the way, than teaching managers about coaching styles, problem solving, cooperation, team building, stress reduction, morale, and motivation. You are wise to put your time and effort into a performance-management program, because it gets more results.

Project Analyzer (1.1)

What do managers think about the current performance-management program?

What do employees think about the performance-management program?

How do you know?

Is your opinion based on fact (such as an attitude survey or grievances) or estimate?

What happened to make you consider installing or changing your organization's performance-management program?

Why change now?

Have you dug deeply enough for information to understand the events that precipitated that change?

What do you think you need to accomplish in order to make your program right?

What positive effects can result from a new program?

What negative effects might result?

1.2 Goals of a Performance-Management Program

Why do organizations manage performance? They do for many reasons—sometimes so many that the real purpose of the program is clouded. When the program serves too many masters, it suffers in design and implementation.

Remember our definition, set forth at the beginning of this chapter: The basic purpose of performance management is for managers and employees to accomplish the following three objectives:

1. Understand what work is to be accomplished
2. Plan together how the work will be accomplished
3. Determine together whether performance achieved the agreed-upon plan

Notice a substantial difference from the typical genre of magazine articles on how to make performance appraisals successful. The ultimate goal, they proclaim, is to improve employee performance. Not so. Look what can happen to a manager's behavior when improvement is the only, or the major, goal. The manager may continue to ask how performance can be improved even though performance is already meeting, or even exceeding, expectations. The manager is forced to struggle to produce a plan for future progress even though present performance is everything, or more than, the organization wants.

Performance management means that a manager plans and appraises work. The manager presents job expectations and later examines whether performance met those expectations. If performance did, wonderful, let's keep it up. If it did not, *then* improvement becomes the topic of discussion. Why not let employees be successful when they do what is expected, even though they are not striving to be better? Additional goals for the program are appropriate when they do not subordinate the basic purpose of performance management.

Here are some specific reasons you might incorporate into a performance management program in your organization:

- *To Control Current Performance*

    — Motivate employees to improve their own performance
    — Promote self-learning among employees
    — Determine individual counseling needs
    — Diagnose individual and organizational performance problems
    — Warn employees about unsatisfactory performance
    — Document disciplinary action taken against employees
    — Decide who is to be transferred, promoted, laid off, or terminated
    — Establish and coordinate organizational and individual objectives
    — Control employee performance in the pursuit of organizational objectives
    — Achieve consistent and equitable performance-management decisions among managers throughout the organization
    — Strengthen manager–employee relationships
    — Open communications between managers and employees

- *To Plan for Individual and Organizational Growth*

    — Develop employees' potential for promotion
    — Encourage employees' personal growth
    — Encourage employees' professional growth
    — Determine individual and organizational training and development needs
    — Identify individual and organizational education requirements
    — Identify the organization's exceptionally talented people
    — Plan the organization's human resources needs or succession schemes
    — Plan individual careers
    — Apply unique employee knowledge, skill, and ability to the organization's requirements

- *To Determine Rewards and Recognition*

    — Divide pay budgets among employees
    — Award pay bonuses to individual employees or groups
    — Recognize exceptional efforts of individuals or groups

Developing managers is a goal that requires special mention. Most managers were promoted into management on the basis of their technical skills, not their interpersonal and managerial abilities. Along the way, they were thrown a few training bones to help them "understand" their role. But such "help" is not good enough.

Managers learn to manage performance properly when the techniques they are required to use are presented in tangible, applicable job terms. Talking about performance management is one thing; doing it is another. The structure offered in this book is designed to demonstrate in specific ways how managers can interact with their employees for mutual benefit.

One survey after another finds that management is not satisfied with its performance-management program. Other surveys find that employees welcome an opportunity to talk with their managers about job performance. Management and employees want the system to work well; they want their work to be a worthwhile experience. Most programs suffer from a multitude of maladies. Fortunately, once some of the essential structural changes proposed in this book are made in a program, many of the problems disappear.

What can an organization expect when it makes the investment to focus on performance management? It can expect increased individual productivity, and improved organizational performance, with an understanding of why each happened. Managers will be better decision makers, because performance issues will be clearer. Employees will agree more often with appraisals, because there will be no surprises. Rapport between managers and employees will be strengthened.

Project Analyzer (1.2)

In what ways does the nature of your organization's business influence the policies and procedures of its performance-management program?

_____

_____

What are management's assumptions about employee behavior and potential?

_____

_____

What will change in your organization as a result of introducing an effective performance-management program?

_____

_____

What are the goals of your organization's performance-management program?

_____

_____

How will the goals be published?

_____

_____

Who else needs to be involved in writing these goals?

_____

_____

Whose support and influence are necessary to implement these goals?

_____

_____

Who needs to approve these goals?

_____

_____

_____

When do you need the approval?

_____

_____

_____

1.3 Managing the Project To Install a Performance-Management Program

Keep in mind the importance of timing. Do not start your project when it is in conflict with other pressing needs of the organization and thus doomed to failure. Your organization must want to do this project now.

Writing job descriptions and performance criteria (or rewriting them), plus having them edited and approved, is time consuming—calculate eight hours per job description and related criteria. Get the time involved out on the table where managers can look at it and know what they are up against. That way, they can plan their time. Too many projects are unsuccessful not because they are burdensome but because managers, who have other responsibilities, are not given the courtesy of advanced warning so they can plan an efficient schedule.

As you step through the program elements in your first overview of the book, begin to make some estimate of the time involved to complete the project.

1.3.1 Obtaining Needed Information

You will need a lot of information to prepare and implement your performance-management program. Some information will be fact; other information will be opinion. Knowing who the information traffic managers are is equally essential. Traffic managers direct information on *formal* and *informal* levels.

Formal information managers are those whose names appear on the organization chart and on the official memos; *informal information managers* are the subculture figures who meet in the hallways and lunchrooms, talk on the telephone, or drop by offices unexpectedly. You must find the information traffic managers on both levels in order to make your program a success.

1.3.2 Employee Participation: The Program Task Force

Some organizations use a program task force successfully to gather information and opinions that will be used in the project. The task force has a limited life (usually only a few months); its charter is to make the initial planning decisions for installing the performance-management program. Most members are senior managers so that the project has credibility, but lower-level managers who deal with performance-management issues daily should also be included.

1.3.3 Clarifying Your Authority

The nature of the questions that will be asked during the project—about the definition of job expectations, personal qualifications to fulfill the expectations, an equitable rate of pay for the person performing a particular job, or measures of quality job performance—may provoke consternation among managers and job-incumbents. Given the controversial nature of some expected adjustments and corrections, you will be wise to define your authority at the beginning of the project.

Authority comes in only three dimensions:

1. You can act at your own discretion.
2. You can act at your own initiative but must tell someone promptly.
3. You can act only after receiving prior approval.

In the Master Project Planner (see section 1.4), identify your authority for each project issue; then verify it with your manager.

1.3.4 Costs

Eventually, somebody will ask how much the project will cost. The decision to inaugurate a program is a choice among rival opportunities for the use of limited organization resources, not just a matter of actual dollars to be spent.

Actual expenses can be direct external expenditures for the purchase of services, equipment, and materials, or internal expense transfers from your budget for services performed by other departments. One cost to be calculated is the time people spend on the project.

1.3.5 Consultants

Having purchased this book, you are probably inclined to design and implement your performance-management program by yourself—and you will be able to do so. Or perhaps this book will give you the background you need to work intelligently with a consultant. You may intend to accomplish most of the work yourself but will want to obtain some expert opinion from time to time about the options presented to you.

When time is short, consultants can help by doing some of the tedious and time-consuming work—but it will cost you. Consultants are helpful when you need someone to present the structure and the guiding principles of the performance-management program to managers and employees. Consultants can provide quality training—for instance, on how to write job descriptions.

You can hire a consultant to accomplish specific work for you. You can hire a consultant to teach you. You can hire a consultant to teach you as you accomplish specific work. Generally, learn everything you can and achieve independence.

Project Analyzer (1.3)

Who has the information you need to design and implement a performance-management program?

_____

_____

Whose opinions are important?

_____

_____

How will you obtain the information and opinions that you need?

_____

_____

When is the best time to begin the project?

_____

_____

When are busy times for the organization?

_____

_____

When are slow times?

_____

_____

_____

What other responsibilities do you have?

_____

_____

_____

What kind of help will be available to you?

_____

_____

Will you use a consultant to help you with the project?

_____

_____

What do you want the consultant to do?

_____

_____

1.4 Master Project Planner

After you have studied this book, this Planner will help you identify the information you need to complete your project, organize and schedule the project elements, plan communication, resolve authority, and estimate costs.

Phase 1: Identify Goals and Get Commitment

1. Identify performance-management program goals (form a task force if appropriate).
2. Obtain approval of program goals from top management.
3. Obtain commitment to program goals from all managers.

Phase 2: Plan, Schedule, and Announce the Project

4. Study options to implement the project.
5. Select the options that best satisfy organization requirements.
6. Schedule and announce project implementation.

Phase 3: Get the Basic Job Information

7. Gather information about jobs and performance criteria.

Phase 4: Write Job Descriptions and Performance Criteria

8. Train writers to prepare job descriptions and performance-criteria profiles.
9. Verify job descriptions and performance-criteria profiles with employees.

10. Obtain approval of job descriptions and performance-criteria profiles from managers.
11. Obtain approval of job descriptions and performance-criteria profiles from senior managers

Phase 5: Develop Documentation and Train

12. Prepare a policies and procedures manual for managers.
13. Train managers to conduct performance-management conferences.

Phase 6: Introduce and Demonstrate the Program

14. Introduce performance management to employees.
15. Review completed "dry-run" conference plans.
16. Inaugurate the program with dry-run conferences.

Phase 7: Monitor the Program

17. Review completed performance-management documents before conferences are conducted.
18. Maintain consistent application of performance ratings by managers.
19. Review pay decisions related to performance before they are announced.
20. Maintain consistent application of pay rewards by managers.
21. Review disciplinary actions recommended by managers before they are taken.
22. Maintain consistent application of disciplinary policy by managers.

Phase 8: Maintain the Program

23. Update job descriptions and performance-criteria profiles as changes occur.
24. Audit and evaluate the effectiveness of the performance-management program at least annually.

(text continues on page 38)

Master Planner: Schedule

Project Completion Date: _____

How long will each activity take to complete? When must it be completed? When must it be started?

	How Long?	When Due?	Start Date	Who Will Do It?
Phase 1: Identify Goals and Get Commitment				
1. Identify performance-management program goals (form a task force if appropriate).				
2. Obtain approval of program goals from top management.				
3. Obtain commitment to program goals from all managers.				
Phase 2: Plan, Schedule, and Announce the Project				
4. Study options to implement the project.				
5. Select the options that best satisfy organizational requirements.				
6. Schedule and announce project implementations.				

	How Long?	When Due?	Start Date	Who Will Do It?

Phase 3: Get the Basic Job Information

	How Long?	When Due?	Start Date	Who Will Do It?
7. Gather information about jobs and performance criteria.				

Phase 4: Write Job Descriptions and Performance Criteria

	How Long?	When Due?	Start Date	Who Will Do It?
8. Train writers to prepare job descriptions and performance-criteria profiles.				
9. Verify job descriptions and performance-criteria profiles with employees.				
10. Obtain approval of job descriptions and performance-criteria profiles from managers.				
11. Obtain approval of job descriptions and performance-criteria profiles from senior managers.				

Phase 5: Develop Documentation and Train

	How Long?	When Due?	Start Date	Who Will Do It?
12. Prepare a policies and procedures manual for managers.				
13. Train managers to conduct performance-management conferences.				

Phase 6: Introduce and Demonstrate the Program

14. Introduce performance–management to employees.			
15. Review completed "dry-run" conference plans.			
16. Inaugurate the program with dry-run conferences.			

Phase 7: Monitor the Program

17. Review completed performance-management documents before conferences are conducted.			
18. Maintain consistent application of performance ratings by managers.			
19. Review pay decisions related to performance before they are announced.			
20. Maintain consistent application of pay rewards by managers.			
21. Review disciplinary actions recommended by managers before they are taken.			
22. Maintain consistent application of disciplinary policy by managers.			

	How Long?	When Due?	Start Date	Who Will Do It?

Phase 8: Maintain the Program

	How Long?	When Due?	Start Date	Who Will Do It?
23. Update job descriptions and performance-criteria profiles as changes occur.				
24. Audit and evaluate the effectiveness of the performance-management program at least annually.				

Master Planner: Communication

Who is the target audience? What communication techniques should be employed? Who will communicate?

	Target Audience	What To Do	Who Will Do It?

Phase 1: Identify Goals and Get Commitment

	Target Audience	What To Do	Who Will Do It?
1. Identify performance-management program goals (form a task force if appropriate).			
2. Obtain approval of program goals from top management.			
3. Obtain commitment to program goals from all managers.			

Phase 2: Plan, Schedule, and Announce the Project

4. Study options to implement the project.		
5. Select the options that best satisfy organizational requirements.		
6. Schedule and announce project implementations.		

Phase 3: Get the Basic Job Information

7. Gather information about jobs and performance criteria.	

Phase 4: Write Job Descriptions and Performance Criteria

8. Train writers to prepare job descriptions and performance-criteria profiles.			
9. Verify job descriptions and performance-criteria profiles with employees.			
10. Obtain approval of job descriptions and performance-criteria profiles from managers.			
11. Obtain approval of job descriptions and performance-criteria profiles from senior managers.			

Target Audience	What To Do	Who Will Do It?

Phase 5: Develop Documentation and Train

12. Prepare a policies and procedures manual for managers.		
13. Train managers to conduct performance-management conferences.		

Phase 6: Introduce and Demonstrate the Program

14. Introduce performance management to employees.		
15. Review completed "dry-run" conference plans.		
16. Inaugurate the program with dry-run conferences.		

Phase 7: Monitor the Program

17. Review completed performance-management documents before conferences are conducted.					
18. Maintain consistent application of performance ratings by managers.					
19. Review pay decisions related to performance before they are announced.					
20. Maintain consistent application of pay rewards by managers.					
21. Review disciplinary actions recommended by managers before they are taken.					
22. Maintain consistent application of disciplinary policy by managers.					

Phase 8: Maintain the Program

23. Update job descriptions and performance-criteria profiles as changes occur.		
24. Audit and evaluate the effectiveness of the performance-management program at least annually.		

Master Planner: Communication Authority

	Provide or Obtain	Interview or Investi- gate	Interpret or Advise	Persuade or Teach	Authorize or Arbitrate	Decide or Determine
Phase 1: Identify Goals and Get Commitment						
1. Identify performance-management program goals (form a task force if appropriate).						
2. Obtain approval of program goals from top management.						
3. Obtain commitment to program goals from all managers.						
Phase 2: Plan, Schedule, and Announce the Project						
4. Study options to implement the project.						
5. Select the options that best satisfy organizational requirements.						
6. Schedule and announce project implementations.						
Phase 3: Get the Basic Job Information						
7. Gather information about jobs and performance criteria.						

Phase 4: Write Job Descriptions and Performance Criteria

8. Train writers to prepare job descriptions and performance-criteria profiles.							
9. Verify job descriptions and performance-criteria profiles with employees.							
10. Obtain approval of job descriptions and performance-criteria profiles from managers.							
11. Obtain approval of job descriptions and performance-criteria profiles from senior managers.							

Phase 5: Develop Documentation and Train

12. Prepare a policies and procedures manual for managers.		
13. Train managers to conduct performance-management conferences.		

	Provide or Obtain	Interview or Investigate	Interpret or Advise	Persuade or Teach	Authorize or Arbitrate	Decide or Determine
Phase 6: Introduce and Demonstrate the Program						
14. Introduce performance management to employees.						
15. Review completed "dry-run" conference plans.						
16. Inaugurate the program with dry-run conferences.						
Phase 7: Monitor the Program						
17. Review completed performance-management documents before conferences are conducted.						
18. Maintain consistent application of performance ratings by managers.						
19. Review pay decisions related to performance before they are announced.						
20. Maintain consistent application of pay rewards by managers.						
21. Review disciplinary actions recommended by managers before they are taken.						
22. Maintain consistent application of disciplinary policy by managers.						

Phase 8: Maintain the Program

23. Update job descriptions and performance-criteria profiles as changes occur.		
24. Audit and evaluate the effectiveness of the performance-management program at least annually.		

Master Planner: Decision Authority

What actions can you take at your own discretion? Which actions do you have to tell someone about? For which actions do you need prior approval?

	Your Discretion	Tell Someone (Who?)	Prior Approval (From Whom?)

Phase 1: Identify Goals and Get Commitment

1. Identify peformance-management program goals (form a task force if appropriate).			
2. Obtain approval of program goals from top management.			
3. Obtain commitment to program goals from all managers.			

	Your Discretion	Tell Someone (Who?)	Prior Approval (From Whom?)

Phase 2: Plan, Schedule, and Announce the Project

	Your Discretion	Tell Someone (Who?)	Prior Approval (From Whom?)
4. Study options to implement the project.			
5. Select the options that best satisfy organizational requirements.			
6. Schedule and announce project implementations.			

Phase 3: Get the Basic Job Information

	Your Discretion	Tell Someone (Who?)	Prior Approval (From Whom?)
7. Gather information about jobs and performance criteria.			

Phase 4: Write Job Descriptions and Performance Criteria

	Your Discretion	Tell Someone (Who?)	Prior Approval (From Whom?)
8. Train writers to prepare job descriptions and performance-criteria profiles.			
9. Verify job descriptions and performance-criteria profiles with employees.			

No.	Task			
10.	Obtain approval of job descriptions and performance-criteria profiles from managers.			
11.	Obtain approval of job descriptions and performance-criteria profiles from senior managers.			

Phase 5: Develop Documentation and Train

No.	Task		
12.	Prepare a policies and procedures manual for managers.		
13.	Train managers to conduct performance-management conferences.		

Phase 6: Introduce and Demonstrate the Program

No.	Task		
14.	Introduce performance management to employees.		
15.	Review completed "dry-run" conference plans.		
16.	Inaugurate the program with dry-run conferences.		

Phase 7: Monitor the Program

	Your Discretion	Tell Someone (Who?)	Prior Approval (From Whom?)
17. Review completed performance-management documents before conferences are conducted.			
18. Maintain consistent application of performance ratings by managers.			
19. Review pay decisions related to performance before they are announced.			
20. Maintain consistent application of pay rewards by managers.			
21. Review disciplinary actions recommended by managers before they are taken.			
22. Maintain consistent application of disciplinary policy by managers.			

Phase 8: Maintain the Program

	Your Discretion	Tell Someone (Who?)	Prior Approval (From Whom?)
23. Update job descriptions and performance-criteria profiles as changes occur.			
24. Audit and evaluate the effectiveness of the performance-management program at least annually.			

Master Planner: Costs

For what items are expenditures anticipated? Who will incur them? How much will each item cost?

What Items?	Who?	How Much?

Phase 1: Identify Goals and Get Commitment

What Items?	Who?	How Much?
1. Identify performance-management program goals (form a task force if appropriate).		
2. Obtain approval of program goals from top management.		
3. Obtain commitment to program goals from all managers.		

Phase 2: Plan, Schedule, and Announce the Project

What Items?	Who?	How Much?
4. Study options to implement the project.		
5. Select the options that best satisfy organizational requirements.		
6. Schedule and announce project implementations.		

Phase 3: Get the Basic Job Information

What Items?	Who?	How Much?
7. Gather information about jobs and performance criteria.		

What Items?	Who?	How Much?
Phase 4: Write Job Descriptions and Performance Criteria		
8. Train writers to prepare job descriptions and performance-criteria profiles.		
9. Verify job descriptions and performance-criteria profiles with employees.		
10. Obtain approval of job descriptions and performance-criteria profiles from managers.		
11. Obtain approval of job descriptions and performance-criteria profiles from senior managers.		
Phase 5: Develop Documentation and Train		
12. Prepare a policies and procedures manual for managers.		
13. Train managers to conduct performance-management conferences.		

Phase 6: Introduce and Demonstrate the Program

14. Introduce performance management to employees.				
15. Review completed "dry-run" conference plans.				
16. Inaugurate the program with dry-run conferences.				

Phase 7: Monitor the Program

17. Review completed performance-management documents before conferences are conducted.					
18. Maintain consistent application of performance ratings by managers.					
19. Review pay decisions related to performance before they are announced.					
20. Maintain consistent application of pay rewards by managers.					
21. Review disciplinary actions recommended by managers before they are taken.					
22. Maintain consistent application of disciplinary policy by managers.					

What Items?	Who?	How Much?

Phase 8: Maintain the Program

	What Items?	Who?	How Much?
23.	Update job descriptions and performance-criteria profiles as changes occur.		
24.	Audit and evaluate the effectiveness of the performance-management program at least annually.		

Master Planner: Information/Opinion Access _____

	Who Has Information?	Who Has Opinion?	How Best To Get It?

Phase 1: Identify Goals and Get Commitment

	Who Has Information?	Who Has Opinion?	How Best To Get It?
1.	Identify performance-management program goals (form a task force if appropriate).		
2.	Obtain approval of program goals from top management.		
3.	Obtain commitment to program goals from all managers.		

Phase 2: Plan, Schedule, and Announce the Project

4. Study options to implement the project.			
5. Select the options that best satisfy organizational requirements.			
6. Schedule and announce project implementations.			

Phase 3: Get the Basic Job Information

7. Gather information about jobs and performance criteria.	

Phase 4: Write Job Descriptions and Performance Criteria

8. Train writers to prepare job descriptions and performance-criteria profiles.			
9. Verify job descriptions and performance-criteria profiles with employees.			
10. Obtain approval of job descriptions and performance-criteria profiles from managers.			
11. Obtain approval of job descriptions and performance-criteria profiles from senior managers.			

	Who Has Information?	Who Has Opinion?	How Best To Get It?

Phase 5: Develop Documentation and Train

	Who Has Information?	Who Has Opinion?	How Best To Get It?
12. Prepare a policies and procedures manual for managers.			
13. Train managers to conduct performance-management conferences.			

Phase 6: Introduce and Demonstrate the Program

	Who Has Information?	Who Has Opinion?	How Best To Get It?
14. Introduce performance management to employees.			
15. Review completed "dry-run" conference plans.			
16. Inaugurate the program with dry-run conferences.			

Phase 7: Monitor the Program

	Who Has Information?	Who Has Opinion?	How Best To Get It?
17. Review completed performance-management documents before conferences are conducted.			
18. Maintain consistent application of performance ratings by managers.			

19. Review pay decisions related to performance before they are announced.			
20. Maintain consistent application of pay rewards by managers.			
21. Review disciplinary actions recommended by managers before they are taken.			
22. Maintain consistent application of disciplinary policy by managers.			

Phase 8: Maintain the Program

23. Update job descriptions and performance-criteria profiles as changes occur.			
24. Audit and evaluate the effectiveness of the performance-management program at least annually.			

1.5 Strategic Planning

On your first quick walk through the book, record your initial thoughts on policy issues that will have to be decided.

_____

_____

_____

_____

_____

Any notes on tactical procedures?

_____

_____

_____

_____

Chapter 2

Where Individual
Performance
Management
Begins

2.1 Defining the Organization's Purpose

Individual performance management begins with the answer to the question,
"What is the purpose of the organization?" The organizational purpose gives
meaning and direction to individual efforts. Performance gaps between organizational purpose and individual performance, including the improvements necessary to close the gaps, are identified when the follow-up question "How well
is the organization achieving its purpose?" is answered.

The attention an organization gives to the development of its purpose statement offers helpful insights into its current state of performance. All organizations have a purpose. Some organizations state their purpose formally (see
Figure 2-1); others operate with only an informal understanding of the purpose
among members of the organization. Some statements, whether formal or informal, are vague. Some formal statements are subverted by a hidden purpose.

2.1.1 A Hierarchy of Organizations

Organizations can use purpose statements to develop operating objectives
and strategies for guiding individual performance within the organization. Or-

Figure 2-1. Sample formal statement of organizational purpose.

POLICE DEPARTMENT PURPOSE

A safe society free from crime, hazards, and disorder remains an unachieved ideal; nevertheless, consistent with the values of a free society, it is the primary purpose of the [*city*] Police Department to approach as closely as possible that ideal. The motto "To Protect and To Serve" states the essential reason for being of the [*city*] Police Department. The Department protects the right of all persons within its jurisdiction to be free from criminal attack, to be secure in their possessions, and to live in peace. The Department serves the people of [*city*] by performing law enforcement and public safety functions in a professional manner, and it is to the people of [*city*] that the Department is ultimately responsible. The specific purposes of the Department are:

1. To prevent and control conduct widely recognized as threatening to life and property
2. To aid individuals who are in danger of physical harm, such as the victim of a criminal attack
3. To facilitate the movement of people and vehicles
4. To protect constitutional guarantees, such as the right of free speech and assembly
5. To assist those who cannot care for themselves—the intoxicated, the addicted, the mentally ill, the physically disabled, the old, and the very young
6. To resolve conflict, whether it be between individuals, groups of individuals, or individuals and their government
7. To identify circumstances that have the potential for becoming problems for citizens, police, or government
8. To create and maintain a feeling of security in the community
9. To promote a cooperative effort between the police and the community to accomplish the Department's purposes
10. To protect life and property through public safety fire suppression efforts

---

ganizations can work without written purpose statements, if they at least understand their purpose informally. However, they will perform better when published statements serve as a reference to guide all organizational activities.

Here is a model you can use to analyze your organization's use of its purpose statement. The model parallels Abraham Maslow's theory, which identifies a hierarchy of human needs from basic, or physical, needs to higher-order, or self-actualizing, needs. Thus, in this model, organizations can be identified as functioning at one of these levels:

- Synergistic
- Solid

- Social
- Secure
- Surviving

Synergistic organizations have carefully developed purpose statements, require all divisions and departments to plan operating objectives in consort with organizational purposes, tie opportunities for individual development to individual objectives, appraise organizational and individual performance in relation to objectives, and reevaluate the stated purpose continually to ensure that the organization's potential is being maximized.

Synergistic organizations have:

- A formal purpose statement
- Departmental and individual objectives
- Individual development opportunities
- A system for managing and maintaining organizational and individual performance
- Purpose reevaluation

Solid organizations are secure in their reason for being; they are open to scrutiny, sometimes deliberately creating challenge within the organization in order to "be all that they can be." They welcome the opportunity to reevaluate the purpose of the organization against day-to-day functional operations. Although evaluation is organization-wide, it is not systematic as in a synergistic organization.

Solid organizations have:

- A formal purpose statement
- Departmental and individual objectives
- Individual development opportunities
- Purpose reevaluation

They do *not* have:

- A system for managing and maintaining organizational and individual performance

Social organizations plan and provide opportunities for employees to develop within job functions, but development is not tied to specific performance objectives. Management of performance is not systematic.

Social organizations have:

- A formal purpose statement
- Departmental and individual objectives
- Individual development opportunities (though not tied to individual objectives)

They do *not* have:

- Regular reevaluations of their purpose
- A system for managing and maintaining organizational and individual performance

Secure organizations have purpose statements that are not well-developed or maintained. These organizations realize an annual profit but do not look beyond the obvious for potential markets.

Secure organizations have:

- An informal purpose statement
- Departmental and individual objectives (though not tied together in a unified plan)
- Individual development opportunities (though not tied to individual objectives)

They do *not* have:

- Regular reevaluations of their purpose
- A system for managing and maintaining organizational and individual performance

Surviving organizations do not prepare purpose statements. These organizations barely realize annual profits, and occasionally show no profit.

Surviving organizations have

- No consensus on purpose

Organizations desiring to improve their effectiveness can use the foregoing model to identify the level at which they are currently functioning, as well as the higher-level elements they need to introduce.

A missing or poorly developed purpose statement is a good starting place, an anchor for improving an organization. Ineffective or inappropriate performance can usually be traced to an unclear organizational purpose. The purpose statement is disseminated to all organizational units so that subordinate purpose statements can be written in consort with the organization's purpose and made compatible with the purpose of other units.

What do you do if your organization does not have a purpose statement? First, recognize that every organization has a purpose, even if it is not written. The process of writing a purpose statement is, therefore, one of clarification, not creation.

Who should be involved in writing the purpose statement? One approach is to create a task force of managers or employees in each department to write a departmental purpose statement. Writers should be selected because of their ability and skill to think both concretely and abstractly. All layers of management within the department should revise and approve the work created by the task force until a document is approved by the department manager. The statements in all departments are then collapsed into a broad statement of overall purpose for the organization. (Even if the organization chooses not to develop a statement, a department can use its own statement for its own benefit.)

Another approach is to have top management start by developing the statement and distributing it to departments for interpretation and clarification. A task-force manager, or an outside consultant, can structure the process and manage discussions so participants are free to focus on the content of the discussion.

2.1.2 What To Consider When Writing a Purpose Statement

An effective starting point when writing a purpose statement is to compare "where we are" to "where we have been." Performance indicators in this comparison are either people-related or product- or service-related. Let's look at both.

People considerations relate to levels of customer satisfaction.

- *Customers.* Regardless of the organization's product—tangible item or intangible service—the fundamental purpose issue is always: How is the product being consumed, and by whom? Who are our customers? Where are they? Why do they use our product? What trends exist in their use of our product? Can we influence the trends? What realities influence the sale of our product? Answers to these questions provide information about who the organization's customers are (as opposed to who the organization would like them to be).

- *Complaints.* A valuable source of information is found in the analysis of complaints about products and services. When and where are complaints made? Are they targeted toward one product or a single geographic location? What is the nature of the complaints? What trends are apparent in the flow of complaints? Answers to these questions provide information about possible differences in the way management and customers view the organization.

- *Public service.* To what extent does the organization extend its contribution into the community? What are some examples of public service? How do employees feel about being a part of the organization?

Product or service considerations relate to the development, production, and delivery of the product or service, including sales or services requested, profits (or operation within or better than budget in not-for-profit organizations), market research, new products or services, and trends analysis.

- *Sales/profits.* How profitable is our organization? Which are our most profitable products? Which are the least profitable? What analysis has been done to understand nonprofitable areas?

- *Market research.* Does our organization study its market? How are research findings used?

- *New products/services.* When was the last time our organization created a new product or service? What internal mechanisms ensure that new products or services are planned for and encouraged?
- *Trends analysis.* Does our organization analyze trends in products purchased or services used? Who is responsible for analyzing trends? How is the information used?

Product- or service-related questions are easier to answer than people-related questions, because they involve tangible, objective measures. People-related issues involve a large number of variables, often less identifiable. Skillful analysis of both performance indices provides a data base for understanding how well the organization is performing now. Compare these data with the way the same questions were (or would have been) answered five or ten years ago. Understanding how the organization has responded to changing conditions over the years helps write your organization's current purpose statement.

2.1.3 Using the Organizational-Purpose Statement To Focus on Performance

Systematic questioning in the organization identifies performance needs and maintains the organizational purpose. Figure 2-2 shows the eight key questions to ask. As the figure suggests, the questioning process is circular in that question one must be answered in order to answer question two, and so on to question eight, which, when answered, starts the series of questions over again.

1. *What is our purpose?* The organizational-purpose statement defines what the organization intends to accomplish.

2. *How well do we achieve our purpose?* Purpose evaluation identifies whether the organization's performance is achieving the purpose. General or vague purpose statements permit only a vague evaluation: "We're probably doing it." Specific objectives are needed to understand performance precisely.

3. *How well do we want to achieve our purpose?* Organizations must ask: "Is our purpose correct?" "Is this as well as we can or want to do?"

4. *What needs to be done to achieve our purpose?* To answer this question, the organization must be aware of *what* might be done. Organizations can determine what might be done by following trends in the industry, studying the literature of the industry, and looking at comparable models of excellence. Without a written, planned commitment to achieve the organizational purpose, an organization tends to be reactive instead of proactive.

5. *How will we know that we are doing what is necessary to achieve our purpose?* An organization knows that it is accomplishing its purpose when employees are achieving results that fit into the overall purpose of the organization.

6. *What do employees need to do to achieve their purpose?* At this point, the

Figure 2-2. Circular model for identifying performance needs.

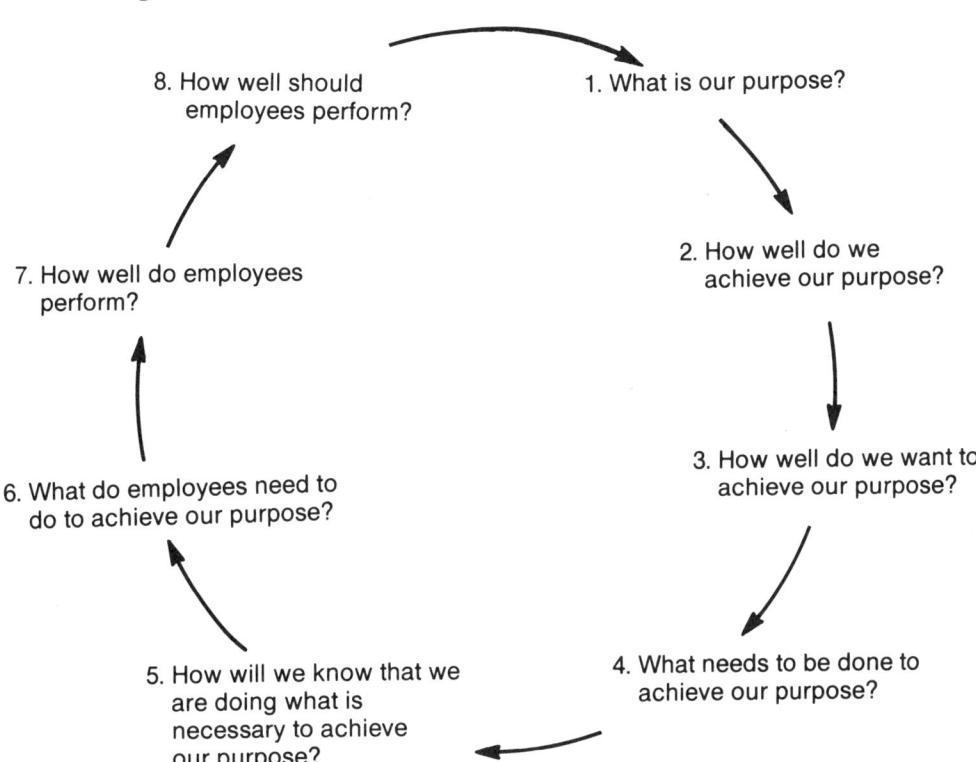

performance-management process focuses on the individuals who make up the organization. Previous questions are "big picture" questions. The organization's plan for carrying out its purpose includes the specific role of each department, which in turn is translated into performance objectives for individual employees.

7. *How well do employees perform?* Performance appraisal is the process of identifying whether individual performance is achieving individual objectives.

8. *How well should employees perform?* After performance has been compared to expectations, the organization must ask: "Is this as well as we want to perform?"

The cycle of questions begins with a look at what the organization wants to achieve, whether it is achieving it, and back again to what it wants to achieve—but now with more understanding. The analysis of information from purpose to performance leads to effective performance management.

Understanding *what* we are and *how well* we're doing is best achieved by looking at past and present performance. Needed changes refer to the future and to planning. Organizations cannot talk about needs without relating to the future and to change. When change must take place, the future becomes a reference point that gives meaning to the present. The criterion by which an organization will be appraised is future accomplishment.

2.1.4 Techniques for Analyzing Organizational and Individual Needs

Specific techniques for determining organizational and individual needs and potential include structured interviews, surveys/questionnaires, report/log analysis, and observations.

Structured interviews involve appointments with key managers for the express purpose of answering the question, "What would you like your department to be doing that it is not?" Secondary issues include what individual or organizational development is needed, and what additional resources must be considered.

Surveys and questionnaires are generally an indirect means to obtain opinion and information. They may be written or oral, formal or informal, anonymous or signed.

Logs and reports record low and high points of performance and show trends.

Observation can show how products or services are used and how employees perform their jobs.

Needs identified must be analyzed to determine if they are issues of purpose or performance. Here are three kinds of needs to consider:

1. *Information needs*—service- or product-related knowledge that affects the ability to produce, sell, or deliver the service or product.
2. *Structure needs*—the way information is moved within an organization. It also refers to the storage and control of the organization's inventory of human and material resources.
3. *Training needs*—the process of developing the human resources within the organization.

In summary, identifying the organizational and individual needs and potential by studying past and present performance starts with acknowledging the purpose of the organization, and then analyzing organizational and individual performance. If the purpose is not clearly stated, or is inaccurate, then the statement, or at least its informal understanding, should be clarified.

2.1.5 Individual Performance Management

Job descriptions serve the same purpose for the individual as the purpose statement serves for the organization. The same hierarchical model used to analyze the state of the organization purpose can be used to analyze the state of the individual employee's participation in the organization. Individuals within organizations have a variety of reasons for working. Some people are very clear about their reasons. Others are not—and consequently they are less clear about what they expect from the organization.

Employees at the *synergistic* level find a total blend of personal, professional, and organizational goals in the work place—a blend that accommodates the employee's sense of worth and productivity.

These employees operate from an individual development plan that addresses specific performance and growth objectives. The plan is a joint product of the employee and the manager that systematically looks at objectives, what appraisal techniques would ensure accomplishment of objectives, and what the employee needs to learn in order to achieve the objectives.

Employees at the *solid* level have a sense of direction and accomplishment related to personal, professional, and organizational growth, but the system for accomplishing and appraising performance is not well defined. Some attention is given to learning, but not as a predictable part of the system.

Not only are these employees allowed to develop professionally, but opportunities for personal development are also made available. These employees expect more than to satisfy merely their basic needs; they need challenges to remain productive to the organization.

Employees at the *social* level participate in the opportunities made available to them for self-development. Their needs as employees go beyond receiving a paycheck and benefits; they want personal challenge and development.

While employees operating at this level integrate personal, professional, and organizational needs, no system exists to identify growth needs. What happens with such employees is the result of their own initiative, not a result of the system.

Employees at the *secure* level do not expect or look for more from a job than basic pay and benefits. These employees do what they are told to do but do not grow beyond the job. They make only minimal efforts to integrate personal, professional, and organizational interests.

Employees at the *surviving* level put in the required work time and take home their pay. These employees are not quite sure what their needs are and have little interest in the needs of the organization. They do not take advantage of opportunities made available to them unless they are required to do so.

When performance is valued by an organization, the purpose statement guides organizational and individual effort, and systems ensure that the purpose is carried out. Along the way, the organization examines its actions to make certain that its original concept was accurate, and examines the marketplace to determine whether a new or altered mission purpose is required. Employee development is a natural ingredient in the process to ensure that the organization purpose is accomplished. Employees are the organization; what they do is what the organization is. In respected organizations, managers are appraised on how well they encourage their employees to perform and grow.

Project Analyzer (2.1)

What is the purpose of your organization?

_____

_____

How well is the purpose understood by the members of the organization?

_____

_____

At which level is your organization functioning?
- ☐ Synergistic
- ☐ Solid
- ☐ Social
- ☐ Secure
- ☐ Surviving

Why does your organization function at this level?

_____

_____

Does your organization have:
- ☐ A formal purpose statement?
- ☐ Departmental and individual objectives?
- ☐ Individual development opportunities?
- ☐ Purpose reevaluation?
- ☐ A system for managing and maintaining organizational and individual performance?

What must happen for your organization to build a foundation for managing performance?

_____

_____

Who would be involved?

_____

_____

_____

Should development start with senior executives or at the department level?

_____

_____

_____

_____

2.2 Strategic Planning

On your first quick walk through the book, record your initial thoughts on policy issues that will have to be decided.

_____

_____

_____

_____

_____

_____

Any notes on tactical procedures?

_____

_____

_____

_____

Chapter 3

Identifying Expected Job Performance

3.1 Methods of Job Analysis

Jobs are analyzed to:

- Establish expected job results
- Set performance criteria
- Determine a base for managing performance

Jobs are also analyzed to:

- Define authority and relationships with other jobs
- Establish hiring and testing requirements
- Develop orientation and training programs
- Determine fair remuneration
- Assess the need for, and plan the use of, human resources

Job analysis is misunderstood when it does not flow from a statement of organizational purpose and is considered only a process of information gathering. Most of the time spent analyzing jobs is for identifying and recording information;

but along the way, job content, performance criteria, authorities, hiring requirements, and relationships among jobs must be questioned to ensure that they make sense. Management uses the information identified and recorded to make decisions about what jobs it wants performed and how well it wants them performed.

In order to analyze a job, information must be collected. Methods of information collection include questionnaires, interviews, logs, and observation of work in progress. The technique selected depends on what will work in a given situation. Some jobs are difficult to describe; seeing is understanding. Some executives prefer to be interviewed; others want a questionnaire in order to fill waiting time in an airport. Employees in distant locations cannot be observed or interviewed personally without extra expense.

3.1.1 Who Is a Resource for Information?

Experience demonstrates that the person performing the job usually knows the most about it. Sometimes the supervisor knows best. When the job is a new outgrowth of other jobs in the organization, the incumbents of the jobs that gave rise to the new job are a resource.

Outside resources include other organizations with the same or similar jobs; descriptions published in pay surveys; the *Dictionary of Occupational Titles* published by the Department of Labor; books of sample job descriptions; professional associations; and certification requirements.

3.1.2 How Many People Should Be Surveyed?

Theoretically, every job-incumbent should be queried to ensure discovery of every distinct job duty (important when defending hiring requirements, performance criteria, and pay levels). Practically speaking, where 200 people are performing nearly identical jobs, not each incumbent needs to be invited to respond.

What are your goals? If you intend to maximize employee participation in the project—in particular, to develop commitment to job results and performance criteria—ask all 200 employees to fill out a questionnaire. Otherwise, identify a random sample of job-incumbents and ask them to participate. Or have all incumbents complete the questionnaire, but read only a random sample.

Interviewing is almost always on a sample basis because of the time involved, and observation is used mainly when the job cannot be understood readily from written and oral descriptions.

3.1.3 Getting Management's Approval of Job Descriptions and Performance Criteria

Regardless of the information-gathering process, all job content and performance criteria must be approved by management—usually the job manager and one or two higher levels of management. There are several reasons for this. Management and employees do not always communicate clearly with each other about job expectations. Management may have something else in mind for the job in the future. Employees may exaggerate. Management may exaggerate. The person who collects the information (the job analyst) may misunderstand.

A draft job description and performance-criteria profile written from the information gathered during the job analysis process should also be used later with incumbents and management to verify that the job and criteria are defined accurately.

3.1.4 Job Results, Job Activities, and Performance Criteria

Good job analysis must pay attention to the distinctions among *what* the incumbent does (job duties), *why* he or she does it (job results), and *how* work performance is assessed (performance criteria).

Most employees think of their jobs in terms of the duties they must perform; employees are not routinely educated to think in terms of the effect, or result, of the activities performed. You'll see how important this is when we examine the definition of performance criteria in Chapter 5. Generally, job analysts gather a mixture of results and duties—sometimes undifferentiated, sometimes mislabeled.

Gathering information on job responsibilities can be approached in several ways:

1. Ask the job-incumbent to identify all job duties, then identify all job results, and then correlate duties and results.
2. Ask the job-incumbent to identify the major job results and then list the duties necessary to accomplish each result.
3. Ask the job-incumbent to identify duties and corresponding results together.

Information on performance criteria is gathered after job results have been defined clearly.

3.1.5 Questionnaires

Questionnaires are an efficient technique because they allow the respondent time to answer carefully without the constraint of an interviewer waiting for a response. Questionnaires also save the job analyst time, because he or she only needs to read answers instead of having to participate in a slower, sometimes rambling, interview.

Effective questionnaires are understood by the respondents and obtain the specific information required. Language must be chosen carefully, because the respondent has no one to clarify the intent of a question. Pretesting the questionnaire is a worthwhile precaution.

A questionnaire should reflect the flavor and style of your organization. Casual language, jargon, and colloquialisms are quite permissible when they make questions clearer to the people who need to understand them.

Separate questionnaires are usually required if there are different job families with different "compensable factors," or job requirements. Otherwise, some questions will be extraneous or awkward.

A sample questionnaire that you can adapt to your organization's needs and preferences appears in Fig. 3.1.

3.1.6 Interviews

Jobs described in writing are not always perfectly clear to the reader; talking to the writer may be necessary to obtain an accurate understanding.

Interviewing a job-incumbent without the benefit of a completed questionnaire takes a lot of time—time to build rapport, to listen to the descriptions of job goals, tasks, and results, and to engage in extraneous discussion. Still, personal credibility is essential to a human system, especially one involving appraisal of performance and pay.

Make the most of the interview time. Prepare by gathering whatever information you can and structuring the questions you want to ask. Follow the questionnaire format. Complete the questionnaire during the interview if it helps guide the dialog.

Make an appointment and arrange for uninterrupted time, wherever convenient. Many interviewers prefer the incumbent's office or work area, because it is more relaxing for the interviewee and information and examples are at hand.

Develop a conversation, not an inquisition. Let the job-incumbent talk approximately 80 percent of the time. Record information for future reference: take notes, draw diagrams, tape-record discussions, videotape actions, collect written examples.

Do not overlook telephone or television interviews when job-incumbents travel a lot or are in distant locations.

3.1.7 Observation

Even though the job-incumbent and the job analyst work hard to clarify the information exchanged in writing and in person, some job events have to be seen—or touched, heard, or otherwise sensed—to be understood. Here are examples of statements that might call for observation:

> "We climb a tall ladder."
> "I gather and assemble information."
> "We meet with irate customers all day long."
> "It's noisy and hot."

(text continues on page 62)

Figure 3-1. Model job-analysis questionnaire.

The information you provide by completing this questionnaire will be used to write a clear and complete job description, as well as to define performance criteria and special job characteristics. Answer as thoroughly as you can, and don't worry about anyone "grading" your answers; the basic information about the job is what is important.

Your Job Title: _____ Date: _____

Name of Person to Whom You Report: _____

Department: _____ Shift: _____

Your Name: _____ Phone Ext.: _____

Amount of Time in This Job: _____

1. Summarize in one or two sentences what your basic job purpose is. (What is the principal reason your job exists? What is your job designed to accomplish?)

_____

_____

_____

_____

2. List the major responsibilities of your job, including the approximate percentage of time spent on each. Job responsibilities can be described in two ways:

What You Do	*Why You Do It*
(the *duties* people can watch you perform)	(the *result* you accomplish)

EXAMPLE:

A waiter, for example:

Places silverware, plates, and glassware (*duties*)	Provides a ready table for customers (*result*)

It may be helpful to first list duties and then identify the results involved; or, if you prefer, list the major results expected of your job and then the duties required to accomplish each result. Remember, sometimes two or three duties combine to produce the same result.

Also identify the *criteria used to determine job performance* for each job result. These criteria, either positive or negative, must answer the question of how someone can tell when the job is performed well.

Rank the responsibilities in numerical order, according to their importance to the organization.

Duties	Results	Percentage of Time Spent Performing Each Duty	Criteria

(Use additional pages as necessary.)

Mark by a D the most difficult part of the job.

Mark by a C the responsibilities involving confidential data.

3. What formal course of instruction is required by law to perform this job?

_____

a. What formal courses of instruction might be helpful?

_____

b. What license or certification is required by law to perform this job?

_____

4. What specific experiences or skills, other than formal education, do you feel a person must have in order to start this job today?

_____

_____

a. What jobs must a person have worked in before this job?

_____

_____

Figure 3-1. (*continued*)

5. Given your answers to the above, how long do you feel it should take a qualified new person to perform this job competently?

_____

6. The way your job is performed affects other people in terms of quality and quantity of service, as well as time and money gained or lost.

People Affected	What would be the positive results of good work on each type of person?	What typically might go wrong for each type of person if job performance were poor? (*Don't think of only the rare catastrophe.*)
a. Customers		
b. Public		
c. Employees in your own department		
d. Employees in other departments		
EXAMPLE:		
a. Customers	Customers receive service, as ordered, on time.	Customers lose time and money.

7. What part of your job entails the greatest chance for error?

_____

_____

   a. How often does this occur (daily, weekly, monthly)?

_____

_____

Figure 3-1. (*continued*)

8. What confidential information do you have access to?

_____

_____

_____

_____

   a. What could happen if this information were released?

_____

_____

_____

_____

9. Can you authorize money to be spent? ☐ No ☐ Yes
   If yes, how much? _____

10. Do you prepare a budget? ☐ No ☐ Yes
    If yes, what is the amount? Revenue $_____
                                           Expenses $_____

11. Describe the contacts with other persons that you normally make while performing your job.

Description of Contact	How Often? (daily, weekly, monthly)	Principal Reason for Contacting Them
With customers:		
With public:		
With employees in your department:		
With employees in other departments:		

Figure 3-1. (*continued*)

12. For which of the following reasons do you generally use communication in your job? (Check all reasons that apply.)

   ☐ Provide or obtain information.   ☐ Persuade or teach.
   ☐ Interview or investigate to   ☐ Authorize or arbitrate.
      identify and discover information.   ☐ Make decisions when policy
   ☐ Interpret or advise to help others   guidelines are not available.
      understand more clearly.

13. Are there any working conditions—such as noise, temperature extremes, or odors—involved in your job that might be described as uncomfortable or disagreeable?

   Condition   *How Often Encountered
                                               (daily, weekly, monthly)*

   _____   _____

   _____   _____

   _____   _____

14. What physical exertion is required to perform this job?

   *Exertion
   (such as pounds to be lifted)*   *How Often
                                               (daily, weekly, monthly)*

   _____   _____

   _____   _____

   _____   _____

15. Describe any unusual time demands on a person in this job, such as travel or being on call. Include the percentage of time each demand requires.

   Demand   *Time Percentage*

   _____   _____

   _____   _____

   _____   _____

Figure 3-1. (*continued*)

16. Are there any hazardous conditions involved in this job that could result in serious injury? □ No □ Yes If yes, explain:

_____

_____

_____

_____

17. Describe any other special conditions involved in this job.

_____

_____

_____

_____

18. What equipment must you be able to operate? How often?

Equipment	*How Often Operated*
_____	_____
_____	_____
_____	_____
_____	_____
_____	_____

19. If you supervise others,
    a. List the titles of the jobs supervised:

_____	_____
_____	_____
_____	_____
_____	_____

Figure 3-1. (*continued*)

b. Check those activities you do:

☐ Hiring/terminating
☐ Promoting/demoting
☐ Transferring
☐ Training
☐ Writing performance appraisals

☐ Determining or recommending salary increases
☐ Disciplining
☐ Assigning work
☐ Checking work for accuracy and completeness
☐ Other: _____

c. How many employees do you supervise?
   • Number reporting directly to you: _____
   • Number reporting to people who report to you: _____
d. Percentage of your time spent supervising: _____
e. ☐ I do not supervise anyone but I:
   ☐ Provide some work direction to other employees.
   ☐ Regularly make recommendations to people's supervisors regarding their job performance.

20. Where do you get the information you use in your job?

   _____
   _____
   _____
   _____

21. Give examples of the independent decisions you make in your job:

   _____
   _____
   _____
   _____

a. What guidance (policy, procedure, supervision) is available to help you with these decisions?

   _____
   _____
   _____

Figure 3-1. (*continued*)

b. Which describes your authority responsibility:
  ☐ Must follow established steps and procedures.
  ☐ May make some alterations when following established steps and procedures.
  ☐ Select specific steps from established options.
  ☐ Develops options by which work can be accomplished.
  ☐ Sets priorities and performance standards.

22. Under what circumstances is your work checked and reviewed by your supervisor?

_____

_____

_____

_____

_____

23. What personal traits are required to perform this job?

_____

_____

_____

_____

_____

24. Is there anything else you want to record in order to help others understand your job better?

_____

_____

_____

_____

_____

25. Attach any documents or examples which may be helpful to explain any of your remarks.

Figure 3-1. (*continued*)

MANAGER'S REVIEW AND COMMENTS:

_____

_____

_____

_____

_____

_____

_____   _____

Manager's Signature   Date

_____   _____

Reviewer's Signature   Date

Being observed can be threatening to some people, but as a rule, people enjoy talking about their work and "showing off." Visiting the job can be a real employee-relations boost.

3.1.8 Logs

When events need to be recorded over a period of time, job-incumbents can be asked to keep a log: number of telephone calls, nature of personal interaction, number of requests for information and reasons for inquiries, pounds lifted and how often, use of equipment, and so forth.

Logs must be designed to minimize the inconvenience to the recorder. Provide for a checkoff rather than essay responses wherever possible. Figure 3-2 shows an example.

3.1.9 Model Approach to Job Analysis

In most situations, you will find it appropriate to begin data gathering with an explanation of the process to the respondents, either in writing or in person.

Figure 3-2. Sample telephone activity log.

Time	Purpose of Call
	1 Obtain standard information
	2 Obtain information requiring research
	3 Place an order
	4 Complain
	5 Request repair
	6 Other
[Check for each call]	*[Enter appropriate number below]*
EXAMPLE	
9:00 A.M. x x	**4, 5**
9:00	
9:05	
9:10	
9:15	
9:20	
[etc.]	

Let people know why they are participating. Here are 11 steps of a model approach:

1. Send questionnaire and log to respondents, usually the job-incumbents, for completion.
2. Have the information collected on a questionnaire and log approved by management before writing a draft job description and performance-criteria profile.
3. Study information returned to understand the job; identify unclear statements.
4. Gather job-content information from other sources inside and outside the organization to develop a clear understanding of the job.
5. Interview the job-incumbent to clarify your understanding of the job.
6. Interview management to understand expectations and requirements for the job.
7. Observe the job to understand what has been written and stated and to verify the accuracy of the statements.
8. Clarify any misunderstandings about the job.
9. Prepare a draft job description and performance-criteria profile (depending on the scope of your project, you might also prepare a draft of job qualifications, plus job-evaluation documentation).
10. Review the draft with the job-incumbent to check its accuracy.
11. Obtain management's approval of the document.

Project Analyzer (3.1)

Who has job-content information needed to understand the jobs?

_____

_____

What outside resources are available?

_____

_____

Is the organizational philosophy to involve all employees in the process, or will management develop job content?

_____

_____

_____

How many people are in the organization?

_____

_____

What is the most efficient method of obtaining information from them?

_____

_____

_____

Is a questionnaire appropriate?

_____

_____

Are personal interviews appropriate?

_____

_____

Are logs appropriate?

_____

_____

_____

Is observation appropriate?

_____

_____

_____

Should information be sampled?

_____

_____

Can the same method be used for all jobs?

_____

_____

What adjustments will be required for which jobs?

_____

_____

_____

How will approval be built into the information-gathering method?

_____

_____

_____

Who will approve job content?

_____

_____

3.2 Strategic Planning

On your first quick walk through the book, record your initial thoughts on policy issues that will have to be decided.

_____

_____

_____

_____

_____

Any note on tactical procedures?

_____

_____

_____

_____

Chapter 4
Writing Results-Oriented Job Descriptions

4.1 The Job Description Defined

When you explain to an employee the duties you want performed and the results you expect, you are describing a job. When you explain how well you want the job performed, you are defining performance criteria. Without such explanations you cannot have an effective performance-management program.

A job description explains how each employee's participation accomplishes a portion of the organization's purpose. A job is the smallest identifiable structure within the organization. Add all the jobs together and you have defined the organization.

It is management's right and responsibility to define jobs and performance criteria, as well as to change them as organizational requirements demand. This right can be exercised at any time, unless it is given away.

A job description is an agreement, much like a contract, between the organization and the employee—except that management always has the right to change the "contract" at its discretion. Treating jobs like "contracts" makes good interpersonal-communications sense, because it creates an understanding between two parties. The courts in some states have held that a job-description contract is a legal contract and that an organization cannot change the terms of the agreement without proper notice to the employee. A problem usually arises when management changes the terms of the agreement for frivolous or discriminatory reasons.

The structural elements of a job description include:

- Title
- Supervisor title
- Jobs supervised
- Purpose statement

- Results expected
- Qualifications required
- Approval authority and date

Job descriptions may also include:

- Authority of the incumbent
- Relationships with other jobs
- Frequency of performance of duties
- Percent of time allocated to each result

- Salary grade and range
- Equipment operated
- Special demands
- Career progression
- Budget authority
- Exempt/Nonexempt status

plus anything else that you believe will help employees and managers collaborate to fulfill the responsibilities needed to make the organization successful.

Job procedures are not normally included in a job description. A job description is a guide or overview to the results to be achieved by the incumbent; procedures are too detailed to be included in the job description and would duplicate operating manuals.

4.1.1 The Many Uses of Job Descriptions

A description of the jobs in the organization is one of the most important documents management needs to accomplish the organization's purpose. Unfortunately, job descriptions are typically viewed only as an exercise required by the personnel department in order to hire somebody—a laborious effort to write out what everybody knows already and will ignore anyway. Incredible as it may seem, many performance appraisal forms are generic and do not include any specific reference to the job description.

Job descriptions are an essential ingredient for managing performance. Job descriptions are also used to:

- Define or revise the organizational structure
- Plan human resources requirements
- Advertise jobs and recruit job candidates

- Determine job pay
- Determine exempt/nonexempt status, as defined by the Fair Labor Standards Act
- Establish career progressions
- Analyze work flow and methods

- Post jobs
- Interview and select job candidates
- Orient new employees
- Identify training requirements
- Train employees
- Evaluate relative job value

- Conduct pay surveys
- Prepare affirmative action plans
- Comply with equal-pay laws
- Establish a base for incentive plans
- Bargain with unions

As you can see, job descriptions are a focal point in the process of managing organizations.

4.1.2 Generic and Specific Job Descriptions

Generic job descriptions describe responsibilities in broad terms so that similar jobs can be defined by one description. This avoids having to write a description for each job. For example, where secretaries perform nearly identical tasks in the same or different departments, the distinctions among jobs might be made more easily in departmental procedure manuals than in job descriptions. Similarly, computer programmers need not have different job descriptions just because they work on different applications of the same programs.

Specific job descriptions are needed when the differences among jobs are sufficient to cause miscommunication if the differences are not delineated clearly in separate job descriptions.

Secretaries who do have vastly different responsibilities from other secretaries should have separate job descriptions and performance-criteria profiles. Computer programmers who work with more complex languages than other programmers must have separate job descriptions (job qualifications) and performance-criteria profiles.

If you keep in mind that a job description must clearly and accurately convey the meaning of the job, you will have no trouble deciding whether to include more than one job under a single description.

Project Analyzer (4.1)

What is management's perception of the value of job descriptions?

_____

_____

What are employees' perceptions?

_____

_____

Do both management and employees understand the relevance of job descriptions to a performance-management program?

_____

_____

Do job descriptions exist for all jobs?

_____

_____

Are job descriptions kept current?

_____

_____

In what ways are job descriptions used now?

_____

_____

_____

Are job descriptions specific enough to communicate job content accurately?

_____

_____

_____

Are job descriptions too specific, so that there are too many of them?

_____

_____

How should job descriptions be used?

_____

_____

4.2 Who Should Write and Approve Job Descriptions?

Tradition has it that the person who gathers and studies the job information, has it fresh in mind, and is expert (usually a human resources professional) will write the job description. But writing implies ownership, so in a sense the job analyst will own the job description—an undesirable scenario.

The job description is primarily an instrument of communication between a manager and an employee. These are the people who should fashion the document or at least edit a model. Certainly, they can obtain advice from the "expert" on technique and expression, but the exercise will be much more meaningful to them when they struggle with the words to say what they mean. Then they will mean what they say and be more committed to the performance-management program.

What this requires, of course, is training people to write job descriptions in the style chosen by the organization. There is a proper writing technique, and it is not complicated, as we will see in section 4.3.

Employees should identify job information. Managers should approve job content—adding or subtracting results and duties as necessary—and write the first draft of the job description and performance-criteria profile. Although writing the criteria in tandem with the job description means a larger investment of time all at once, writing the two together helps the writer clarify each. Writing performance-criteria profiles is examined in Chapter 5.

The job analyst should critique the style and format of the job description and the performance-criteria profile. The employee and the manager should finalize the first draft together. The manager's manager should approve the description and performance-criteria profile for content and integration of results and criteria with the objectives, policies, and standards of the organization. The human resources manager should review the description and performance-criteria profile for organizational consistency and legal compliance.

Obviously, each organization will process job descriptions according to its own style, resources, and time demands. In most organizations, however, human resources departments have typically taken the burden on themselves and have suffered the consequences, as department managers have disowned or failed to maintain the product because they have no investment in it.

Sometimes, consultants are hired to write job descriptions and performance-criteria profiles. You can see that ownership is now even further away from the organization, plus the cost is high. The descriptions and performance-criteria profiles will be expertly written, but may not match the interactive style of managers and employees. It's better to have documents that do not receive an A in style but convey a clear message to the parties involved.

There is nothing wrong with moving the process along by having writers with more experience contribute their ability. But do not forsake a thoughtful, meaningful product for efficiency.

Where job descriptions and performance-criteria profiles are produced by people other than the manager and the employee, it would be prudent to have the employee review the document to create understanding and have the manager approve the document to create ownership.

Project Analyzer (4.2)

Who writes job descriptions now?

_____

_____

Is this the best way to have them prepared?

_____

_____

Who should be involved?

_____

_____

Will training be required?

_____

_____

Who will conduct the training?

_____

_____

Who approves job descriptions?

_____

_____

Are the appropriate people included in the approval process?

_____

_____

Who needs to be included?

_____

_____

4.3 Writing in a Results-Oriented Style

A job description should tell an employee what to do, right? Yes, but that's only part of what an employee needs to know.

Why do managers get so frustrated with employees? Because they get tired explaining and reexplaining **why** certain aspects of a job should be performed.

Jobs are traditionally described in terms of the duties, tasks, or activities to be performed by the incumbent. Expressed in such a laundry-list fashion, job descriptions are not much fun; actually, they're rather boring and demotivating, if not unmanageable.

Why unmanageable? Because an employee "doing" duties does not always produce the results management desires. A report may be filed, but it may not provide the required information. Equipment may be inspected, but an inspection report may not answer the question of whether equipment replacement is necessary. Candidates may be interviewed, but the questions asked of them may fail to identify critical selection information.

Thus, an employee may "do" the job, endlessly, but not achieve the results that management requires. The employee would be "entitled" to a high performance rating for "doing" the job, even though a low rating for not accomplishing desired results would be appropriate.

Employees can psychologically escape accountability, because their job description only requires them to file, inspect, and interview; there is no statement to identify what these duties are intended to accomplish.

Yes, you must tell employees what to do—file, inspect, and interview—but more important, you must tell them why they do what they do. You have to focus them on the results that must be accomplished. Obviously, employees can make the connection, you say. Yes, they can; but will they? Not after years of "do what you're told" conditioning. The natural inclination of people to do what is necessary for the good of the enterprise has been stifled because traditional job descriptions, without painting the big picture, say: do these little things.

When employees are told only what to do, they are unable to integrate that duty with other duties. More important, they are unable to see other possibilities of performing the work in order to accomplish the desired result.

4.3.1 Results-Oriented vs. Duty-Oriented Style

Here are some specific job-description examples to demonstrate the difference between results and duties. First, read the duties only (they're all you find in traditional job descriptions in most organizations). Then read the results and notice the more complete understanding of the job. A thorough job description, of course, must include both results and duties.

These are results:		*These are duties:*
Fills vacant positions	*by*	recruiting through newspaper ads and placement agencies, and interviewing and testing candidates.
Provides secretarial services	*by*	typing correspondence, procedures, interoffice memos, and announcements.
Produces house newsletter	*by*	soliciting, gathering, editing, and arranging articles.
Monitors benefits program	*by*	acting as liaison between users and providers and reviewing and updating records, bills, and employee lists.
Aids in anticipating cash flow related to material purchases	*by*	projecting purchase order commitments.
Helps maintain a perpetual inventory system	*by*	recording receipt of materials against open purchase orders, proofreading receiving reports, and recording inventory.
Maintains inventory	*by*	projecting production requirements, analyzing discounts, and tracking materials used.
Ensures material availability	*by*	approving payment to processors and authorizing movement of materials.
Determines availability, price, and sources of materials	*by*	placing special materials inquiries with domestic mills and international brokers.
Formulates investment programs	*by*	reviewing account objectives and restrictions and projecting the direction of financial markets, interest rates, and the economy.

What is your reaction to the two writing styles? Yes, the duties-only style is a shorter way to write, and yes, it is how we have always written job descriptions. But which writing style would you prefer for your own job description?

4.3.2 Using Job Descriptions To Educate Employees

Job descriptions and performance-criteria profiles have been used for their "contractual" purposes: if you do these things, in this manner, I will pay you. Job descriptions and performance-criteria profiles have not been viewed as a method of education, an opportunity to help employees understand why and how the organization works. Instead of explaining and reexplaining, let's tell employees up front, from day one, why their work is important to the organization, what it is designed to accomplish, and how well it needs to be accomplished.

Let us give employees a sense of purpose and participation in the organization; let us show employees their place in the purpose of the organization. We have relied on managers to fill in the gap between the job duties we have required of employees and the integration of these activities into an organization. Perhaps we have assumed that employees won't comprehend the total organization, that only management is capable of balancing inputs to achieve the desired outcomes.

Surprise! Managers do not always understand the outcomes, either. We have bemoaned the managerial inadequacy of the many technicians who have been promoted to the rank of manager—technicians who do a poor job of integrating the requirements and purposes of managerial action, particularly requirements involving human resources considerations. And we ask these same managers to explain to employees why management does what it does to fulfill the purposes of the organization!

4.3.3 Gaining Clarity Through Job Descriptions

The development of a results-oriented job description gives a manager an opportunity to clarify why job duties are performed—why they are important. Writing job results forces a manager to think through the essence of the job, and then defend that understanding to higher-level or peer managers. Imagine the clarity and consistency of management thinking that we might derive from such conversations.

Think about the increased clarity of manager–employee relationships when jobs are understood and agreed upon for their intent instead of only their practice. Writing jobs in terms of results is not just a method of expression; the educational principle is one of defining the purpose first so that the instructions—in this case, job duties—make sense as they are joined into a unified whole. Without this focal point of concentration, an employee must continually search for meaning in the relationships of job duties. "Why am I important?" may sound terribly philosophical, but in practical terms, the answer guides employees' efforts to accomplish the organization's goals.

Job descriptions were born in an era when employee involvement was not as prominent an issue as it is today. Employees were simply told what to do; if they did not do what they were told, they could go somewhere else. The old factory term "hired hands" tells much about the mentality of the era. Of course, even then employees asked themselves about the value of their work, but today we encourage them to do so.

4.3.4 Where to Begin Writing

The information gathered during job analysis, as described in Chapter 3, determines the content of the job description. Essentially, the writing process reorders the information gathered into a different, crisper format. Much of the information gathered during the analytical process is used for job evaluation.

Begin by crystallizing your thoughts; identify the major job-result areas. Rules of thumb about how many result areas there should be are misleading, since the number of results identified is determined by the job content. Very simple jobs may have only one result area; complex jobs may have ten or so. One-half dozen generally sounds reasonable; 15 or 20 is too many.

Or, instead of identifying major job results first, simply list duties and results as they are remembered and then arrange them into several results with subordinate duties (see Figure 4-1). Use current job descriptions as a start if they are available.

Job descriptions typically are long because they list duties separately rather than clustering them with related duties under a germane result. You will find that the results-oriented structure is succinct, efficient, and orderly.

Once the results have been identified, arrange them in a logical sequence that helps the reader consider the job, such as order of importance, steps in a process, or frequency of performance.

Figure 4-1. Sample arrangement of mixed job duties and results into several results.

New Job Results

1. Remains aware of the company's needs for materials and parts.	2. Maintains the company's competitive cost position.	3. Prepares information for others as needed.
↓	↓	↓

Mixed Job Duties and Results

1. Is aware of requirements for materials and parts.

2. Keeps competitive.

3. Monitors production reports.

4. Provides information.
5. Prepares reports.

6. Investigates new materials.

7. Reviews inventory reports.

8. Maintains record transactions.

9. Negotiates with vendors.

4.3.5 The Basic Structure of the Results-Oriented Job Description

A job-result statement involves three elements:

1. An action verb
2. What the action described by the verb produces
3. How the action is performed

Here is a job result written correctly:

Determines needed drapery repair and replacement by making inspections.

Here it is incomplete:

Inspects draperies.

Notice that the correct version tells us up front what the result is and goes on to indicate how the result can be accomplished. The "target" is very clear.

The incorrect version identifies only the duty involved. An employee could "successfully" inspect draperies without ever accomplishing the expected result.

The remainder of this chapter includes examples to demonstrate how to translate duties-oriented job descriptions into results-oriented ones. Compare the thinness of the duties-oriented description with the more complete understanding achieved when the results are clarified. Notice also that—typical of many job descriptions—some of the results are stated in the duties-oriented descriptions, but buried in verbiage; occasionally, some results are implied, though not explicitly stated.

Here is a duties-oriented job description for an accounting clerk, followed by an improved results-oriented version.

DUTIES-ORIENTED DESCRIPTION

JOB TITLE: Accounting Clerk II

REPORTS TO: Accounting Manager

JOB PURPOSE: Performs accounting functions associated with data requiring the application of basic theory of accounting involving clerical tasks.

WORK PERFORMED:

1. Reviews data for posting to journals and ledgers, making closing entries, applying or verifying account transfers, summarizing totals and balances.
2. Assists in the preparation and issuance of reports, statements, and statistical data, making preliminary analyses and investigations.

3. May prepare monthly reports or analyses for a particular area of accounting.
4. May initiate correspondence or telephone other locations concerning discrepancies and other questionable charges.
5. Maintains records of source documents and accounting-detail backup data.
6. Performs calculation on standard calculating machines.
7. May be assigned a particular section on a repetitive basis, such as payroll, accounts receivable, taxes, etc.

RESULTS-ORIENTED DESCRIPTION

JOB TITLE: Accounting Clerk II

REPORTS TO: Accounting Manager

JOB PURPOSE: Records company income and expense by posting journal entries and preparing reports as directed.

JOB RESULTS:

1. Records accounting transactions by posting to journals and ledgers, making closing entries, applying or verifying account transfers, and summarizing totals and balances.
2. Prepares reports, statements, and statistical data as assigned by making preliminary analyses and investigations.
3. Resolves discrepancies and questionable charges by corresponding with and telephoning vendors.
4. Maintains accurate accounting-resource information by adjusting and correcting backup data.
5. Calculates data by using standard calculators.

Look at the Accounting Clerk job descriptions closely to understand why the two examples are different. Notice the addition or clarification of the expected results in the improved version. Study the distinction between the results (before the *by*) and the duties (after the *by*).

The correct version focuses on the result and helps explain to an employee why it is important to do certain things.

Here are some other typical duties that are given meaning when they are expressed in relation to the results desired:

Duty	*Result*
Conducts laboratory tests.	Provides diagnostic data to physicians.
Polices buildings and grounds.	Keeps residents safe.
Recruits and screens applicants.	Hires qualified employees.
Maintains electrical equipment and systems.	Supplies power for building and equipment.

Try this writing format: *result to be accomplished* **by** *performing duties.* When you use that format, the complete statement would be:

Provides diagnostic data to physicians *by conducting laboratory tests.*
Keeps residents safe *by policing buildings and grounds.*
Hires qualified employees *by recruiting and screening applicants.*
Supplies power for building and equipment *by maintaining electrical equipment and systems.*

Incidentally, some writers prefer to state the duties which are performed "in order to" accomplish an expected result (for example, "Polices buildings and grounds *in order to* keep residents safe"). You might find this style preferable. However, it is better to put the statement of purpose up front than to let it trail at the end, because the initial position encourages both the writer and the reader to pay more attention to the desired job result.

4.3.6 Duty vs. Result—A Simple Test

No one learns to write job descriptions by reading about the subject; you have to practice to get the feel of the flow of words and the relationship of duties to results.

One tip: When you are struggling to say just what you mean, you may wonder whether you are writing a duty or a result; try placing your thought both before the "by" and after it to gain a sense of proportion and understanding. For example:

Inspects draperies by . . .
vs.
. . . by making inspections.

A result answers the question, *Why are we doing this?* "Inspects draperies" is not the *why* of anything; if we tried to complete this statement, we would be describing job procedures or protocols—(1) set up a ladder, (2) climb the ladder; (3) remove the drapery from the rods, and so on. That's much too detailed for a job description.

Such job procedures and protocols are essential management tools and form the basis of job training programs, but they normally are not included in the job description. When might they be? When the job is simple and contains only one or two results.

When you flip the statement around and try "by making inspections," you can fit in the missing piece of the puzzle and achieve an understanding of the situation that you did not have before.

One other tip: Do not try to write the perfect job description on the first shot. Good writing has much more trial and error than most people understand. Go ahead and get something down on paper and then try out different possibilities.

Work intensely for a while and then put the writing away. Come back later, when you have regained your objectivity, and do your editing then.

Try this next duties-oriented job description and see what you can do to identify and include job results; an improved version follows.

Remember:

. . . by . . .

JOB TITLE: Senior Buyer

REPORTS TO: Materials Manager

JOB PURPOSE: Secure and maintain optimum level of parts and materials for the efficient production of the company's product in accordance with established policies and procedures.

WORK PERFORMED:

1. Remain cognizant of the company's needs for materials and parts to promote efficient production. This is done through monitoring data reflecting inventory needs, stores, warehousing, and change orders. Search out, investigate, select, and negotiate new and tried vendors supplying the company's needs and maintain the company's competitive position insofar as materials cost is concerned.
2. Prepare reports and maintain data on the company's transactions.
3. Coordinate with engineering and production in the changing needs of the company and its products with regard to new products, product innovations, and quality control.
4. Negotiate in the company's best interest for price and delivery of needed materials and parts, consistent with the quality and service required.
5. Coordinate pricing and cost determinations with interested company representatives, e.g., cost accountants, inventory analysts, etc.
6. Lead and direct others in the procurement of goods and services.

Job-Description Writing Practice

Job Title: Senior Buyer

Job Purpose: _____

_____

_____

1. _____

_____

_____

2. _____

_____

_____

3. _____

_____

_____

4. _____

_____

_____

5. _____

_____

_____

6. _____

_____

_____

Here is the improved, results-oriented job description of the Senior Buyer position:

JOB TITLE: Senior Buyer

REPORTS TO: Materials Manager

JOB PURPOSE: Supports the production of products by purchasing and maintaining an optimum level of parts and materials.

JOB RESULTS:

1. Remains aware of the company's needs for materials and parts by monitoring production reports and inventory.
2. Maintains the company's competitive cost position by investigating, selecting, and negotiating with vendors.
3. Provides information to others by preparing reports and maintaining data on company transactions.
4. Keeps aware of new products, product changes and innovations, and quality control by coordinating with engineering and production.
5. Obtains quality and service required by negotiating for price and delivery of needed parts and materials.
6. Participates in pricing decisions by accumulating cost information and providing it to others, such as cost accountants, inventory analysts, and market analysts.
7. Accomplishes departmental work in the procurement of goods and services by directing others.

4.3.7 The Job-Purpose Statement

Every job description should begin with a job-purpose statement. The job-purpose statement follows the same writing structure as a job result. It is a synthesis of the intent of the job in its entirety. This section might also be named the *Job Objective*. The job purpose, then, is the ultimate overall result expected from the job.

4.3.8 Verbs, Verbs, Verbs

Selecting the verb that most accurately describes the action is one of the major concerns when writing a job description. As you might expect, job-description writing has something of a jargon of its own. Figure 4-2 lists verbs describing job actions, arranged under useful major categories.

After writing a first draft of a job description, edit it to make it clear and

Figure 4-2. List of verbs describing job actions.

Controls	*Teaches*	*Recommends*	*Counts*	*Studies*
decides	trains	advises	adds	examines
determines	instructs	apprises	totals	audits
directs	guides	consults	balances	investigates
authorizes		counsels	bills	analyzes
signs	*Records*	submits	invoices	reviews
approves	registers	suggests	figures	ascertains
assumes	receives	proposes	extends	inspects
conducts	codes	promotes	inventories	observes
executes	notes	contributes	measures	samples
delegates	describes	interprets	calculates	estimates
represents	outlines		reconciles	tests
manages	summarizes	*Contacts*	computes	surveys
supervises	writes	calls	compiles	scans
administers	composes	notifies	pays	screens
schedules	drafts	visits	remits	searches
selects	copies	informs	disburses	
assigns	circulates	corresponds	sells	*Designs*
acts for	distributes	discusses	collects	develops
acts	disseminates	interviews	appraises	plans
orders	lists	refers	evaluates	organizes
initiates	issues	attends		establishes
implements	furnishes	collaborates	*Compares*	institutes
releases	renders	participates	checks	selects
oversees	posts	cooperates	proofreads	defines
arranges	prepares	conducts	edits	prepares
anticipates	processes	facilitates	catalogues	creates
coordinates	enters	consults	indexes	originates
routes	attaches	confers	classifies	formulates
employs	deletes	requests	affirms	
secures	itemizes	requisitions	revises	*Operates*
obtains	arranges		verifies	centers
contracts	merges		rates	aligns
requires	places			clears
follows up	files			stacks
expedites	transfers			opens
corrects	tabulates			carries
keeps	charts			handles
ensures	lays out			collates
maintains	amends			disassembles
cancels	locates			assembles
closes	finds			feeds
adopts	traces			types
	consolidates			processes
				batches
				sorts

concise. For example, words such as "ensure," "make sure," "assure," or "provide" can often be deleted. Modifiers such as "good," "efficiently," "accurately," "properly," and "timely," which are intended to remind employees how well something must be done, are unnecessary, since they are commonly implied or are better stated as performance criteria.

Change this:	*To this:*
Processes payroll and taxes by . . .	Pays wages and remits taxes by . . .
Makes sure that shipments are complete by . . .	Completes shipments by . . .
Ensures payment by . . .	Obtains payment by . . .
Keeps customers informed by . . .	Informs customers by . . .
Keeps customer accounts up to date by . . .	Maintains customer accounts by . . .
Ensures that automobile fleet is in good condition by . . .	Maintains automobile fleet by . . .
Ensures that fleet cars are properly registered by . . .	Registers fleet cars by . . .
Ensures quality and timeliness of administrative services by . . .	Provides administrative services by . . .
Ensures accuracy of data by making sure that each manifest is balanced and that product codes agree with customer's order	Verifies data by balancing manifests and correlating product codes with customer order.
Provides support to inside and outside salespeople and branches by coordinating and maintaining all activities relating to specific product lines.	Manages and coordinates a product line by managing inventory and providing sales information.
Ensures that customers are billed accurately by entering appropriate information in the system.	Inputs billing data by operating computer terminal.

Here is another example of a duties-oriented job description. Try to rewrite the description, including the Job Purpose section, into a results-oriented format.

JOB TITLE: Commercial Illustrator II

REPORTS TO: Marketing Manager/Commercial Illustrator I

JOB PURPOSE: Performs graphic-arts activities for publications and brochures relating to the company's products and activities.

WORK PERFORMED:

1. Creates artwork that will graphically illustrate the features of the company's products; this will include sketches, drawings, isometric displays, photographs, and color representations.
2. May be called upon to use a variety of photography equipment including both cameras and processing.
3. Assists in the paste-up and layout of brochures and publications.
4. May be called upon to make detail drawings, proposals, catalogs, and other graphics.
5. May be called upon to make charts, graphs, overlays, slides for formal presentations.
6. Assists in the coordination of graphic-arts needs with vendors and agencies.

Job-Description Writing Practice

Job Title: Commercial Illustrator

1. (*Result*) _____

   by (*Duties*) _____

   _____

2. (*Result*) _____

   by (*Duties*) _____

   _____

3. (*Result*) _____

   by (*Duties*) _____

   _____

4. (*Result*) _____

   by (*Duties*) _____

   _____

5. (*Result*) _____

   by (*Duties*) _____

   _____

6. (*Result*) _____

   by (*Duties*) _____

Here is the results-oriented version of the Commercial Illustrator job. Besides the results, verbs, and general editorial changes, notice the substitution of "through" and "using" for "by."

JOB TITLE: Commercial Illustrator II

REPORTS TO: Marketing Manager and Commercial Illustrator I

JOB PURPOSE: Represents the company's products by preparing layouts for publications and brochures.

JOB RESULTS:

1. Illustrates the features of the company's products by preparing sketches, drawings, and photographs as directed.
2. Produces illustrations by using photography equipment including cameras and processors.
3. Prepares layouts for printing by pasting up camera-ready copy and illustrations.
4. Produces formal presentations by preparing charts, graphs, and slides.
5. Maintains graphic-arts supplies by requisitioning from vendors.

Here are a few more improved job descriptions.

JOB TITLE: Executive Secretary

REPORTS TO: Vice President or Director

JOB PURPOSE: Facilitates the work of an executive of the company by performing secretarial and administrative duties.

JOB RESULTS:

1. Provides secretarial support for an officer of the company, by typing, taking dictation, and maintaining files.
2. Provides administrative support for supervisor by managing projects as authorized.
3. Acts for supervisor by initiating and answering correspondence within limits of authority.
4. Facilitates smoothly conducted meetings by making arrangements, preparing agenda, and acting as recording secretary as requested.
5. Prepares reports and presentations by collecting, assembling, and analyzing data and preparing information for use in graphics.
6. Administers a program such as the pension plan, the profit sharing plan, personnel recordkeeping, patent administration, or the insurance program by completing reports and clerical requirements.
7. Accomplishes secretarial and clerical work of the department by directing other secretaries and clerks.

JOB TITLE: Receptionist

REPORTS TO: Community and Public Relations Manager

JOB PURPOSE: Offers welcome and direction to guests and visitors by greeting and referring them.

JOB RESULTS:

1. Provides information and direction by greeting guests and visitors, contacting company employees when visitors arrive, and routing visitors to company offices.
2. Secures company premises by preventing trespassing into company offices by unauthorized persons.
3. Helps others by performing clerical duties such as sorting, filing, typing, and assembling reports.
4. Maintains lobby and reception area by arranging magazines and calling for janitorial services as needed.
5. Keeps switchboard open by filling in for switchboard operator as needed.

Project Analyzer (4.3)

Are your job descriptions duties-oriented or results-oriented?

_____

_____

How well are job results understood?

_____

_____

What would it take to get managers to think in terms of job results?

_____

_____

What training would be required to write job descriptions in a results-oriented style?

_____

_____

4.4 Strategic Planning

On your first quick walk through the book, record your initial thoughts on policy issues that will have to be decided.

_____

_____

_____

_____

_____

_____

Any notes on tactical procedures?

_____

_____

_____

_____

Chapter 5

Stating Performance Criteria in Four Dimensions

5.1 Reasons for a Four-Dimensional Performance-Criteria Profile

Managers and employees alike have been conditioned to use a one-dimensional performance scale that ranges in gradation from good to bad. The conditioning has been wrong, as we will see shortly. The problem is intensified when performance scales are substituted for pay scales so that pay budgets can be distributed from "a lot" to "a little." The relationship between job results and performance criteria can be conveyed more clearly and accurately with a different arrangement.

Magazine article after magazine article, book after book, have heralded the need for performance standards if performance management is to be successful. Yes, performance standards are essential—but standing alone, they frequently do not give enough information to ensure understanding of the performance possibilities in a situation. More criteria than just a standard are required to help employees understand—three more, in fact.

The job result, as shown in section 4.3, clarifies what the employee must accomplish. The four-dimensional performance-criteria profile clarifies performance possibilities by expressing them in specific job-language terms tied to the result; this reduces the interpretation errors resulting from generic labels and imprecise language. Personal interpretation of the scale is minimized.

For example, here is one job result for an employee who works on a kitchen food-tray line:

JOB RESULT: Prepares meals for delivery by placing food on trays.

For each job result, a four-dimensional profile of performance criteria is written. In our example, the performance-criteria profile might look as follows:

> *Performance Standard* [*what management wants to have happen*]: Trays are assembled and ready for delivery to the patient areas on schedule.
> *Problem* [*the effect when what management wants is not accomplished*]: Patients eat late, become upset, and complain.
> *Improvement* [*what an employee needs to learn/do in order to accomplish the results desired by management*]: Needs to organize activities in order to have all preparations completed before the tray line is scheduled to start; needs to read menu selections while trays are moving and memorize layout of serving table.
> *Performance Option* [*what an employee does who is giving management more that it desires*]: Finishes preparation for tray line early and helps co-workers; makes the tray line operate more efficiently by volunteering ideas and encouraging teamwork.

Words may fail to communicate clearly because of the structure in which they are presented. When a one-dimensional scale is used to appraise human performance from effective to ineffective, the rater must apply modifiers (adjectives and adverbs) to a single criterion to distinguish between levels of the criterion.

Let's look at a common (and real) example to understand the problem:

Outstanding:	Performance far exceeds the normal requirements of the position and leaves little room for further improvement in the job.
Superior:	Performance consistently exceeds that of most others in this behavior area, particularly others doing similar work.
Acceptable:	Performance is not harmful to the organization in this behavior, but the individual could be more effective if further improvements were made.
Marginal:	Performance in this behavior area must improve to meet the requirements of the position.

Notice, for instance, that the modifiers "far exceeds" and "consistently exceeds" in the scale do not establish a clear and precise meaning to help the rater and ratee understand the difference between the two.

Words may also fail to communicate when they do not mean the same thing, or at least nearly the same thing, to each person who reads them. Words are defined uniquely by each person according to his or her accumulation of life experiences. People are able to understand each other when the nuances of different definitions are not significant, or when they use more words to clarify what they mean.

The use of the generic word "performance" in the example scale raises the question of what specific performance is meant. Discussions about performance between manager and employee are useful only when they involve the use of specific job-language terms—say, accounting terms for accountants, or bus-driving terms for bus drivers.

Similarly, what the writer of the scale means by "normal requirements" of the job is anybody's guess.

Some statements are not only vague but decidedly distracting. "Is not harmful to the organization" and "Leaves little room for further improvement in the job" are backhanded support. These statements certainly do not motivate an employee to perform better.

When the definition specifies performance as compared to "most other employees in this behavior area, particularly others doing similar work," one has to ask why the writer singles out others doing *similar* work. Will there be comparisons with others who do dissimilar work? How would these comparisons be made? Would they be fair?

You would think that "acceptable" should be, well, acceptable, but according to the scale, acceptable means that the "individual could be more effective if further improvements were made." Interestingly, the one definition conspicuously absent from this scale is what the organization actually expects from its employees—the performance standard.

In the "marginal" category, that performance "must improve" at least gives the employee a warning that performance is inadequate. Unfortunately, there are no clues at all as to what behavior would help the employee improve.

The two major faults of this type of scale are that many of the words are subjective, not objective, and that they do not relate to a specific job. In addition, the top of this one-dimensional scale obviously describes better performance than the bottom. Employees being rated with this type of scale will naturally want to be rated as high on the scale as possible, even if their performance does not warrant it. Employees will want better ratings even more if the higher rating is tied directly to higher pay.

5.1.1 A Four-Dimensional View of Performance

Figure 5-1 shows the four-dimensional view of performance. As the figure suggests, the four views of management's expectations are tied together by the same job result. The performance profile should be read as an integrated set of different views of the same event, each view supporting the other to provide a harmonious totality. The purpose of the profile is to help managers and employees clarify job results required and performance expectations, and to provide a logical concept of performance management (see Figure 5-2).

Figure 5-1. Four dimensions of performance.

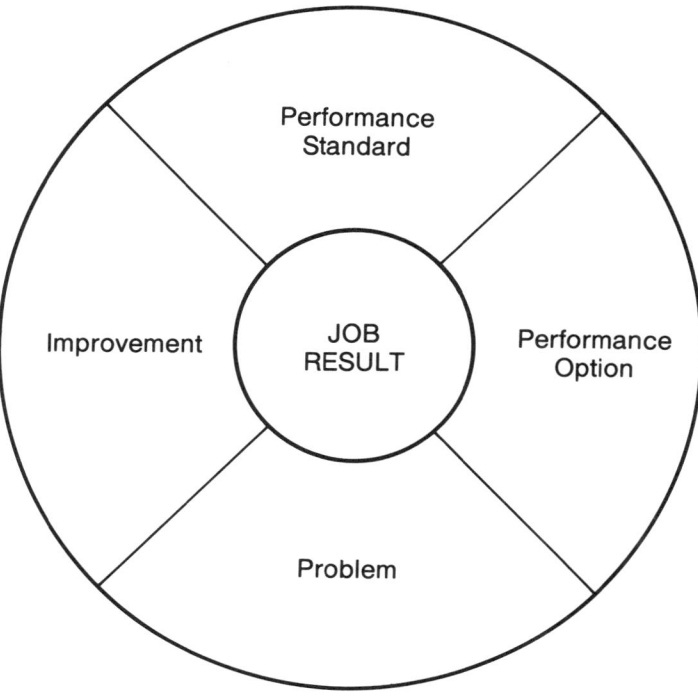

The *Performance Standard* is the central element of the profile, a clear statement of the effect when the job result is accomplished the way management wants it to be accomplished. It is the purpose of performance, or the result of behavior. In short, it is what management wants to have happen.

However, as we have all experienced, what is expected may not be clear until we state what is *not* expected.

The *Problem* states what goes wrong—the bad effect—if the Performance Standard is not met. It is what management does not want to have happen.

The Problem is presented immediately after the Performance Standard in the profile for reasons of communication. Sometimes we may not be able to express clearly in the Performance Standard what we want, but we can usually be *very* clear about the Problem we don't want. An employee who is problematic is at the lowest level of performance and is near, or in, disciplinary action.

Sometimes an employee does not perform up to the Performance Standard, but the performance is not so bad that it causes a Problem. The *Improvement* describes the knowledge, skill, or ability an employee *typically* needs in order to be able to perform up to the Performance Standard. Not every possible learning need has to be listed here, only a representative sample.

Figure 5-2. Job results and the performance-criteria profile.

A. Performance Requirement	B. Clarification Expectation	C. Learning Opportunity	D. Incentive	Levels of Performance
			Performance option	1. High
Job result	Performance standard			2. Expected
		Improvement		3. Somewhat below expectations
	Problem			4. Low

A. *Performance Requirement:* Performance-management communication between a manager and an employee begins when the manager describes the job results that must be accomplished by the employee.

B. *Clarification of Expectation:* The manager must also tell the employee how well the work must be performed, for the employee may have performance standards different from the organization's. Performance expectations should be stated in two ways: (1) "Do this" (Performance standard) and (2) "Don't let that happen" (Problem).

C. *Learning Opportunity:* When an employee does not perform quite up to the standard, the manager must tell the employee what new skills need to be learned and how to learn them in order to bring performance up to standard (Improvement).

D. *Incentive:* Recognizing that some employees will choose to perform better than the manager requires, the manager can encourage outstanding performance by identifying exemplary behaviors (Performance option).

"Improvement" is the designation for employees who are not performing up to standard but are not so ineffective that they are causing problems. Employees who need to improve their performance are not living up to the manager's expectations but do not warrant disciplinary action. The Improvement statement offers the manager and the employee guidance for the development of a corrective performance plan. Employees who are problematic certainly need to improve their performance, and their improvement is logically guided by the learning opportunities listed in the Improvement statement.

The assumption underlying the development of most rating scales is that employees who do not perform up to the standard intentionally choose to perform poorly. Although this may be true of some employees, the assumption in our Improvement category is that employees would perform better if they knew how.

Performance Option states what a model employee does that is above and beyond management's expectations. It is model performance worthy of imitation by other employees. It is a defined *opportunity* for employees to perform above and beyond the requirements of the Performance Standard, to earn recognition—and reward—if they so choose.

The profile, although presenting four views of the same job-result, is essentially based on only two conditions: expectations met (Performance Standard) or not (Problem). The other two conditions (Performance Option and Improvement) follow from this observation. The construction of the profile specifically avoids any middle or "average" degree common in odd-numbered scales.

Specific techniques are used to write each statement; instructions for writing them will be presented in section 5.2.

5.1.2 Relabeling the Profile

The four dimensions of the profile may be labeled as you prefer. Here are three options besides the terms used in this book:

	Option 1
Performance Standard	*Expected Performance*
Problem	*Critical Incident*
Improvement	*Corrective Action*
Performance Option	*Incentive Option*

Option 2	*Option 3*
Desired Effect	*What we want*
Unacceptable Outcome	*What we don't want*
Learning Opportunity	*What you need to learn*
Bonus Opportunity	*Better than what we want*

5.1.3 Inventory of Methods for Planning and Appraising Performance

Management may choose from a variety of methods to plan and appraise performance. The four most common methods are (1) Job Requirements, (2) Peer Comparison, (3) Personal Traits, and (4) Unstructured Systems. Each is based on different concepts and techniques. The categories are defined in Table 5-1.

Each method has advantages and disadvantages, depending on the situation in which it is applied. However, the principal reasons for systems failure are (1) the lack of relatedness between jobs and performance criteria and (2) inconsistent decisions among managers when they apply the criteria. The performance-management approach presented in this book is based on job requirements and a

Table 5-1. Methods for planning and appraising performance.

Area	*Method Used by Rater*
1. *Job requirements*	
a. Assessment center	Conducts laboratory simulations of actual job requirements.
b. Behavioral anchoring	Describes employee behaviors in terms ranging from effective to ineffective.
c. Committee review	If manager has contact with employee, achieves a consensus on a performance.
d. Critical incidents	Notes when they actually occur.
e. Essay	Writes an unstructured narrative of employee's performance, including strengths, limitations, and potential.
f. Objectives	Sets or negotiates performance targets, including plans to achieve them.
g. Work standards	Predetermines yardsticks of performance.
(1) Forced choice	• Selects yardsticks from specific choices that best describe the employee's performance.
(2) Mixed standards	• Selects performance yardsticks, but does not know value of yardsticks selected.
(3) Graphic range	• Selects from yardsticks arranged in a scale from acceptable to unacceptable.
2. *Peer comparison*	Measures performance as better than, the same as, or worse than the performance of other employees.
a. Paired	Measures performance against only one other person at a time; employees are finally ranked from best to worst.
b. Ranked	Measures performance against all other employees at the same time; employees are finally ranked from best to worst.
3. *Personal traits*	Assesses employee characteristics regarding how well they help or hinder job performance.
4. *Unstructured systems*	Establishes whatever system seems workable.
Systems may be augmented with these methods:	
a. Forced distribution	Only a predetermined number of employees can receive each rating.
b. Weighted	Factors rated can be valued so that each has a different impact on final rating.

graphic range of criteria augmented by a record of critical incidents; performance objectives set to meet specific job requirements; essay commentary; and weighting.

5.1.4 Investing Time To Save Time

Some managers revolt at the thought of having to write a separate profile for each job result instead of simply using a generic scale. Yes, we agree that there will be a lot of writing to inaugurate this structure, but the time spent brings big advantages.

Whereas managers waste huge amounts of time trying to translate generic scales into understandable job language and explaining their point of view to employees who dispute their opinion, a performance-criteria profile sets forth job-specific words before the work begins. Conversations are easier and less time-consuming. Once written, criteria need not be rewritten until the job changes.

Furthermore, the very nature of jobs is that they all differ from one another; therefore, they demand unique profiles. We train employees differently to do each job. Each job is expected to accomplish a different result. Logically, then, we cannot ignore this difference when job performance is appraised. Separate criteria must be designed for each different job.

The true value of the profile is the increased dialog between manager and employee about important job issues. More time is spent discussing performance, productivity, costs, quality, methods, and so forth—the issues that managers and employees should be talking about.

5.1.5 A Complete Job Description With Performance-Criteria Profiles

Here is a job description with related performance-criteria profiles for each job result to give you a complete picture of the document and the relationship between job description and performance criteria. Performance criteria may be printed on a separate document from the job description, or the two elements may be combined into one document. Additional excerpt examples from job descriptions are presented in Appendix A. Examples of universal profiles applicable to employees in all jobs, such as performance criteria for attendance, are presented in Appendix B.

JOB TITLE: PRESIDENT, COMMUNITY SERVICE AGENCY

1. Identifies community service requirements, both actual and anticipated, by active personal contact and rapport with potential and actual clients and other persons in a position to understand the needs of the community.

Performance Standard:	Community human service needs of families and individuals are met at the time that services are needed; information about community problems is assembled through a network of viable, accurate sources.
Problem:	Indices of family problems do not improve or are growing; potential clients seek help from other agencies that may not be able to give appropriate or equal help; clients ask for help which should, but is not, being delivered.
Improvement:	Needs to develop methods and contacts which identify symptomatic information about community problems.
Performance Option:	Perceives issues before they become public problems and community demands.

2. Addresses changing community and professional trends by inaugurating progressive programs.

Performance Standard:	Changes in client needs are anticipated and met with modern, accepted counseling/service methods.
Problem:	Complaints are voiced about the lack of appropriate, up-to-date services.
Improvement:	Needs to keep in touch with other professionals in social work and related disciplines who are working with new concepts in family and individual counseling/service.
Performance Option:	Participates in innovative studies and research which uncover unidentified needs or counseling/service methods.

3. Develops a competent, productive, and satisfied staff by supervising, directly and through delegation, all personnel; supervisory responsibilities include hiring, transferring, promoting, demoting, disciplining, counseling, coaching, appraising performance, and terminating, as well as providing educational and experiential growth opportunities and maintaining morale.

Performance Standard:	Agency maintains a reputation as a desirable place to work.
Problem:	Staff complains about personnel practices or seeks employment elsewhere.
Improvement:	Needs to study and apply personnel management practices.
Performance Option:	Helps employees accomplish innovations in their work.

4. Plans for and protects the physical and financial resources of the corporation by

budgeting, controlling, and auditing, and by initiating and participating in fund-raising activities, including the submission of grants.

Performance Standard:	Agency costs are within the overall budget, and new sources of funding are sought.
Problem:	Uncontrolled expenses exceed budget.
Improvement:	Needs to review requests and planned expenditures to discover out-of-line situations.
Performance Option:	Acquires additional funds.

5. Maintains Agency operations by formulating and enforcing program, operational, and personnel policies and procedures.

Performance Standard:	Agency staff solves routine problems independently.
Problem:	Clients and employees complain of disparate treatment.
Improvement:	Needs to identify issues that need corporate guidance or where guidance is unclear; needs to publish required policies or procedures.
Performance Option:	Perceives and addresses issues before they become problems.

6. Maintains the stability and reputation of the agency by complying with, or influencing the development of, legal and accreditation requirements.

Performance Standard:	Agency receives accreditation certificate.
Problem:	Agency is cited for deficiencies; clients lose confidence in the agency's ability to serve them.
Improvement:	Needs to study legal and accreditation requirements and make necessary changes to comply.
Performance Option:	Institutes changes that improve accreditation requirements and/or the accreditation process.

7. Maintains Agency credibility by working with the President and staff of the funding agencies, with other sponsoring groups, and with other related service agencies.

Performance Standard:	Agency maintains amenable and cooperative contacts with the funding agency, other sponsors, and related agencies.
Problem:	Agency does not receive funds for all programs; opportunities to contribute expertise are lost.
Improvement:	Needs to apply rapport-building techniques.
Performance Option:	Is recognized and sought out for creative collaboration.

8. Promotes agency image by ensuring that the community understands what program services are available, publicizing accomplishments, and conducting himself or herself according to a professional code of ethics.

Performance Standard:	Agency is perceived by the public and clients as needed and effective.
Problem:	Potential clients are not aware of the agency's services.
Improvement:	Needs to spend more time in the community explaining the agency's services.
Performance Option:	Receives compliments from clients and the community at large.

9. Contributes to the effectiveness of the Board of Directors by identifying short-term and long-range issues that must be addressed; providing information and commentary pertinent to the Board's deliberations; recommending options and courses of action, especially where professional considerations are involved; implementing directives; and recruiting candidates.

Performance Standard:	Board has necessary information to make informed decisions.
Problem:	Board's decisions are ill-informed.
Improvement:	Needs to study the Board's functions and discuss requirements with the Chair.
Performance Option:	Anticipates Board requirements and gathers appropriate information.

Project Analyzer (5.1)

What type of scale do you use to appraise performance now?

_____

_____

What reactions have you had to it from managers?

_____

_____

What reactions have you had to it from employees?

_____

_____

What are its strengths?

_____

_____

What problems have you had with your current system?

_____

_____

Have managers and employees disagreed over the interpretation of criteria?

_____

_____

_____

Have appraisal decisions been appealed because employees thought they were unfair?

_____

_____

_____

In all fairness to employees and managers, is the structure of the system, rather than the people who use it, at fault?

_____

_____

_____

5.2 Writing Instructions for the Four-Dimensional Performance-Criteria Profile

The performance-criteria profile is designed to produce a positive conversation about work performance between managers and employees. The key to the design is strict grammatical rules.

Try writing the Performance Standard first, because it is most closely tied to the job result, which you already have in the job description. The Performance Standard sets a reference for writing the other criteria. Sometimes, however, you will have a better understanding of another criterion—perhaps the Problem, which describes the outcome you don't want. Start with whatever criterion is clearest to you.

Remember, the four criteria are a single unit—four different perspectives of the same job result. If you are not certain what you are trying to describe in some criterion, look to the others for another perspective.

If the job result is not stated correctly, as when a job duty is mistaken for a job result, writing the Performance Standard will be difficult if not impossible. Thus, a struggle to state the Performance Standard may signal that the job result should be rewritten. When you view the job result and the Performance Standard together, writing one helps clarify the other.

5.2.1 Writing Performance Standards

Start writing the statement with a *noun*, and write in the present tense. Do not start with a verb or adverb or use modifiers that are imprecise (for example, "usually").

Here is a job result, as published among several in a job description, that we will use to write example performance criteria in this section:

JOB RESULT: Prepares typed letters, memos, reports, manuscripts, and other departmental correspondence and records by transcribing dictation, written notes, or printed matter.

The Performance Standard would be written *correctly* this way:

Documents are typed as dictated and returned without error on time.

It would be written *incorrectly* this way:

Types [*verb*] errorlessly and returns work quickly [*imprecise*].

The Performance Standard is written as a results statement—the condition that exists when the job result is accomplished. The Performance Standard specifically avoids describing the employee's behavior that produces the result. Behavioral statements focus the attention of the conversation on the employee instead of the work. That focus can be particularly damaging, as we will see soon when we look at the construction of the Problem statement.

The more tangible the job, the more tangibly the criterion can be stated—for example, frequency, time, number, speed, or errors allowed can be spelled out. Don't shy away from identifying less tangible human values, such as tact, but don't focus directly on the value. Instead, focus on what the value *produces*. Tact, for example, produces rapport or ameliorates disagreements. Don't focus on creativity; instead identify the production of new products or methods. Look at what you get, not what you do.

Sometimes, you will start to write a vague term, such as "promptly." Catch yourself and use the opportunity to clarify the condition. For example, "promptly" might be better stated as "by the third working day of the month." Still, you may find that it simply makes more sense to describe the condition you want as "on time" and make it clear that the deadline must be specified to an employee when work begins and kept up to date as circumstances change.

Consider the basic performance criteria as rather stable references of expectation that do not change much during the history of the job. Specific changes in expectations can usually be dealt with in performance plans for a specific performance period. For example, a Performance Standard for an accounts receivable clerk may require that "receivables are at the fewest possible days." A specific Performance Standard for the next performance period would state the exact target in number of days.

Writing Practice for Performance-Standard Statement

As instructions for writing each criterion are presented in this section, it will be helpful for you to practice writing the criterion. Follow the grammatical instructions (such as "start with a noun") *precisely*. A suggested solution will be presented at the conclusion of this practice exercise.

Here is a job result for you to use in this section:

Fills retail clerk vacancies by recruiting candidates from the company or from external sources.

Performance Standard: [*start with a noun*] _____

_____

_____

_____

_____

_____

Writing Tip: Study the job result. What is an observable event that tells you that the result has been accomplished? Do not start with a verb, because it forces you to write about employee behaviors.

Application Project for Performance-Standard Statement

Now select a job result from a job that you know well. Following the writing instructions, write the Performance Standard for this job result.

Job Result: _____

_____

_____

_____

Performance Standard: [*start with a noun*] _____

_____

_____

_____

5.2.2 Writing Problem Statements

Start writing each statement with a *noun.* Do not start with a verb. Do not merely state the opposite of the Performance Standard (for example, "Deadlines are met"/"Deadlines are not met"). Do not use modifiers (as in "Deadlines are *frequently* missed").

The Problem would be written *correctly* this way:

Time is wasted as documents must be returned for correction.

It would be written *incorrectly* this way:

Commits [verb] too many [modifier] errors and doesn't give work back soon [modifier] enough; does not type documents as dictated [opposite of Standard].

It is not always possible to identify all the Problems that might occur as a consequence of failing to produce up to the Performance Standard. The description of the Problem can be explained to employees as a representative indicator rather than an all-inclusive statement.

The Problem is intentionally not written in behavioral terms (that is, the duty or activity the employee does not perform) but instead is written in objective result terms (that is, the conditions that will exist after the employee performs the duty or activity).

Behavioral statements implicate the employee as the cause. Because these statements start with verbs, the implied subject of the sentence is the employee. Results statements are grammatically different; the subject of the sentence is the work, not the employee. To illustrate this point, here is an example:

[*Stated Behaviorally*]	[*Stated as Results*]
Does not meet deadlines	Deadlines are not met.

The differences can be subtle. It may be argued that "Does not meet deadlines" says the same thing as "Deadlines are not met." However, behavioral statements make the employee the *sole* reason for not meeting the deadline. Being so accused is likely to trigger a defensive reaction in the employee. Obviously, a variety of other factors may influence whether deadlines are met.

By focusing dialog on the result, the manager and the employee are able to look at the circumstances as two adults trying to understand what happened and find ways to prevent it from occurring in the future. Managers are more likely to be effective communicators when they start with the irrefutable, objective fact that the deadline was not met, and work back to the reasons for the deadline not being met. Conversations in behavioral terms put managers at a disadvantage when they confront employees about unmet job requirements.

Many people have been conditioned to become defensive when a problem has been created. Pointing to the few pieces produced (instead of pointing at the employee who presumably is slow to produce the pieces) gives the employee an opportunity to look at the situation and deduce why the expected number was not produced. Was the cause an external influence? The employee's choice? A lack of training? Inadequate supervision?

Writing Practice for Problem Statement

Job Result: Fills retail clerk position by recruiting candidates from the company or from external sources.

Problem: [*start with a noun*] _____

_____

_____

_____

    Writing Tip: It's easy to fall into the trap of writing something that is only the opposite of the Performance Standard. Keep asking yourself: What will go wrong if the standard is not met?

Application Project for Problem Statement

Continue with the job result that you selected.

Job Result: _____

_____

_____

_____

Problem: [*start with a noun*] _____

_____

_____

_____

5.2.3 Writing Improvement Statements

Start writing the statement with "Needs to . . ." Do not describe what a person should do "more" of or be "better" at, or what "knowledge of" or "understanding of" a subject is needed. Do not write personal statements aimed at getting a message to a certain person. Do not state the same as in the Performance Standard.

The improvement statement would be written *correctly* this way:

Needs to consult the dictionary for correct spelling of unfamiliar words; needs to review operation of dictation equipment; needs to learn or practice typing skills; needs to confirm special instructions.

It would be written *incorrectly* this way:

Needs to learn how to type better [*better*], understand [*understand*] instructions, not become defensive [*personal admonishment*] when suggestions are made on how to improve, and type documents as dictated [*same as Performance Standard*].

The Improvement Statement articulates a key concept of the profile. Some managers seem more intent on catching employees in the act of not performing their jobs than in teaching employees how to improve their job performance. Once employees are caught, the logical extension is to punish them for noncompliance.

The human theory behind the profile is that employees respond better when they perceive that their managers want them to learn more in order to perform better. The assumption guiding the Improvement criterion is that employees who do not perform well do not know *how* to perform well, not that employees deliberately choose to perform poorly.

Now, certainly, some employees are motivated by forces other than a desire to perform up to standard. However, a manager will generally obtain better performance from employees by making the positive assumption instead of the negative one. Furthermore, publishing typical learning requirements when performance falls below standard makes management's intent to foster learning that much more obvious.

Finally, the Improvement statement recognizes that employees are adult learners who can recognize their deficient performance, find out for themselves what they need to know by reading the published statements, and decide to learn what is required for better job performance.

In the example, an employee will be able to recognize when time is being wasted, because documents are being returned for correction. With the profile, the employee can review learning opportunities and choose the one that will correct the situation.

Writing Practice for Improvement Statement

Job Result: Fills retail clerk vacancies by recruiting candidates from the company or from external sources.

Improvement: [*start with "Needs to . . ."*] _____

_____

_____

_____

Writing Tip: Be as specific as you can when describing behaviors that will improve performance. Let the employee know exactly what he or she can learn in order to perform up to the standard. Some typical statements begin with "Needs to review and apply . . ." or "Needs to practice and demonstrate . . ." or "Needs to reorder priorities in order to . . ."

Application Project for Improvement Statement

Continue with the job result that you selected.

Job Result: _____

_____

_____

_____

Improvement: [*start with "Needs to . . ."*] _____

_____

_____

_____

5.2.4 Writing Performance Option Statements

Start writing the statement with a verb. Do not start with a noun. Do not state superlatives (as in "Makes the clearest presentation").

The performance option would be written *correctly* this way:

Recognizes incorrect information, grammar, or other errors and corrects them.

It would be written *incorrectly* this way:

Documents [*noun*] are always [*superlative*] typed perfectly [*superlative*]; does her [*sexist*] best [*superlative*] to help out and offer suggestions.

In some cases, the Performance Option may be defined as more of the same as the Performance Standard. For example, if the Performance Standard is 800 items produced per day, the Performance Option might be 1,000 items produced per day. However, the Performance Option is more likely to be qualitatively different from the Performance Standard. For example, if the Performance Standard is to total store receipts daily, the Performance Option may be to identify trends in store receipts. Sometimes, performance that is optional for an employee is the Performance Standard for the employee's manager, so look at that position for some ideas.

Performance Option statements are compliments to the employee, recognition of commendable performance. Statements begin with a verb in order to make the employee the subject of the sentence, because compliments mean more to a person when they are personal.

Writing Practice for Performance Option Statement

Job Result: Fills retail clerk vacancies by recruiting candidates from the company or from external sources.

Performance Option: [*start with a verb*] _____

_____

_____

_____

_____

Writing Tip: This is the role-model employee. Look to the manager's job for clues, because outstanding performers frequently do things for their manager so that the manager can get on with other responsibilities. You may start with "Anticipates . . ." or "Identifies the need for and recommends necessary changes or improvements . . ." or "Develops improved methods to . . ."

Application Project for Performance Option Statement

Continue with the job result that you selected.

Job Result: _____

_____

_____

_____

Performance Option: [*start with a verb*] _____

_____

_____

_____

Answer for the Writing Practice

Job Result: Fills retail clerk vacancies by recruiting candidates from the company or from external sources.

Performance Standard:	Position vacancies are filled from a selection of qualified candidates, with no lost job time.
Problem:	Work is interrupted; sales are lost; customers complain because of slow service.
Improvement:	Needs to identify employees who are interested in transferring into the retail clerk position; needs to identify labor market resources where candidates are likely to be found.
Performance Option:	Maintains a roster of candidates who are immediately available for work.

5.2.5 Examples of First and Edited Drafts of Performance Criteria

Here are several first drafts of performance criteria, followed by the edited versions, to demonstrate common mistakes made when writing performance criteria. Although you may wish to write the criteria perfectly for the first time you use them, such perfection is usually not achievable or necessary.

JOB TITLE: Receptionist [*original draft*]

JOB RESULT: Facilitates department communications through relationships with customers, co-workers, and others.

RELATED PERFORMANCE CRITERIA:

Performance Standard: Telephone is answered promptly and courteously and calls are handled or routed appropriately. Arrangements are made for the phone to be answered promptly at all times. Co-workers are treated with professional respect. Customers are treated with courtesy and respect.

Problem: Customers or co-workers complain of rude responses; telephones are not answered by the third ring; unresolved staff friction hampers teamwork of the department, and low staff morale results.

Improvement: Needs to be familiar with all aspects of telephone courtesy, needs to demonstrate a polite and courteous attitude to customers, co-workers, and others; needs to solicit direction from supervisor. Needs to be familiar with the concept of teamwork.

Performance Option: Strives to increase individual competence through continued improvement of verbal and interpersonal skills through continuing education and constructive exchange of knowledge and concepts.

JOB TITLE: Receptionist [*edited draft*]

JOB RESULT: ~~Facilitates~~ [Accomplishes] department [al work and] communications [by helping] ~~through relationships with~~ customers, co-workers, and others.

RELATED PERFORMANCE CRITERIA:

Performance Standard: Telephone is answered ~~promptly~~ [by third ring] and courteous[ly] [in a manner,] and calls are ~~handled or routed appropriately~~ [referred to the appropriate person]. Arrangements are made for the phone to be answered ~~promptly at all times~~ [in receptionist's absence]. ~~Co-workers~~ [All persons] ~~are treated with professional respect. Customers~~ are treated with courtesy and respect.

Problem: Customers or co-workers complain of rude responses [or inconvenience]; ~~telephones are not answered by the third ring;~~ unresolved staff friction hampers teamwork of the department, and low staff morale results.

Improvement: Needs to ~~be familiar with all aspects~~ [practice and apply techniques] of telephone courtesy, [and personal] ~~needs to demonstrate a polite and courteous attitude to customers, co-workers, and others~~; needs to ~~solicit direction~~ [seek advice] from supervisor [when the situation is unclear; apply concepts.] ~~Needs to be familiar with the concept of~~ teamwork.

Performance Option: ~~Strives to increase individual competence through continued improvement of verbal and interpersonal skills through continuing education and constructive exchange of knowledge and concepts.~~ [Serves as a resource to other people in the department to resolve conflicts.]

Job Title: Nursing Technician [*original draft*]

Job Result: Provides documentation on patient care activities, procedure and treatments performed and observations by completing the surgical checklist, using orderly task sheet, making appropriate notes in Nursing Notes regarding tasks to be performed; uses approved abbreviations.

Related Performance Criteria:

Performance Standard: Documentation is concise, accurate, and completed in a timely manner, in appropriate location.

Problem: Patient care cannot be substantiated, failure to follow patient needs and progress and increase legal risk to oneself and hospital decrease financial reimbursement.

Improvement: Needs to know medical abbreviations, learn proper information to record and proper location.

Performance Option: Maintains, reviews and updates unit manual.

Job Title: Nursing Technician [*edited draft*]

Job Result: ~~Provides documentation on patient care activities~~, procedure and treatments performed ~~and~~ observations by completing the surgical checklist, using orderly task sheet, making ~~appropriate~~ notes in Nursing Notes regarding tasks to be performed; uses approved abbreviations.

[handwritten edits: "Documents" inserted; "procedure's and"; "observations" circled; "performed." with "with" inserted]

Related Performance Criteria:

Performance Standard: Documentation is concise, accurate, ~~and~~ completed shortly after observation of performance, and recorded on the appropriate form. ~~in a timely manner, in appropriate location.~~

Problem: Patient care cannot be substantiated, ~~failure to follow patient~~ patient needs cannot be followed, and progress ~~and increase~~ legal risk to oneself and hospital ~~decrease~~ financial reimbursement is increased; is lost.

Improvement: Needs to ~~know~~ medical abbreviations, ~~learn proper information to record pertinent information; needs to review appropriate form for documentation record and proper location.~~ [handwritten: memorize and use] [handwritten: ∧ needs to identify and] [handwritten: record pertinent information; needs to review appropriate form for documentation]

[handwritten: Identifies need for and recommends necessary improvement in documentation procedure.]

Performance Option: ~~Maintains, reviews and updates unit manual.~~

JOB TITLE: Food Service Aide [*original draft*]

JOB RESULT: Contributes to patient satisfaction by preparing and delivering late trays.

RELATED PERFORMANCE CRITERIA:

Performance Standard: Late trays are correctly assembled and delivered to nursing units as requested.

Problem: Patients receive incorrect or delayed trays.

Improvement: Needs to concentrate on assembly and delivery of late trays. Needs to check tray for correct contents before delivery.

Performance Option: Helps others with late trays. Notices and corrects late tray errors prior to delivery. Notifies nursing staff of tray arrivals.

JOB TITLE: Food Service Aide [*edited draft*]

JOB RESULT: ~~Contributes~~ to patient satisfaction by preparing and delivering late trays. [handwritten: Serves meals] [handwritten: ∧s]

RELATED PERFORMANCE CRITERIA:

Performance Standard: Late trays are ~~correctly~~ assembled and delivered to nursing units as requested.

Problem: Patients ~~receive incorrect or delayed trays~~. [handwritten: are hungry and dissatisfied, and they complain.]

Improvement: ~~Needs to concentrate on assembly and delivery of late trays~~. Needs to check tray for correct contents before delivery.

Performance Option: Helps others with late trays. Notices and corrects late tray errors prior to delivery. Notifies nursing staff of tray arrivals.

JOB TITLE: Engineering Coordinator [*original draft*]

JOB RESULT: Work orders are prepared for dissemination by reviewing each order for required work, establishing estimate of completion time, and entering information into the database.

RELATED PERFORMANCE CRITERIA:

Performance Standard: Database is noticeably complete. Work orders contain accurate information. Time estimates are accurate.

Problem: Workers become confused on what the job is. Information is not available for responding to requestor inquiries.

Improvement: Needs to review relationships of department function interactions. Needs to take initiative with requestors for better details of need. Needs to take more care in interpreting input and seek collaberation with management to improve alignment with goals.

Performance Option: Actively sustains high level of detail and accuracy in record keeping and analysis. Actively searches out, suggests improvements, and successfully complete changes to procedures. Actively instructs peers in proper documentation procedures.

JOB TITLE: Engineering Coordinator [*edited draft*]

JOB RESULT: ∧ Work orders ~~are prepared~~ for ~~dissemination~~ by reviewing each order for required work, ~~establishing~~ estimate of completion time, and entering information into the database.

Prepares ... *distribution* ... *-ing*

RELATED PERFORMANCE CRITERIA:

Performance Standard: Database is ~~noticeably~~ complete. Work orders ~~contain ac-curate information~~ are verified. Time estimates are ~~accurate.~~ calculated correctly.

Problem: Workers ~~become~~ are confused ~~on what the job is~~ about the work to be done. Information is not available for responding to requestor inquiries.

Improvement: Needs to review ~~relationships of~~ interaction between department ~~function interactions~~ s. Needs to ~~take initiative with~~ ask requestors for ~~better~~ complete details of need. Needs to ~~take more care in interpreting~~ study input and ~~seek~~ collaberate ~~collaberation~~ with management ~~to improve alignment with goals~~ as needed.

Performance Option: ~~Actively sustains high level of detail and accuracy in record keeping and analysis. Actively~~ searches out and suggests improvements, and successfully complete ~~s~~ changes to procedures. ~~Actively~~ instructs peers in proper documentation procedures.

JOB TITLE: Payroll Clerk [*original draft*]

JOB RESULT: Prepares payroll by tabulating timecards and noting backup information.

RELATED PERFORMANCE CRITERIA:

Performance Standard: Timecards are consistently completed in accordance with organization policy.

Problem: Inaccurate interpretation of organization policy or timecard notation has serious effect on staff satisfaction.

Improvement: Needs to become familiar with policies and consistently follow procedures, seeking assistance as needed.

Performance Option: Proposes new methods for record maintenance. Recommends new system on policy methods.

JOB TITLE: Payroll Clerk [*edited draft*]

JOB RESULT: Prepares payroll by tabulating timecards and noting backup information.

RELATED PERFORMANCE CRITERIA:

Performance Standard: Timecards are ~~consistently~~ completed in accordance with

organization policy.

Problem: ~~Inaccurate interpretation of organization policy or timecard notation has~~ Timecards must be recalculated.

~~serious effect on~~ staff satisfaction. is dis-~ied ⊙

Improvement: Needs to ~~become familiar with~~ review and apply policies and ~~consistently follow~~ pro-

cedures, seeking assistance as needed.

Performance Option: Proposes ~~new~~ improved methods for record maintenance. Recommends

~~new~~ improved system on policy methods.

Remember, criteria will probably never be as precise as we want them. Managers and employees will occasionally disagree on what is or was expected. At the beginning of section 5.1, we looked at a common example of words failing to convey their writer's meaning. The performance-criteria profile cannot eliminate all communication problems between managers and employees, but it is designed to minimize them.

The profile gives the manager more time to think about *how* to say what he or she wants to say instead of deciding *what* to say. The *what* is already written. The profile opens doors to conversations and makes clarity, not measurement, the focus of attention.

Editing can be made a part of introducing the program to managers and employees. Certainly, during the initial writing process, the profiles can be edited by human resources specialists, trainers, senior managers, and consultants. After that round of editing, however, the profiles should be used by managers and employees in dry-run conferences. Managers and employees can test the accuracy of the words by using them in an actual conversation—except that the results will not be used for actual performance-management decisions.

Here is the complete four-dimensional performance-criteria profile for the job result we discussed throughout section 5.2:

JOB RESULT: Prepares typed letters, memos, reports, manuscripts, and other departmental correspondence and records by transcribing dictation, written notes, or printed matter.

Performance Standard:	Documents are typed as dictated and returned without error on time.
Problem:	Time is wasted as documents must be returned for correction.
Improvement:	Needs to consult the dictionary for correct spelling of unfamiliar words; needs to review operation of dictation equipment; needs to learn or practice typing skills; needs to confirm special instructions.
Performance Option:	Recognizes incorrect information, grammar, or other errors and corrects them.

5.2.6 A Final Thought on Language

Human language, without reference to real experience, is inadequate. The novice cook may read, "Blend the ingredients well," "Heat over a moderately high heat," or "Cook until tender," but rare is the person who can read a recipe and, without experience, prepare a fine meal. A chef's training includes the experience of recognizing when ingredients are blended well, when heat is moderately high, when meat is cooked to tender, and so forth.

Although we can correct vague language by being more precise, we should not be so precise that we lose flexibility. The same food ingredients may be assembled time after time according to the recipe, but they will not be identical in freshness, texture, or consistency. Thus, preparation for each meal is different depending on the quality of the ingredients. Blending, for instance, will occur at a slightly different rate each time ingredients of a different quality are mixed.

Similarly, people may be the same "ingredients" in all organizations, but they apply themselves differently to the work at hand. Performance criteria point us in the direction of expected results, but, given the quality of the participants, the manager and the employee must adapt the specific way the work will proceed.

Project Analyzer (5.2)

If you use performance standards in your performance-management program now, are they written objectively or subjectively?

_____

_____

Do vague and imprecise words confuse intended meaning?

_____

_____

Is a clear statement of unacceptable performance in each job available to the job-incumbent?

_____

_____

What resources do employees have to guide improved job performance?

_____

_____

Do managers view appraisal as catching and correcting bad performance, or maintaining expected performance and encouraging outstanding performance?

_____

_____

Do employees know what to do if they want to win extra reward and recognition?

_____

_____

5.3 The Performance-Management-Conference Form

The job description and its related performance-criteria profiles are the key documents that guide the performance-management conference. Regardless of where and how the documents are presented, they must be included in the process.

Preferably, the job description and the performance-criteria profiles are included together in the form.

Figure 5-3 shows a model form that you can adapt to your organization's needs and preferences. If you prefer not to print the full job description and profiles on this form, an abbreviated form is presented in Figure 5-4. When using the abbreviated form, the job description and the profiles are simply included in the process as supporting documents.

Figure 5-3. Model performance-management-conference form.

PERFORMANCE-MANAGEMENT CONFERENCE

Name: _____   Conference date: _____
Job title: _____   Type of conference: _____
Department: _____   Date of hire: _____
Manager: _____

Purpose

Our organization works best when managers and employees have a common and consistent understanding of:

1. Work that needs to be accomplished
2. How it will be done
3. The criteria used for examining work performance
4. Whether or not performance has achieved the agreed-upon plan

We believe that employees are entitled to know how they are performing in relation to expectations, what they can do to excel, and what they must do to improve if improvement is required. Employees should know this, not just once a year, but throughout the year.

However, formal Performance-Management Conferences are held at least once a year to review organizational and personal requirements and to develop performance plans to meet organizational and personal objectives. The conference is an opportunity for the manager and the employee to exchange opinions about the employee's job performance and the help offered by the manager. Employees are encouraged to write their reactions to the conference in Section IV (Comments) of this form.

For new employees, conferences will be held at the end of 30, 60, 90, and 180 days following employment to help them become thoroughly familiar with job expectations.

Performance will be examined according to criteria related to each major job result as published on a job description (Section I), as well as to other, universal criteria applicable to all employees (Section II).

Performance is defined on four levels: (1) Performance Standard; (2) Problem; (3) Improvement; and (4) Performance Option.

Figure 5-3. (*continued*)

An employee is entitled to know which definition best matches his or her job performance for each job responsibility. For each responsibility or job result, the level that best matches the employee's performance for the appraisal period is marked. When *Improvement* or *Problem* is marked, a specific performance plan, including steps required to improve or correct performance together with target dates for reviewing progress is required. The four levels are defined as follows:

1. *Performance Standard:* Job performance meets management's expectations.
2. *Problem:* Job performance is seriously below expectations; comments are required in the space provided for this purpose to specify what behavior must be stopped, what must be learned, when it must be learned, and what consequences will result from noncompliance.
3. *Improvement:* Job performance must be improved; comments are required in the space provided to specify what the employee needs to learn in order to bring performance up to management's expectations, how it will be learned, and when it will be learned.
4. *Performance Option:* Job performance exceeds expectations; employee is a role model for other employees.

Are the job description and the performance criteria up-to-date?   Yes □   No □
If not, edit and attach revisions.

Section I
Job Description and Related Performance Criteria

Job Description

---

1. Maintains boilers and emergency generators by installing new equipment, repairing defective equipment, and conducting preventive maintenance inspections.

    □ *Performance Standard:* Power is provided in the building as needed. Inspections are documented.

    □ *Problem:* Equipment requiring power is unable to function and production is lost; deadlines are missed.

    □ *Improvement:* Needs to study and follow equipment maintenance manuals; needs to sudy causes of equipment failures; needs to study time-management techniques in order to conduct inspections.

    □ *Performance Option:* Anticipates extraordinary power requirements and possible breakdowns; maintains supply of hard-to-get parts.

    Learning Plan, or comments:[1] _____

[Insert all other categories that are appropriate to include.]

Figure 5-3. (*continued*)

(The job description and performance criteria profile are the base from which performance plans are written to meet current organization objectives for a specific performance period. See Figure 5-5 for an example of a performance planning format. See Chapter 7 (Figure 7-1) for an example of a complete plan.)

Section II
Universal Performance-Criteria Profiles
Applicable to All Jobs

1. Punctuality
   PS = Work starts on time.
     P = Other employees' schedules are disrupted.
      I = Needs to reduce late time.
   PO = Takes extra precautions to be on time.
   Learning Plan or comments: _____

_____

[*Insert all other categories that are appropriate to include.*][2]

Section III
Performance Summary

A. Enter number of items marked as
   Performance Standards Met: _____
   Problematic: _____
   Improvement Needed: _____
   Performance Option: _____

B. Written Summary: (In your own words, briefly summarize the employee's performance during the performance period, including the employee's greatest strengths.)[3]

_____

_____

_____

C. Career planning interest[4] pertinent to current performance: _____

_____

_____

Figure 5-3. (*continued*)

Section IV
Employee Comments, Authorization, and Approval[5]

This appraisal and plan has been discussed with me, and I would like to say: (You are not required to write any statement.)

_____

_____

_____

_____

_____

_____

_____

_____

_____

_____

Employee's signature: _____   Date: _____

Manager's signature: _____   Date: _____

Reviewer's signature: _____   Date: _____

The information on this form is confidential. The information is for the express purpose of identifying and guiding the employee's job performance in the current job or on subsequent jobs within the organization. The information may not be divulged to other persons who have no need to know it. Any release of information can be made only with the approval of the employee.[6]

---

1. An example of a completed Learning Plan, or comments, is presented in Chapter 8, Section 8.1.1.
2. In the same way that job-specific profiles may be printed as a part of this form or in separate documents, the universal profiles may be printed on this form or in separate supporting documents. Only those profiles applicable to all jobs are reproduced on the form. Other categories besides punctuality, that might be included are listed in Figure 5-4.
3. An example of a completed written Summary is presented in Chapter 8, section 8.1.2.
4. A space to check whether the employee is or is not promotable is uncalled for on the conference form. A commitment to promote may be premature for the manager to make at this time. The opposite choice (unpromotable), even if true, is particularly bad. Career planning—a broader topic than promotability—is useful and should be made the subject for a separate conference.
5. The Employee Comments section is reviewed in section 11.1.1, Guideline #5.
6. Because fair-information practices vary from state to state, any statement about confidentiality should be reviewed with an attorney.

Figure 5-4. Abbreviated performance-management-conference form.

PERFORMANCE MANAGEMENT CONFERENCE

Name: _____   Conference date: _____
Job title: _____   Type of conference: _____
Department: _____   Date of hire: _____
Manager: _____

Purpose

Be sure to review the Statement of Purpose of Performance Management found in the organization policy manual.

Are the job description and the performance criteria up-to-date?   Yes ▫   No ▫
If not, edit and attach revisions.

Section I
Job Description and Related Performance Criteria

Job Result No. From Job Description	*Performance Level* (circle one)	*Learning Plan or Comments* (required where Improvement or Problem Is indicated; use extra pages where necessary)
No. _____	PS P I PO	_____
		_____
		_____
		_____
No. _____	PS P I PO	_____
		_____
		_____
		_____

Figure 5-4. (*continued*)

No. _____ PS P I PO _____

_____

_____

_____

Section II
Universal Performance-Criteria Profiles
Applicable to All Jobs[1]

1. Punctuality	PS___	P___	I___	PO___
2. Attendance	PS___	P___	I___	PO___
3. Personal appearance	PS___	P___	I___	PO___
4. Supplies and equipment	PS___	P___	I___	PO___
5. Work-area cleanliness	PS___	P___	I___	PO___
6. Employee/visitor safety	PS___	P___	I___	PO___
7. Confidentiality	PS___	P___	I___	PO___
8. Security	PS___	P___	I___	PO___
9. Planning	PS___	P___	I___	PO___
10. Organizing	PS___	P___	I___	PO___
11. Decision making/problem solving	PS___	P___	I___	PO___
12. Downward communications	PS___	P___	I___	PO___
13. Development of subordinates	PS___	P___	I___	PO___
14. Cost control/budgeting	PS___	P___	I___	PO___

1. Only those profiles applicable to all jobs are reproduced on the form.

Figure 5-5. Performance planning format.

Our Objective Is: _____

_____

Our Performance Criteria Are:

   a. What do we want? _____

     _____

   b. What don't we want? _____

     _____

   c. What snags can be anticipated? _____

     _____

   d. What's better than what we want? _____

     _____

What Resources Do We Need? _____

_____

Who Does What? _____

_____

When Do We Check Progress? _____

_____

Project Analyzer (5.3)

What forms do you use to manage performance now?

_____

_____

What reactions to them have you had from managers?

_____

_____

What reactions to them have you had from employees?

_____

_____

What are the strong points of the forms?

_____

_____

What problems have you had with the forms?

_____

_____

In all fairness to employees and managers, is the form, rather than the people who use it, at fault?

_____

_____

_____

How could you use the model Performance-Management-Conference Form to improve or revise the system you now have in place?

_____

_____

_____

5.4 Strategic Planning

On your first quick walk through the book, record your initial thoughts on policy issues that will have to be decided.

_____

_____

_____

_____

_____

_____

Any notes on tactical procedures?

_____

_____

_____

_____

Chapter 6

Interpreting Performance Standards

6.1 Developing Consensus Among Managers on the Meaning of Performance Standards

Each manager has a unique set of values. No amount of training will change a manager's personal values if he or she does not want to change them. However, the degree to which the personal values of managers can be blended with the organization's values determines how well performance management works. Managers must interpret and apply performance standards consistently, though not identically, throughout the organization.

Organizations fail to develop consensus when they don't allow thorough discussion of the options, don't recognize that their managers have individual value systems, or don't communicate to new managers the values developed in the past by other managers.

Large organizations can use task forces throughout the organization to elicit information and opinion. Videotapes can be made of these discussions and used to initiate discussions among other managers instead of merely issuing written policy.

What may seem obvious when you state performance criteria may not be so easily applied. What may seem easy to apply may not be so easily stated. The following case study illustrates how consensus among managers was developed in a small, new organization where all the managers could meet in face-to-face discussions. The managers in this organization were examining the criterion of *attendance.*

The organization stated the universal attendance-criteria profile as follows:

Performance Standard: Required work is accomplished each day.

Problem: Absences cause a serious disruption to work flow.

Improvement: Needs to reduce absences.

Performance Option: Takes extra precautions to be present.

In this organization, employees received pay for two weeks' vacation, five days' sick leave, two days' funeral leave, five days' jury duty, and two weeks' military-reserve duty.

6.1.1 Performance Option

In meeting after meeting, the managers struggled with issues such as: Should the Performance Option mean perfect attendance? Is perfect attendance an option or luck? If the employee is absent to the extent of the benefits provided, can he or she still qualify for the Performance Option, or would that encourage employees to take five days' sick-leave pay, whether or not they were ill?

The managers needed to decide: What does the organization really want to communicate to employees about attendance and accomplishing the organization's work? How many absences are too many? How do we deal with the employee who had perfect attendance for four years but this year had major surgery and was out three months on disability? It may seem cruel, for instance, to tell that employee that his three-month absence caused a serious disruption of work flow when he nearly died. Should we praise him instead for stockpiling his sick leave for a time when he truly needed it? Still, he wasn't at work, so we can't treat him as if he was.

Do you begin to see the complexities with a seemingly obvious criterion?

In discussion, the manager of an 80-person department was far more laissez-faire about attendance than the manager of a three-shift, three-person department. The manager of the 80-person department had to do a little shuffling of personnel when someone was absent, but the manager of the three-person department frequently had to work a double shift when an employee was absent. These two managers had different values because of their different environments and because of the different impact of absenteeism on them personally.

The manager of the three-person department suggested that the Performance Option should be reserved for employees who put in extra time, or gave weekends to solving problems that would have caused downtime on Monday. Other managers argued that their people could never reach Performance Option under such a definition, because their departments never had that kind of need to be met.

After much agonizing, the managers finally arrived at a consensus, of sorts: The Performance Option demanded perfect attendance. You may be thinking, that's only attainable by a few employees. Yes, it is, but that's the point of the Performance Option, these manager decided; it has to stretch employees. If anyone can achieve it with only a little extra effort, it is not outstanding performance, by definition, they said.

6.1.2 Performance Standard

Some managers argued that the Performance Standard meant a day or two of work missed; some thought that three was O.K.; some said four; and some were willing to accept five. Still others thought a number couldn't be used at all. As you might expect, the manager of the three-person department felt that any missed workday was a Problem.

Because the company allowed five days paid sick leave, the managers felt compelled to treat absences up to the five-day benefit as meeting the Performance Standard.

But then, what about employees who were away for weeks on disability? Recall the employee who had major surgery. Work was definitely disrupted. One manager could not agree that this employee should be marked less than the Performance Standard; he argued for a difference between planned and unplanned disruptions of work flow. Because the employee scheduled the surgery, the manager was able to plan to offset the impact of the employee's absence.

An employee who reports for work one day but may or may not report for work the next gives the manager no opportunity to plan. Yes, an employee could have emergency surgery for which there could be no planning, but at least the recuperative time is something definite to plan for. Excused absences became the key to defining the Performance Standard for these managers.

These managers didn't realize it at the time, but they were accepting their responsibility, as well as their right, to manage. If an employee missed work on the basis of a day here or there, and those numbers started to mount up, it was the manager's responsibility to correct the situation. Even though needs varied by department, generally accepted values were being developed for the organization, and consistency would be the rule.

In another organization, where consistency about attendance had not been established, an employee requested a transfer to another department. When the two department heads conferred, the receiving manager told the transferring manager, "You may allow this kind of attendance in your department, but the candidate's attendance does not meet my department's standards." What do you say to the employee who didn't get the transfer? "Your attendance is O.K. for Department A but not good enough for Department B"? This is confusing not only for the employee but for all other employees.

6.1.3 Improvement

The managers in the first organization we discussed had little difficulty defining which employees would be marked as needing Improvement ("Needs to reduce absences"). The employee who missed work on a sporadic basis, giving the manager no way to anticipate the absence and no time to plan for it, qualified easily for this category. Then the managers had to decide whether they would allow an employee more absences than the benefit program (five days) and still mark the employee as meeting the Performance Standard. They decided that more than five days' absence meant that Improvement was required.

How many days beyond defined benefits would be interpreted as needing Improvement? Where would the cutoff be before the number of days became a Problem? The managers concluded that Improvement meant from one to five days beyond the defined sick-days benefit of five days, for a total of six to ten sick-days' absence. This would be sufficient, they reasoned, not to penalize the employee who caught an occasional cold. Some hard-nosed managers still felt that once an employee exceeded the five-day level of benefits, he or she was a Problem.

But what about the employee with the ten-day virus, the managers wondered, who missed fewer days of work than the medically disabled person yet couldn't meet the Performance Standard? If the employee with the ten-day virus had a solid record of attendance, Improvement still should be marked they decided but the rating could be softened through explanation in the *Learning Plan or comments* space provided on the conference form—say: "Except for a ten-day virus absence in this performance period, attendance has met the Performance Standard."

If you wonder how you will relate the decisions these managers made to your organization, you are beginning to understand the issue of blending personal values with organizational values, and the hard work it takes for an organization to be consistent.

6.1.4 Problem

In our example, an attendance Problem was defined as "over ten days missed." Why ten? Because this is the answer these managers decided upon, together. Your company could decide on any number. The number itself is not important. What is important is that employees understand what the organization's values are, and that managers are able to administer the organization's values without sacrificing their own. Managers can still talk to employees about the needs of the individual department, and the differing impact of attendance among departments, yet apply the criteria in a way that is consistent with the ratings by fellow managers.

6.1.5 Intangible Standards

Establishing and maintaining organizational consistency is far more complex when the performance criteria involve intangibles. Attendance is relatively easy. How can two managers supervising different groups of receptionists in a health-care facility compare intangible values for greeting patients when they arrive for their appointment? The approach is not so different from the approach used by the managers who defined attendance together.

In the first organization we discussed in this section, the managers first worked together to write the performance-criteria profile:

Performance Standard:	Patients are welcomed to the office.
Problem:	Patients complain about the way they are greeted, or the way information is requested from them.
Improvement:	Needs to ask questions to understand patient's situation; needs to observe and respond to problems that patients appear to have; needs to demonstrate personal interest in patients by smiling, engaging them in conversation, making eye contact.
Performance Option:	Verbally reaches out to patients who are distressed when they arrive for their appointment.

Next, the two managers compared their interpretations of a receptionist who met the Performance Standard. They were encouraged by their manager to visualize successful performance and state their perceptions. (You would benefit by taking a few moments to think through this process yourself, and then compare your opinion with what the managers in this organization decided.)

These managers felt that an employee would meet their expectations by: smiling, making eye contact, engaging the patient in pleasantries, and welcoming the patient to the medical facility as they would to their home.

The managers defined a Problem as: complaints from patients about rudeness, briskness, inattentiveness, or curtness by the receptionist; or patients not relaxed when they see their doctor; or patient satisfaction surveys that rate welcome by receptionists as "poor."

For Improvement, the managers specified the behaviors they had already identified for the Standard. Employees who needed to improve typically did not use these rapport-building techniques. (From your personal experiences, think of the receptionist who only looks up for a moment as if interrupted from other duties, briefly acknowledges your presence, and perfunctorily checks you in. You wish that you were being checked out.)

To attain the Performance Option, the managers wanted the receptionist to go the "extra smile," to sense patient distress, anxiety, and fear, and to alleviate these feelings by verbally and emotionally reaching out to the patient—the kind of performance that frequently elicits compliments.

It's easy to agree that a receptionist should smile. How many times in a conversation should he or she smile—once, twice, continually? What one person views as friendly, another may perceive as forward.

We have tried, mistakenly, to measure human performance explicitly. We can easily measure the number of water meters an employee reads, but we cannot measure as easily the rapport a receptionist establishes. We are a technological society. We search for quantifiable measurements in every aspect of life, but we have erred. It is a worthy goal, however, to bring the extremes of human performance into a reasonable range of understanding, to help two human beings improve the prospect of understanding each other. Nonetheless, we cannot guarantee that two people, observing the same event, will describe the event in identical terms.

Having managers observe each other's subordinates and talk about various perceptions of the same behavior and results achieved is one of the best approaches to establish criteria and maintain consistent application. Too many managers work in a vacuum, never realizing how much help they can be to one another.

In one organization, each manager selected the written performance appraisals of certain of his or her employees—a superstar, a problem employee, and an employee who was difficult to read. The managers then observed each other's employees perform their jobs, without knowing which employee was which. The managers then compared notes to develop a consensus about interpreting the criteria. Sometimes, observing employees is awkward and inconvenient, and case-study discussions will have to suffice instead.

A great deal of work? Definitely! This process separates the managers who want to manage from those who only want to be called managers without performing the necessary work. Learning about each other's values is a *growth opportunity* for each manager. An organizational commitment to manage performance fairly means that managers must put a great deal of effort into establishing and administering performance criteria, and then making sure that employees understand the criteria.

Managers may complain at first: "I haven't got the time to spend on this." The question for these managers is: Do you want to spend your time preparing for performance, or chasing around picking up the pieces when employees don't perform the way you want them to? A clear performance-criteria profile puts the issues on the table early and points employees in the direction the organization wants to go. Without clear communication up front, employees are free to interpret criteria as they wish, which means that managers (and customers) will suffer the consequences.

Once managers accept the difference between chasing behaviors and accomplishing results, they will find the time to prepare for performance, and will then build consensus among employees about the values imbedded in performance standards. For some managers, waiting to deal with behavior until it appears seems to be easier than anticipating performance problems, because then the behavior can be directly confronted. However, waiting locks a manager into a style of reaction instead of proaction. By being forced to discuss criteria up front with employees, managers soon realize the less-than-advantageous implications of only reacting to employee behavior when it occurs.

6.1.6 Exchanging Opinions

In one other example organization, a performance standard for managers states: "Employees are prepared to accomplish job results at the completion of the 'get-acquainted' period, and throughout their employment." The senior managers who were to use this criterion to appraise the performance of their subordinate managers wondered together in a meeting how they would apply the standard. How will we know that employees are prepared? they asked. Here is some of their dialog.

MANAGER 1: Obviously, we can tell that employees are prepared to do the work if the work gets done.

MANAGER 2: But other influences besides the preparation of the employee may determine whether or not work gets done.

MANAGER 3: Is it fair to hold all managers equally accountable when some jobs are more difficult and more time-consuming to prepare for than other jobs?

MANAGER 1: The work still has to get done. If some job preparation is more difficult and more time-consuming, then we have to put more resources into the preparation. It's the manager's responsibility to come to us and request more resources in order to get the job done.

MANAGER 2: So, if other influences prevent the work from being done, and if we can identify those influences, then we know that the problem was not unprepared employees and we would not hold the manager accountable.

MANAGER 4: Maybe we would hold the manager accountable instead for not identifying and dealing with the outside influences.

MANAGER 3: Wait, we only require in the standard that the "employees are prepared," not that the work is accomplished. "Work is accomplished" is stated as the performance standard for a different job responsibility. Maybe we ought to think about testing employees to determine whether or not they are prepared.

MANAGER 1: You have a point there, although the proof of the pudding is in the eating. Testing is O.K., and maybe we can use a test at the end of the get-acquainted period, but some people can do very well on a test and yet not do well in the actual job situation.

MANAGER 3: You're right. We should look at both tests and actual job performance. So, the performance standards for each employee's job become the manager's performance standards.

In this conversation, the senior managers learned about each other's point of view and came to a helpful agreement on what was important to them. Even from this brief conversation example, the style of some of the managers begins to emerge. The first manager focused on the end result of preparation and helped some of the other managers who were not quite thinking in a results-oriented way.

As the managers are talking among themselves about the meaning of performance criteria, each manager learns from the discussion. While it is important that the words of the performance standard and the other dimensions of the performance criteria are carefully chosen, it is equally important to recognize that the process of discussion *is* the opportunity to examine different opinions. The examination *is* the learning. The final interpretation among the managers *is* the consensus.

The process is not static. The managers will meet again and again to discuss the criteria. They will have their interpretations tested in the appraisals they write. Some of the interpretations will be incomplete or wrong. The managers and the organization will learn from experience. The managers will adjust their thinking when faced with new demands. Still, as they act together, they are in consensus.

In still another example organization, a group of managers looked at a Performance Standard for *subordinate development*: "Subordinates are able to accept new and more challenging assignments." Here is some of the discussion that ensued:

MANAGER 1: Does this mean that a subordinate must be promoted before the standard can be met?

MANAGER 2: I hope not, because there is no job for my employees to be promoted into in the normal job progression.

MANAGER 3: So, new and more challenging assignments does not necessarily mean new and more challenging jobs. If we can document that an employee is doing more on the job, then the employee is meeting the standard.

MANAGER 1: Not just more work, but a higher level of work. For example, something that you do now but instead pass on to your employee because the employee is now capable of doing it.

MANAGER 4: Is the standard met if the employee is *able* to do the work, but someone else is already doing the work and it isn't appropriate to transfer the work to the employee who is now capable of doing it? The performance standard says, "are *able* to accept new and challenging assignments."

MANAGER 5: I don't think that's the point of the standard. I think we want to pay for people who are not only *able* but actually *do* accept new and more challenging assignments, otherwise we'd be paying for a lot of potential but no performance.

MANAGER 6: I agree. Measuring capability instead of actual performance could be very risky. We can observe an employee performing a new and more challenging assignment, but we'd be in a difficult area if we tried to count potential. It's too subjective. Some employees think they have the capability of performing other jobs just because they went to a training session, but they are not really qualified, because they haven't tried those skills on the job.

Some performance standards, as well as the other statements in the profile, are written broadly because they can be satisfied in a variety of ways. The language used is not so precise as to define the various ways work performance can occur in all situations. Aiming at such precision would produce an endless list, which defeats the purpose of the performance-criteria profile to focus attention on the essence of the issue.

Detractors may argue that the application of the statements must be consistent throughout the organization. Consistent, yes, but not absolutely identical. The application must be similar in form, follow from the same principle, and be in harmony with the intent of the statement. However, except in the case of obviously quantifiable measures, the application cannot be absolutely alike. The conditions of human performance typically do not arrange themselves in such an orderly fashion.

Holes may be found in performance-criteria statements, particularly the value-laden issues. Some people will attempt to detract from the concept by pointing out inconsequential details. The case must be made on the principle, not the detail. Of course, where the missing detail is notable, the statement must be changed.

The value of using the four-dimensional performance-criteria profile to communicate performance values to employees is that employees *begin to perform up to the manager's expectations*. Employees who need to learn more about their jobs are able to identify specifically what they need to learn in order to perform up to the Performance Standard. Employees who do not want to work according to organizational standards are obviously and dramatically distanced from other employees. Employees who care to give the organization an extra effort in order to earn extra reward and recognition are given a clear direction.

6.1.7 Consensus Building

Getting managers to agree on organizational values to be held in common is not easy. Each manager wants to manage in his or her own way. Short of complete agreement, they may achieve a consensus. This simply means that each manager has the opportunity to argue for a point of view, yet is willing to accept and respect the group's right and need to decide values for the common good.

Participants in the consensus-building process need interpersonal ability. The more experience they have at achieving consensus, the stronger will be the bond among them. Participants must talk with each other and present their point of view. Where only a few members of the group carry most of the discussion, the consensus is impaired.

In particular, participants need to listen to each other and then clarify what each does not understand. Typically, people take a stand and argue to defend their position. There are precious few communication models that demonstrate respect for, and a polite attitude toward, an opposing point of view.

Group discussions must be managed. So-called leaderless groups have their occasional place in group dynamics, but they are inefficient in comparison with managed discussion. The group manager can help participants express their points of view, as well as help them listen to other points of view, by stopping arguments, preventing one participant from interrupting another, and separating fact from opinion.

Group managers can also ensure that all differences have been put on the table, suggest brainstorming when the conversation bogs down, help the group look at what-if scenarios, propose tests and trial runs, and suggest closure at an opportune moment.

Consensus building follows the same process, built around the same questions, as decision making: What is the problem/opportunity? What are options to solve the problem or achieve the opportunity? What are the advantages and disadvantages of each option? Which is the best option?

In the final analysis, someone has to decide by what standards the organization will operate. Managers—legal agents of the organization—are obligated to enforce the standards for the organization, but they must enforce them consistently and fairly. Employees understand that standards must be established. In fact, they want standards established so that they can feel secure in understanding how to gain rewards and recognition and keep their jobs.

The final result is that the organization begins to pull together in stronger ways. The organization's culture becomes clearer, because managers and employees have whittled away the discrepancies of varying opinions. In sum, employees and managers together now understand what's required on the job and why it is required.

Project Analyzer (6.1)

Do managers in your organization meet to define performance standards?

Are managers more likely to stick to their own opinion instead of trying to achieve a consensus?

Do managers in your organization have effective interpersonal skills?

Have managers been trained to improve their interpersonal skills?

Have managers been trained to improve their decision-making skills?

Are senior managers capable of managing discussions to achieve a consensus?

6.2 Applying Performance Standards Consistently

Once performance standards are established throughout the organization, managers must administer the program consistently, and they must convince employees that performance management is a "way of life," not just an annual occurrence. The program's success depends on how well managers handle these two tasks.

6.2.1 Applying Performance Standards to New Employees

Performance management as a way of life should be introduced to new employees during their orientation—specifically, by giving them the job description and the performance-criteria profiles. The new employee cannot help but be impressed that the manager and the organization want to succeed, and want the employee to succeed as well. The profile gives the employee nearly all the information he or she needs to be successful. What could be more helpful and fairer to the employee?

A new employee's performance should be discussed at least three times during the first 90 days' employment.

First, the frequent review trains the employee to perform according to the organization's standards. Second, the employee learns the organization's approach to performance management. Third, the manager and the employee begin to develop rapport through conversations, and set the stage for continuing dialog throughout the time the employee remains employed.

Fourth, the process guides the manager's monitoring of the employee's progress during the initial "get acquainted" period (formerly known as the probationary period) of employment. Fifth, although in some states employers can summarily dismiss an employee during this initial time, all organizations are advised to protect themselves against possible lawsuits by documenting any counseling or disciplining of probationary employees. In states where employment practices are more tightly controlled by law, managers must be even more careful about their actions during this time.

Some managers are so enthusiastic to encourage new employees to perform well and to help them fit into the organization quickly that they compliment them as exceptional performers from day one. True, some employees grasp new tasks quickly and perform them well; but when job qualifications state that it takes six months' on-the-job training to perform at the Performance Standard, it is contradictory to say that an employee is performing at the Performance Option level in 30 days.

Consider the effect on a new employee who is "encouraged" by being told that he or she is performing above Peformance Standard at 30, 60, and 90 days but then, at the annual review, when his or her performance is compared to the performance of other employees, is told that Improvement is necessary.

If the Performance Standard is defined accurately, then managers must remember that the standard remains the standard and is not *changed* because the employee is new and learning the job. Allowances for new employees are made during this get-acquainted time—that is, the standard is temporarily set aside—but it is not changed.

For example, here is the case of a new employee in a dental laboratory who was employed for 30 days. The performance criteria for *job knowledge* were defined as follows in this organization:

PS = Job knowledge is sufficient to accomplish job responsibilities.
P = Job requirements are unaccomplished or incomplete.
I = Needs to identify job methods that are needed to fulfill all job responsibilities.
PO = Seeks ways to expand job knowledge through formal education or informal learning.

The employee was told that she needed to improve her job knowledge. The manager wrote: "Shirley needs to learn how to trim orthodontic models esthetically in order to perform up to expectations. I feel that she has really caught on to the lab system in the last 20 days."

Encouraging? Yes. Realistic? Yes. Had the manager fallen into the trap of not clarifying the allowance made in the application of the Performance Standard for an employee who is learning the job, the employee would have become frustrated when she learned in a subsequent appraisal that she not only didn't perform on the Performance Option level but actually had not even attained the Performance Standard. Orientation standards can be separated from actual performance standards, but actual standards are always the baseline.

Overrating the new employee also tells the employee that the current performance level is all the organization expects. The employee is likely to adopt an attitude of, "It doesn't take much effort to work here." Of course, some employees come to a job more qualified than others. If they do meet the Performance Standard, they should receive full credit.

Once upon a time, a manager appraised an employee as performing well, but three weeks later was back in his manager's office saying that the employee was "impossible" and that disciplinary action was required. The manager's manager told the manager that *he* was the person with the problem, because he wanted to be the "good guy" earlier when handing out raises. The manager was the one hurt the most, because his credibility was diminished, but the employee and the organization were hurt, too. Employees know when they and other employees are doing a good job and when they are not. Word gets around when reward and recognition do not match performance.

6.2.2 Preventing Manipulation of the System

Any approach to performance management can be subverted, and any aspect of the system can be played with. However, the exacting language of job descriptions and performance-criteria profiles required in the approach offered in this book helps an astute reviewer pick out the manipulations more quickly than with other systems. The toughest part for a reviewer is to pick up on the conversations that occur between the manager and the employee—conversations that the reviewer never hears, except when rebuttals occur.

Let's look at the situation of an employee whose performance was marked by the manager as a Problem on the appraisal form: "Work is frequently bottlenecked or unfinished."

The employee argued in her written appeal that she had not only completed all assigned projects well before the agreed-upon completion dates but also prepared reports anticipating that they would be necessary. She pointed out that reports submitted to her manager had been held with no action for so long that he had to request a revised report, and that her final report could not be finished on time because of this.

By criticizing the employee, the manager thought he could mask his own procrastination. The more open the performance-management system, the more difficult it is for anyone to manipulate it.

Another destructive influence occurs when an employee who meets all Performance Standards is described as "average" in the summary. No one likes to be average, just another cog in the organization wheel. The philosophy of the performance-criteria profile is that the employee who meets the Performance Standard in all areas is a *terrific, valued* employee. Wouldn't you be thrilled if all your employees met the Performance Standard in all areas of responsibility?

Performance management is so much more than filling out a form; it is the essence of the relationship between a manager and an employee. Thoughtful and consistent completion of the criteria becomes the basis for a good, meaningful conversation. Let's look in on a difficult situation, and how a seasoned manager might handle it.

6.2.3 Maintaining Consistency of Standards: A Case Study

An employee (a department manager) was faced with the serious illness of his spouse. His performance, especially in the areas of attendance and punctuality, had slipped. The manager and the employee talked often during the performance period as the employee sought to find adequate care for his wife. He was frequently called away from work for an emergency, and was often preoccupied with a real tragedy in his life. This employee had been a real strength to the management team and a role model to his employees for several years; he had proven himself again and again. Then, the attendance and punctuality of his employees began to slip.

His performance conference was difficult for him and his manager. The performance criteria of attendance and punctuality were clear. The employee had not met them, for obvious and understandable reasons. For how long, with good reason, can a manager allow the employee's lateness and absence? There is always so much more to human performance than just performance standards, and it is only through effective conversations that true understanding can be attained. The conversation between the manager and the employee went like this:

MANAGER: Paul, because we've talked so often these past months, I feel that I understand what you are going through in your personal life. It would be easy if we could separate what's happening in your family from your work performance, but you and I both know that isn't possible.

PAUL: I know, I'm having a great deal of difficulty balancing my personal problems and my work. You know I can't afford to leave my job even temporarily.

MANAGER: When we talk about your attendance and punctuality, it's impossible for me to criticize you, because I have willingly excused you. However, I can't say that you meet the Performance Standard in these areas, because you are not here, or you arrive late, or you leave early. Besides, your work is frequently interrupted during the day to answer telephone calls. I understand the compelling reasons affecting your performance in these two areas, but you are not meeting the Standards.

PAUL: You've been understanding and supportive, and generous in saying that I only need to improve. I personally would have said that my attendance and punctuality were a Problem.

MANAGER: Unfortunately, your personal problem seems to be affecting your department's attendance and punctuality, and some members of the administrative staff have questioned your coming and going. I have respected your wishes to keep your wife's illness private, but we have to address this issue because of its impact on the organization. You have been a role model in the past, but now your personal life makes that impossible. Do you have any ideas to help us through this difficult time so that we can maintain the organization's Performance Standards?

PAUL: I have confided in one other manager, though she promised to keep the information to herself. She agreed to cover for me when I need to leave abruptly.

MANAGER: O.K., that alleviates the coverage problem, but do you think it addresses the perceptions of your employees?

PAUL: No, I've learned that already. One of my supervisors told me just yesterday that she resented a manager from another department stepping in when she's been managing just fine for me in my absence.

MANAGER: Your supervisor isn't aware, then, of why you are being called away?

PAUL: No.

MANAGER: Have you considered telling something about your problem to your employees and your fellow managers?

PAUL: I can't do that.

MANAGER: I accept that. What can we do to minimize the impact of your problem on the organization?

PAUL: I don't know.

MANAGER: We are at a point where we need to find some answers. Your wife's illness is not going to go away, and I believe that you have faced that reality. We have talked about community resources, and you have availed yourself of them. You know your job, and you've been one of my best managers. You have always been there when I needed you, and I've tried to return that loyalty to you now. One of my toughest jobs is balancing what the organization needs with what you need. The organization is being compromised by your personal needs, and we must find a balance soon. I want you to give plenty of serious thought to the problem. I'll be available when you want to talk. We must find a way to alleviate the problem of your attendance and punctuality.

Here are some questions to think about in regard to this conversation. Do you appreciate the extent to which the human element must enter into the application of performance standards? Did you notice that the manager upheld the organization's standards, yet did it in an understanding manner? Had you been Paul, would you have felt "O.K." after the conversation? Had you been the manager, would you have conducted the conversation in the same manner?

Each of us has unique values; each of us will deal with similar situations differently. In the context of an organization, only so many style variations can be allowed. Paul faced a truly difficult situation in his life. Compassion was required and, in this case, was given. At the same time, the organization needed to proceed with its work, and Paul had to know that.

Employees do not dispute the need for consistent application of performance standards. On the contrary, they welcome consistency for the security that it gives them. Organizations err when consistency turns into rigidity. Employees lose faith in the system because there is no justice.

Project Analyzer (6.2)

How well do managers convey performance criteria to employees?

_____

_____

During employee orientation, when are job responsibilities and performance criteria discussed?

_____

_____

Do employees complain that they do not know what is expected of them?

_____

_____

Are managers guilty of filing acceptable performance reports, only to attempt disciplinary action shortly thereafter?

_____

_____

6.3 Strategic Planning

On your first quick walk through the book, record your initial thoughts on policy issues that will have to be decided.

_____

_____

_____

_____

_____

Any notes on tactical procedures?

_____

_____

_____

_____

Chapter 7

Preparing for and Conducting Performance-Management Conferences

7.1 Preparing for the Conference

The job description and the performance-criteria profiles, along with new objectives set by the organization, are the base documents used by the manager and the employee to manage performance. Performance management involves two phases, planning for performance, and then, after work has been performed, appraising it. Though planning and appraising are distinct processes, one is not done without consideration of the other.

7.1.1 Planning

Before work begins, it must be planned. Follow these nine steps to plan for the planning portion of the performance conference:

1. *Review the job description and the performance-criteria profiles.* What are the basic requirements of the job? What are the employee's special talents? Has the employee expressed any desire to become involved in special projects?

2. *Review current organization objectives.* What is the current operational plan for the organization? What are key priorities? What new requirements have

been assigned to your area of responsibility? Which of these would appropriately be assigned to this employee according to routine expectations in the job description? Is this employee better suited than another employee to carry out the objective? Will the employee be interested in carrying out the objective?

3. *Write a draft performance plan for specific issues.* Translate current organization objectives as related to basic job requirements into a plan of action. See Figure 5-5 for a performance planning format. See Figure 7-1 for a completed example.

4. *Put the papers away for a while.* A brief interlude gives you time to regain an objective view of the requirements and goals of your situation.

5. *Reread the plan.* Is it still workable? Can the employee become enthused about it? Is the information correct? Are any adjustments required?

6. *Confer with your manager.* Does your manager support your preparations? Are any adjustments required?

7. *Set up an appointment with the employee.* When is the best time to meet? How will you prevent interruptions? How much time should you allow? Where will you meet? Is the room setup conducive to conversation?

8. *Ask the employee to prepare.* What information does the employee need?

Figure 7-1. Performance plan from a job description result for a specific performance period.

Job Title: Manager of Recruitment and Training

Job Result on the Job Description: Prepares new employees to perform work assignments and understand work rules, organization policy and procedure, and benefits by conducting orientations

Our Objective Is: To improve orientation by developing a video-tape program

Our Performance Criteria Are:
    a. What do we want? Personal presentations are replaced with video; cost associated with personal presentations are reduced; video tape prepared within budget
    b. What don't we want? New employees evaluate the presentation as not helpful
    c. What snags can be anticipated? Production cost overrun; misapplication of current video technology; inaccurate scripts
    d. What's better than what we want? Video wins association award

What Resources Do We Need? Audio-visual consultant

Who Does What? Incumbent prepares budget and script, and selects consultant. Manager approves budget

When Do We Check Progress?   July 1 – budget and program approval
                                     Sept 1 – script outline
                                       Jan 1 – script
                                       Apr 1 – presentation

9. *Set a conversation strategy.* What is the result you would like to have happen? Will you need to move the conversation toward an anticipated conclusion, or should the conversation work around and explore different options? Does the employee understand the purpose of the conference?

Although the manager and the employee must prepare for the conference, care must be taken not to let the preparation become the outcome in the minds of the preparers. The conference is an open dialog to determine whether perceptions and assumptions are accurate and whether proposed plans will produce the results desired.

7.1.2 Appraising

After work has been performed, it must be appraised. Follow these fourteen steps to prepare for the appraisal portion of the conference:

1. *Review the job description and the performance-criteria profiles.* Has any new responsibility been added? Is there any new technology involved? Has the employee received any special training? Does the job still fit organizational needs? Are any changes needed? Is a new job analysis required?

2. *Review the performance plan written during the last conference.* Have any unexpected changes occurred? Were there any uncontrollable events? Should the performance plan be adjusted? Did you provide sufficient resources?

3. *Review progress and incident notes.* Were appropriate adjustments made along the way? How often did you request progress reports? Did you encourage discussion of differences of opinion? Did you encourage performance? Were you available to talk about problems and opportunities? Are you weighing information from the beginning of the performance period equally to information acquired recently?

When appraising performance, review recollections and documentation of the performance period. You know what was to have been accomplished, and how well it was to have been accomplished. The possible conditions of performance are identified in the four dimensions of the profile. For each job responsibility, identify the condition that best describes the employee's performance.

Sometimes, the performance standard will be quite specific—say, "Thirty collections per day"—so that matching will be obvious. Other times, the profile will state a more general condition that should exist, such as "Service is reviewed on a regular basis." The manager must examine the evidence of whether service was reviewed, whether the review was sufficient to identify problems, and how often and regularly the service was reviewed.

Here again, the value of planning is notable. Questions of evidence should be reviewed and decided at the time performance is planned so that there are no surprises or "misunderstandings" at the end of the performance period.

Employee performance below "Twenty collections per day" is Problematic because that is what the profile states. The service profile states that it is a

Problem when "Customers complain about the service they receive." The quantifiable measure of collections per day is obvious. "Customer complaints" needs to be examined for severity and frequency. More judgments are needed again to determine what is a severe complaint and how often complaints will be tolerated, but if these questions were raised and answered during planning, appraisal judgments are not difficult to make.

Furthermore, remember the internal structure of the profile: either performance matched the standard, or it did not. Either "service is reviewed" as stated in the Performance Standard, or "complaints are received" as stated in the Problem. At the start of the conversation between the manager and the employee, there should be little doubt as to which condition exists.

Of course, sometimes performance does not quite meet the standard, or the problems created are quite small. The employee made 29 calls instead of 30, or made the service calls but not regularly, so that occasionally customers called inquiring about missed service. Performance is not Problematic in either case, but Improvement in performance is needed because the standard is what is expected.

On the other hand, the employee may make many more collections than are expected, or may find "imaginative ways to anticipate customer service requirements" so that the manager can identify the performance at the Performance Option level.

Examine the employee's performance in this manner for each job responsibility and universal requirement, and total the judgments for all responsibilities. Conclude with an overall statistical and written summary of performance.

4. *Use your calendar and any other records to refresh your memory.* You may forget to record some observations, but other recorded events may trigger recollections about the circumstances you are appraising.

5. *Get other opinions.* Who else was in a position to observe and comment on the employee's performance? What performance records would offer evidence in lieu of personal observations?

6. *Review previous appraisals and performance plans.* What trends have developed?

7. *Write a draft appraisal.* Do you have sufficient information? Is the written appraisal consistent with comments you made personally during the performance period? Do you have a realistic balance between compliments and suggestions for improvement?

8. *Write a draft performance plan based on the appraisal.* Does the plan suggest improvements for deficiencies? Does it open the door to pursue new opportunities? Does the plan include new organizational objectives?

9. *Put the papers away for a while to let your mind clear.* It's difficult to maintain objectivity when you're working intensely—especially when the work involves making difficult value judgments.

10. *Reread the draft appraisal and plan.* How does it read from the employee's point of view? How would you expect the employee to respond? Do you have your facts correct? What adjustments are required?

11. *Confer with your manager.* Does your manager support your conclusions and plans? What adjustments are required?

12. *Set up an appointment with the employee.* When is the best time to meet? How will you prevent interruptions? How much time should you allow? Where will you meet? Is the room setup conducive to conversation?

13. *Ask the employee to prepare.* What information does the employee need? Should you give a copy of the appraisal to the employee in advance? If not, why not? Should you ask the employee to complete a self-appraisal form before the conference? Would a self-appraisal form be too threatening, or does the employee usually examine his or her own performance formally?

14. *Set a conversation strategy.* What is the result you would like to have happen? Will you need to move the conversation toward an anticipated conclusion, or should the conversation work around and explore different options? Does the employee understand the purpose of the conference? Is your attitude open and exploratory, or closed and in pursuit?

7.1.3 The Manager-Employee Relationship

To be successful, the ongoing relationship between the manager and the employee must be one of psychologically equal participants; it cannot be based on the premise that the manager is superior, or that the manager's role is to judge the employee. The relationship must be structured instead on the essential job issues they share.

Psychologically equal people acknowledge, though not necessarily agree with, each other's view of the world. A relationship is off-center when there is no mutual respect. Managers and employees should plan and appraise performance together, with respect for each other's opinion.

The mood of the performance-management conference is determined by the quality of the relationship between the manager and the employee throughout the period of time between one conference and the next conference. The outcome of the conference is almost completely determined long before, and regardless of, specific preparation for the conference. Preparation begins two or three weeks before the event when specific performance information is gathered and a conversation strategy is developed; but the rapport of the conversation began when performance objectives were set in the last conference.

You are now ready to enter the conference room and conduct a face-to-face conversation.

Project Analyzer (7.1)

How well do managers in your organization plan for performance-management conferences?

Are managers required to have their plans reviewed by their manager or the human resources professional?

Are managers trained to plan their conferences?

What is the general quality of relationships between managers and employees?

Are employees respected for their ability to participate in planning performance?

Are employees asked to participate in planning their performance?

7.2 Conducting the Conversation

As a result of following the steps presented in section 7.1, the manager now has a strategy for conducting the conference. Next, the manager needs to plan for the use of specific conversational techniques.

First, three guidelines for engaging in a conversation will be offered. Then, a model will be presented for analyzing conversations to see where they can be improved.

1. *Put yourself, and the other person, at ease.* Start in a friendly manner. Review the purpose of the conference. Let the discussion develop naturally. Get to the major issues quickly. Don't overuse plaudits so that the employee starts to wonder when the other shoe is going to drop. Pay attention to performance instead of personality. When you feel stress in yourself or in the other person, deal with it. Act promptly before emotions get out of hand. Tailor what you say and how you say it toward building strong rapport with the employee.

2. *Agree whenever you can.* Praise strong points. Show appreciation. Don't put the other person on the defense. Use positive instead of negative words. Make the tone of your conversation positive. Match your nonverbal cues to your oral statements. Resolve disagreements before proceeding. Get additional information if necessary, even if it means rescheduling the conference. Stop the conference if tempers get out of hand, and try again at another time.

Avoid contradicting the other person. State what you understand the other person to have said in order to clarify meaning. Time what you say. Go back and pick up the pieces when conversations go bad.

Remember, however, that the final responsibility for the outcome of the conversation rests with you. You are in charge. When all manner of reasoning and explanation fail, you may have to announce that this situation is the way you see it, period. People can have psychologically equal rapport even though one of them has more authority than the other.

3. *Ask questions until you get all the information you need.* Don't jump to conclusions. Verify the facts. Don't ignore what the other person is trying to say to you. Listen to what the employee says; hear what the employee feels (more about this later in this section). Ask as many questions as you can that start with who, what, where, when, why, and how. Avoid questions that can be answered yes or no as far as possible. Get the employee to comment. Give encouragement where necessary. Take notes.

7.2.1 The Listening-in-Perspective Scale (LIPScale)

Each statement in a conversation contributes to the success or failure of the conversation. When there are too many poor statements in a conversation, or when one of them is extremely poor, the outcome is doomed. A person who knows how to use the LIPScale* is able to plan an effective opening gambit, prepare responses to predictable statements, and respond effectively as the conversation develops.

Three principles, as expressed in the following statements, guide the use of the scale:

* Roger J. Plachy, *When I Lead, Why Don't They Follow?*, rev. ed. (Chicago: Bonus Books, 1986).

1. "I have a choice of eight different ways to talk to another person."
2. "Each degree on the scale is a correct way to talk to another person."
3. "The person with whom I am talking, and the situation that we are in, determine whether the degree used is correct."

With the LIPScale, statements in a conversation are categorized to understand what the speaker intended, how the statement affects the conversation, and what type of response will produce the most effective outcome for the conversation.

The scale categories are:

- Listening
- Agreeing
- Asking
- Persuading
- Giving Orders
- Comforting
- Avoiding
- Criticizing

Because the bottom degrees of the scale are typically less effective than the top degrees, conversations can be improved by using the top degrees as often as possible. This means more use of Listening, Agreeing, and Asking, and less use of Persuading, Giving Orders, Comforting, Avoiding, and Criticizing.

The names of the degrees can be changed to suit personal preference. Substitute words will be offered.

Here are definitions for the degrees of the LIPScale:

Listening is one thing we do when we want to get to know another person. Listening means concentrating on what the other person is saying and not thinking about what we want to say as soon as we get the opportunity.

Substitute words for Listening are:

Accepting	*Being attentive*
Acknowledging	*Being open*
Receiving	*Being aware*
Recognizing	*Summarizing*
Reflecting	*Repeating*
Empathizing	*Paraphrasing*
Identifying	*Verifying*

Listening is expressed as: "Let's talk about it." "I can see that something is bothering you; tell me about it." "You really look upset about this." "You seem to feel as though there's nothing more you can do." "I get the impression that . . ." "Why don't you tell me about it?" "Let's see if I understand what you're saying." "I gather that you mean . . ." "This is obviously upsetting you." "I think you became angry because I . . ."

We listen on two levels. On a *physiological* level, we listen to the words or content of the conversation. On an *emotional* level, we tune in to the feelings of the person speaking the words. Effective communicators listen on both levels in a conversation.

We listen *passively* when we hear the words and watch for nonverbal cues without saying anything in return, or when we use a few words or a gesture occasionally to demonstrate that we are still involved in the conversation. We listen *actively* when we speak out to encourage someone to tell us more, or to ensure that we understand what is said, as well as what is meant.

Agreeing tells another person that you go along, that what he or she is saying or doing is all right with you. Agreeing is more than just allowing the other person to say or do something (which we call accepting) when you disagree. Agreeing means that you would do or say the same thing yourself.

Substitute words for Agreeing are:

Endorsing	*Rewarding*
Confirming	*Harmonizing*
Reinforcing	*Being congenial*
Praising	

Agreeing is expressed as: "I agree with you." "You're doing just fine." "I know what you mean." "Yes." "O.K." "Uh-huh."

Sometimes agreement is *implied* and not stated explicitly, which is acceptable. Implied agreement is disastrous, however, when one person proceeds as if there were an agreement when there was not. Unfortunately, some people have honed their ability not to disagree without ever agreeing.

Asking is questioning, searching through the details and data. Asking looks to reasons, motivations, and background; it inquires of fundamentals.

Substitute words for Asking might be:

Examining	*Exploring*
Investigating	*Inquiring*
Questioning	*Evaluating*
Clarifying	*Interpreting*
Probing	*Discussing*
Searching	*Studying*
Analyzing	

Asking is expressed as: "What happened then?" "Then what did he say?" "When did you start to feel this way?"

Persuading is an attempt to get other people to do what you want them to do, or to believe what you want them to believe. Persuading is also giving reasons to others for what you did.

Substitute words for Persuading are:

Advising	*Explaining*
Selling	*Demonstrating*
Prodding	*Repeating*
Prompting	*Exhorting*
Inducing	*Reminding*
Encouraging	*Counseling*
Convincing	*Manipulating*
Inspiring	*Coaxing*
Stimulating	*Cajoling*
Urging	*Pressuring*
Emphasizing	*Rationalizing*

Persuading is expressed as: "Why don't you wait a little longer before you decide." "You can do it; you have the ability." "You ought to . . ." "I think it should be done this way."

Information presented to inform or to answer questions is routinely categorized as Persuading/Informing, on the belief that people want the information or answer to be accepted, not denied.

Giving Orders means deciding what has to be done and telling others to do it. Giving Orders derives from a position of authority to direct a sequence of events.

Substitute words for Giving Orders are:

Commanding	*Mandating*
Directing	*Dictating*
Instructing	*Demanding*
Telling	*Insisting*
Decreeing	*Compelling*
Prescribing	*Deciding*

Giving Orders is expressed as: "Do this first." "Deliver these papers." "Sit down." "Would you please have these prepared?" "Cheer up."

Comforting is an expression of tenderness at a time when you want to help another person through difficult circumstances. Comforting recognizes that the other person is at some emotional disadvantage and that you have an opportunity to provide some stability or strength.

Substitute words for Comforting are:

Consoling	*Being warm-hearted*
Sympathizing	*Being considerate*

Reassuring
Commiserating
Pitying
Being merciful, kind, or humane

Being compassionate or tender
Being benevolent
Being indulgent

Comforting is expressed as: "Don't worry, things will work out." "I'm sorry to hear about that." "Yes, it can be boring." "Don't let it get you down." "Don't cry."

Feeling sorry *for* someone is different from feeling sorry *with* someone. The first is Comforting—a genuine concern, but not an emotional involvement. The latter is empathy—that is, feeling what the other person is feeling in so far as that is humanly possible. Empathy is the main part of good Listening.

Avoiding is the tactic you use to sidestep an encounter with another person. It may be the safest way to avoid involvement, or it may be a kind way of not opening an emotional wound.

Substitute words for Avoiding are:

Evading
Dodging
Hedging
Abandoning
Withdrawing
Deserting
Shirking

Ignoring
Disregarding
Abstaining
Shunning
Eluding
Escaping
Being indifferent

Avoiding is expressed as: "Let's not talk about it now." Or it may involve changing the subject: "Would you like to see a new project I'm working on?" Avoiding is also walking away from a situation without saying anything, or staying away from someone altogether.

Criticizing is telling another person what is wrong with what he or she did. You may be angry with the person, or trying to get even, or even trying to help.

Substitute words for Criticizing are:

Disapproving
Censuring
Condemning
Threatening
Warning
Intimidating
Menacing
Punishing
Correcting
Disciplining
Penalizing

Forbidding
Deriding
Satirizing
Ridiculing
Degrading
Discrediting
Belittling
Teasing
Minimizing
Regulating
Denying

Rejecting
Jeering
Repudiating
Renouncing
Silencing
Frustrating
Excluding
Blaming
Prohibiting
Admonishing
Scolding

Taunting	*Contradicting*	*Lecturing*
Discounting	*Opposing*	*Preaching*
Chastising	*Inhibiting*	*Controlling*
Castigating	*Prejudging*	*Restricting*

Criticizing is expressed as: "If you do, you'll be sorry." "Do it yourself, if you have so much time." "That's ridiculous." "We've been through this before." "You shouldn't feel frightened when these things happen."

7.2.2 Analyzing a Performance-Management Conversation With the LIPScale

Let's look at an example of an ineffective conversation and analyze it with the LIPScale. Then we'll examine an improved version of the same conversation.

This conversation is between a senior manager (Tom) and a subordinate manager (Sally). It occurs during an annual performance planning and appraisal conference. The names "have been changed to protect the guilty," as they say, but the guilt is obvious. Sally has been in the job for eight months. At the time of her promotion, Tom suggested that "we work along for a while and see how it goes."

There have been several casual conferences held during the last eight months, during which specific work projects were discussed. They were in the vein of: "You're doing fine, but . . ." One brief formal conference was held four months ago. It centered on an employee's complaint about work scheduling. Tom pointed out that employees have a tendency to complain about work schedules, but also remarked that "too many complaints aren't very good, either." "We'll talk about this later," he concluded.

Both managers are now in Tom's office and have just finished a discussion about the installation of some new equipment.

The following codes will be used to identify the various degrees on the scale: Listening = L; Agreeing = AG; Asking = AS; Persuading = P; Information = P/I; Giving Orders = GO; Comforting = CO; Avoiding = AV; Criticizing = CR.

TOM: By the way, I received your annual appraisal form from Personnel the other day. P/I These things take up a lot of time CR but we have to do them. P I knew you were busy with this new installation, so I didn't send you a copy to fill out. P Besides, you're too new in your job to really understand it. CR I thought we'd just talk it out. P I think we have some real problems here, Sally. CR

SALLY: Problems? AS What problems? AS/CR You haven't said anything about problems. CR

TOM: Well, your work with the equipment and the processing is just fine. P In fact, I graded you at the Performance Option level on #4 here on the job description because of the way you anticipated some of the maintenance problems. P Almost all of the rest are marked as meeting the performance standard. P

SALLY: Just one Performance Option? CR I thought I was doing very well in a lot of areas. P You haven't said a word to me. CR

TOM: Wait a minute, Sally, CR we talked a number of times. CR I tried to help you. P Maybe you didn't understand what I was saying. CR Besides, this isn't that big a deal. CO You're new in the job. P

SALLY: It's a big deal to me. CR I worked hard for that promotion. P Now all of a sudden you're telling me I've got problems. CR You've been stringing me along for eight months without warning me that you think I've got some problems. CR What problems do I have, anyway? CR/AS

TOM: Here, item #15 is one of them P:

15. Completes operational requirements by scheduling and assigning employees and following up on work performance.
    - ☐ PS = Work is accomplished on schedule with an efficient complement of staff.
    - ☒ P = Customers are dissatisfied with services rendered; time is wasted and excessive costs are incurred to correct errors.
    - ☐ I = Needs to review and apply scheduling techniques; needs to observe work progress and make adjustments in work assignments in order to meet the work schedule.
    - ☐ PO = Anticipates work interruptions and makes arrangements to accomplish work on schedule. P/I

SALLY: What do you mean, customers are dissatisfied? CR You haven't told me about any customer complaints. CR How come I wasn't told? AS/CR

TOM: There were only a few of them saying that they couldn't get through on the telephone because the lines were busy for a long time. P/I But that's not the real issue. P I'm looking at the high costs because of the scheduling problems you've had. CR We talked about that a few months ago. P

SALLY: Yes, we talked for a few minutes, and you said that we'd talk about this later. CR This is a helluva time to be talking about it when you've already marked the paper. CR

TOM: Well, we're talking about it now, and you'd better listen. CR All the problems you're having are in managing your people. CR I had to mark you down in #16 as well CR:

16. Maintains staff performance by counseling, appraising, and disciplining employees.
    - ☐ PS = Employees accomplish job results according to management's expectations.
    - ☒ P = Customers are dissatisfied with services rendered; excessive costs are incurred to correct errors or to counsel or discipline employees; employees do not understand the problems they are causing.
    - ☐ I = Needs to study and apply counseling and coaching techniques; needs to review and follow legal procedures.

    ☐ PO = Reaches out to employees and helps them solve problems before the problems affect job performance. **P/I**

I only marked you off a little on #17 **P**:

17. Maintains staff by selecting, orienting, and training employees.
        ☐ PS = Employees are prepared to accomplish job results by the completion of their probationary period, and throughout their employment.
        ☐ P = Customers are dissatisfied with services rendered; excessive costs are incurred to correct errors or to retrain employees.
        ☒ I = Needs to review hiring criteria; needs to study and apply interviewing techniques; needs to review and correct orientation and training content and instructional process; needs to identify continuing training requirements among employees to maintain job performance.
        ☐ PO = Helps employees acclimate themselves before they complete one-half of their probationary period; identifies continuing training needs so that employees are able to apply current job methods; develops a team spirit so that employees help train each other. **P/I**

SALLY: This is ridiculous! **CR** You knew I hadn't ever supervised anyone before when you put me into the job, but you said you'd help and send me to some courses. **CR** Some help! **CR** Every time I showed you a brochure for some training, you said that it either cost too much or you couldn't spare me. **CR** What exactly is wrong with me? **AS/CR**

TOM: You're losing control of your employees. **CR** They're out there moaning and complaining about their work schedules. **CR** Some of them just don't show up when they don't like the schedule. **CR** You've got to tell them what's expected and then enforce your rules. **GO** They're beginning to lead you around. **CR**

SALLY: Nobody's leading me anywhere. **CR** I've talked to the people when they didn't show up, and they had good reasons. **CR** All but one of them called in; the other was in an accident. **P/I**

TOM: Who knows that they're not just giving you a story. **CR** Some of these employees have been around for a long time. **P** You're the new kid on the block, and you're young. **P/CR** They're going to test you.   **P** You've got to stand your ground. **GO**

SALLY: It seems to me that trying to understand my employees will get me further along with them instead of nailing them when things don't go right. **P**

TOM: Sometimes you have to hit them over the head with a two-by-four in order to get their attention. **P**

SALLY: Very funny. **CR** How come you didn't rate me as needing improvement in #15 and #16 like you did on #17? **CR** I know that I have a lot to learn. **P** I'm willing to learn, but I can't do it all by myself. **P** And by the way, exactly why did you mark me as needing improvement on #17?   AS/CR   I haven't had to hire anybody yet   P

TOM: That's true,   AG   but it's in the category of supervision, and that's where you need to improve.   P

SALLY: You mean I'm getting marked down on general principles?   AS/CR

TOM: You're getting marked down because you aren't doing well as a supervisor.   CR   You know the work, but you've got to handle the people better.   CR   You've got to toughen up.   GO   You're not one of the troops anymore.   P   You can't pal around with them and be friends with them.   CR   You're the boss.   P

SALLY: I don't know if being the boss is worth it.   P

TOM: Sure it is.   P   It's rewarding to know that through your efforts, you got a lot accomplished.   P   You'll make it.   P   Just try a little harder.   P/CR   Tell you what, let me find some supervision class for you to attend.   P   O.K.?   AS   Just don't bring back any of those be-nice-to-your-employees ideas.   CR   We'll talk when you get back from the class, and I'll help you.   P   And be sure to sign this appraisal form for me, will you?   GO

In the first place, Tom set himself up for a losing situation when he failed to orient Sally properly when she was promoted. In fact, he should have sent her for some training *before* she entered the job. He held no effective performance-management conversations, and the ones that he did hold were incomplete.

Sally has some problems as a new manager. She is trying hard not to offend any of her employees. She wants to be fair to everyone, but she is going overboard. She is mistaking being *nice* to employees for being *fair*. A few employees are taking advantage of her, and then, to avoid being caught in their own web of manipulation, they are complaining about their work schedules.

Tom made a mistake in marking Sally down on all supervisory performance-criteria profiles. He should have given her no rating at all and made a note in the comments section that no events occurred in this area of responsibility during the performance period.

At the time of the conference, with no other conferences having been held, Tom had no choice but to mark Sally as having problems on items 15 and 16, but he probably could have been in a position to mark her as needing improvement had he approached the situation more diligently. Now, Sally is discouraged, and Tom has a motivational problem with her.

Tom's conversational technique needs improvement. His approach is critical (CR) in nature, and he relies on his "good-buddy" attitude to pull him through. Actually, his approach adds up to dishonest interaction, although it would never occur to him that his manner could be interpreted that way.

In principle, effective communicators are positive instead of negative about the subject of the conversation and their attitude toward the other person. They see opportunities instead of problems. They try not to judge or be superior, but instead are accepting of the other person's behavior—even when they disapprove.

Effective communicators pay attention not only to what the other person is saying, but also to what the other person is feeling. They continually position themselves to look at the world from the other person's point of view. Finally, they offer themselves as they are. They are real people with real thoughts, opinions, and emotions—and no games to play.

Being genuine is very important to the developing communicator, for it is the only way to improve. No person is without fault as a communicator. There are no experts—that is, people who make no interpersonal mistakes. However, some people have much more of a knack for carrying on an effective conversation than others.

People who do not improve their ability to communicate have insulated themselves from the effect of their words. They are not willing to look at new ways to communicate. However, when people are genuine and not trying to be someone they aren't, who they are becomes clear—sometimes painfully so. Once people are able to examine their behavior for what it is, and see its effect on others, they can change their behavior if they so choose.

7.2.3 An Improved Conversation

Let's look, now, at how Tom should have prepared for and conducted the conversation.

TOM: [*at the conclusion of a meeting about new orders*]: Sally, you've been in your job for six months now. You're over the initial promotion jitters, as they say. P/I Just as you would do with one of your employees, even though you haven't hired or promoted anyone yet, we should set aside some time to take a good look at what this time has been like for you, where you're heading, and what you need. P You've been through an appraisal as an employee, but now you're a manager, so not only is this an opportunity to look at your own performance, but it's also an opportunity to prepare for the way that you'll conduct your own conferences in the future. P

For one thing, the Personnel Department helps us by sending a reminder when major performance-management times occur for each employee. P/I They send one copy for me to complete so I can prepare for our conversation, and another for you so that you can prepare also. P/I You have the option to let your employees complete the form, but some may not want to do it because they find the self-examination a bit threatening. P/I Mostly, we let employees fill it out. P/I Let's see, is next Tuesday at 10 A.M. O.K. for you? AS That will give you a few days to think about our conversation. P

SALLY: Sure, that sounds fine to me. AG I think it's about time to talk. AG

Tuesday, 10 A.M.

TOM: Come on in, Sally. P Do you want some coffee? AS Only decaf for me now, not the real stuff anymore. P/I

SALLY: That would be great. AG I could use a breather this morning. P

TOM: What's going on? AS

SALLY: Oh, just some small but annoying scheduling problems. P/I In a way, I'm glad they came up this morning, because they're the kind of thing that I wanted to talk to you about. P/I

TOM: Good. AG Here, let me get my chair around to your side of the desk so we can look at these papers together P/I Did you get a chance to complete yours? AS

SALLY: Yes, I did. P/I It was a good review. P/I Reading the words in the results and criteria brought some of the issues into real focus. P/I

TOM: That's fine, because that's just what they're supposed to do. AG So, how do you feel about your performance as a new manager? AS

SALLY: I have real mixed emotions, Tom. P/I There are parts that I enjoy and parts that I don't. P/I

TOM: What would you like to talk about first? AS

SALLY: Well, the good part is the easiest. P/I I think that I handle the technical aspects of my job well. P I feel good about what I'm doing, because I know what I'm doing. P/I I think that I've met the Performance Standard in all cases. P In fact, I think I am at the Performance Option level on #4, Equipment Maintenance, and #8, Work Orders. P What do you think? AS

TOM: Yes, that is the good part. AG One of your strengths we noticed when we considered your promotion was your technical ability. P/I You know this aspect of your job very well. P/I And I agree, you have done a super job on equipment maintenance. AG I, too, marked you at the Performance Option level, AG although I couldn't quite see you there yet on Work Orders. CR Why did you mark yourself there? AS

SALLY: Well, as the criterion states: "Searches out and suggests improvements, and successfully completes changes to procedures. Instructs employees in proper documentation procedures." P/I I devised the new project coding system that will save us a lot of time. P/I Then, I taught my employees how to use it. P/I That's more than the standard, isn't it? P

TOM: Yes, it is. AG I guess I got hung up on the words "and successfully completes changes to procedures." P I think we're still in the test phase to prove that the system will work the way we want it to. P Next year you'll get all of the bugs out and I expect to be looking at a Performance Option rating for you then. P Are you ready to turn the system loose? AS

SALLY: No, not really. P/I I see what you're saying. AG I'm almost there, but not quite. AG

TOM: In fact, I've been wanting to set a date with you when we can give the system a thorough examination with everyone involved. P We'll set a date when we're done talking, for about two months from now. GO

So, that's the good part. P/I What about the not-so-good part? AS You mentioned some scheduling problems when you came into the office. P/I What's the problem? AS

SALLY: You first. GO I'd like to hear what you have to say. P

TOM: Oh, no you don't, I asked you first, P but, since you stepped off the end of the board first, I'll tell you what I think. AG This business of being a manager is new to you. P/I You're trying very hard to be successful because this job means a lot to you.   P/I   I know you've been disappointed that the whole thing hasn't gone the way that you wanted.   L   You said so when we talked a few months ago.   L   So far so good?   AS

SALLY: Right.   AG

TOM: But, there are some snags.   P/I   Now it's your turn.   OG   Where do you think the snags are?   AS

SALLY: I'm not sure, otherwise I would have corrected them.   P   I seem to be getting a lot of flak from some of the people.   P/I   They all want the good schedules.   P/I   Nobody wants the bad ones.   P/I   Everybody all of a sudden has excuses.   P/I   They're not showing up regularly, but they always have plenty of good reasons why they are having problems.   P/I   Why do my employees have all of the car accidents?   AS

TOM: Sounds as though you think you've lost your team.   L

SALLY: Not "lost."   P   I never had one.   P

TOM: Sure you did, in the beginning.   P   Didn't you feel that your employees gave you a lot of support in the beginning?   AS

SALLY: I suppose so.   AG   Maybe it was just a game.   P   Maybe they were setting me up so they could pull this stuff.   P

TOM: Don't get bitter, now.   CR   You were an employee once, too.   P/I   Put yourself in their frame of reference.   P   What do you see?   AS

SALLY: I see a new manager who wants to be successful, and who thinks that we can have a good time doing it.   P/I

TOM: How do they know this?   AS

SALLY: Doesn't everyone want to be successful and have a good time doing it?   AS

TOM: I would hope they would, but still, what have you done to show them?   AS   Have you told them?   AS

SALLY: Yes, I have, more than once.   P/I   You know we have our weekly meetings.   P/I   I've told them many times that we have to be a team, and that if we were, we'd be successful together.   P/I   I admitted that I was new to this business of managing but that I'd do my part to learn my job and that I wanted them to do their part by doing their jobs.   P/I   I said I'd help them any way that I could.   P/I

TOM: Sally, is it possible that some of them are testing you?   AS

SALLY: Testing me?   AS   Why would they?   AS

TOM: You tell me.   GO

SALLY: I can't imagine.   P/I   They know that I want them to succeed.   P/I

TOM: [*silence*]   L

SALLY: This is tough.   P   O.K. They know that I want them to succeed P/I   But they're testing me. They're O.K., but I'm not.   P/I   I'm the new kid on the block.   P/I   They don't know how I'll do.   P/I   So, they have to test me. P/I   But why?   AS   What would I be thinking if I were in their shoes?   AS   Maybe I'd want to know how tough my boss would be under fire.   P/I   I guess I would be worried if I had to be tied to a loser.   P/I   Maybe I'd do some testing, too.   P/I

TOM: And what have they been doing to you?   AS

SALLY: Seeing how far I would bend with their complaints about scheduling. P/I They know the rules, but they want to see whether or not I will enforce them evenly. P/I

TOM: And are you? AS

SALLY: I certainly am trying. P/I Yet, maybe I have been too lenient with some of them. P/I I don't know them all very well yet. P/I I need to understand them better. P/I Some of them have real problems. P/I I want to help them, but if the work suffers, everyone gets hurt. P/I

TOM: So, what you're figuring out is that if you've been too lenient with some of them, it's unfair to the others. L

SALLY: I guess so. AG

TOM: Look, Sally, don't be too tough on yourself. P There's nothing wrong with wanting to be a thoughtful manager. L The line there is very thin. P And besides, I think we can safely say that at least some of the complaining was purely selfish. P If they could get something out of you for nothing, why not? AS But now you're catching on. L

I think you understand the operational scheduling requirements of the job and what you have to do to get the work out, but you've got to learn how to blend operational requirements with employee requirements. P That's why I showed you as needing Improvement on #15 here. P

The issue of staff performance is different, however. P Most new managers have a tough time with counseling their employees. P/I Unfortunately, some of them do not pay enough attention to the problem when they first start out, and it plagues them for years. P/I I'm marking #16 as a Problem area to emphasize its importance to you. P You have to take charge and counsel your employees so that this annoyance stops. GO

When we talked recently, you mentioned that you would like to attend a supervisory course. P/I We agreed when you took the job that your pre-promotion orientation was only a beginning and that you would work in the job for a while before you attended a seminar. P/I This way, what you hear in class will be more useful to you, because you now understand why you need to know what they are talking about. P/I I think we can agree that you're ready now. P I have some brochures about some courses. P/I Stop by tomorrow morning with your calendar, and we'll decide when and where you should go. GO And then we'll set a time to review what you've learned after the class is finished. GO What do you think? AS

SALLY: That's fine with me. AG I'm ready. AG

TOM: Great! AG I'll finish the appraisal form based on what we've discussed today and have it ready for you tomorrow morning to sign. P/I Think about what we've said so that, if you want to, you can write some comments on the form. GO O.K.? AS

SALLY: O.K. AG

Tom had paved the way for the conversation long before he and Sally entered the room. He had been supportive through the performance period. There were no surprises.

Tom knew that Sally was smart enough to figure out her problem all by herself. He didn't have to hit her over the head with it. He wanted her to take the lead so that he could retain all his conversational options. Had she not been prepared to admit any problems, he would have had to work harder to help her understand her actions, and maybe he would have had to put the issues on the table himself. However, if he had taken the lead, Sally might have become defensive. Because she admitted them, there was no need for her to feel defensive.

When she first walked into the office, Sally said that she knew a problem existed in her performance. Tom only needed to bring that point back into the conversation at the opportune moment. He knew from other conversations with her that she wanted to be successful; he reinforced that motivation. The stage for her buying in to the problem was set.

The solution was not so difficult, because Tom and Sally had already talked about the need for supervisory training. Just like any new manager, Sally needs time to adjust to her new role. She needs time to assimilate information about planning, organizing, leading, and controlling—information that most any adult is familiar with—into her new perspective as a manager. Tom will want to pace his approach so that he can help Sally learn as she becomes ready.

The conversational techniques Tom used relied heavily on asking questions (AS) and making his point persuasively (P). He waited for, and took advantage of, opportunities to demonstrate that he was listening (L).

7.2.4 Effective Conversational Techniques

Effective communicators spend more time paying attention to the other person in the conversation and less time thinking about what they intend to say. And as they talk, they avoid certain dangerous types of statements.

1. *Avoid "you" and "your" statements.* Effective communicators are careful about using the word "you" or "your" in conversations, especially when talking about problems with another person's performance. For example, they say:

> *Some employees feel that the work demands are hard on them.*

instead of:

> *You are too hard on your employees.*

Or they might say:

> *Kathy's feelings were hurt today after she talked with you.*

instead of:

> *Your words to Kathy were very rude.*

The ineffective statements are a judgment and do not give credibility to the other person's view of the situation. The statements start out with an accusation and conclusion instead of an opening to explore the reasons the situation occurred.

People on the receiving end of these statements usually become defensive.

After all, people conduct themselves in a manner that makes sense to them at the moment. They thought it was the best way to say what they wanted to say, or they just didn't know how to say it better.

2. *Be careful with "I" statements.* The use of "I" in conversations requires just as much attention as the use of "you" or "your." For example:

I think we ought to do it this way.

could be stated better as:

What other ways can we do this?

3. *Cut out vague statements.* Effective communicators eliminate vague statements from their conversations; they are specific. For example, instead of the generalization:

Your work has been slipping lately.

an effective communicator would say:

The monthly production report has four errors in it.

Effective communicators watch their adjectives and adverbs. For example:

Contact the customer at the appropriate time.

leaves the listener unclear about what time is appropriate. An effective communicator would say:

Contact the customer each time an inquiry is made.

Effective communicators clarify situations with other people by reviewing assumptions, examining options, and anticipating consequences. Wherever possible, they establish a feedback loop in their conversations so that the other person has the opportunity to contribute information that is not obvious.

Project Analyzer (7.2)

What is the quality of rapport between managers and employees as a result of conversations held during performance-management conferences?

_____

_____

What common mistakes do managers make while conversing?

_____

_____

Are managers willing to improve?

_____

_____

What training do managers need?

_____

_____

How can you get them to "buy in" to a need for training?

_____

7.3 Training Communicators

No one is above learning more about communicating with others. Even the smallest amount of training is helpful, particularly when it reinforces the idea that people may have vastly different interpretations of the same words, events, or actions. We all need insight into our prejudices and biases.

Because of the special situation in which managers find themselves—namely, counseling other people—they need the best support an organization can give them to learn conversational techniques. After all, professional counselors receive training up to a master's or doctorate degree to enable them to help others. Although managers are not expected to function at the professional level—and they should be advised not to—they can easily find themselves in demanding interpersonal situations.

Communication training is essential at the beginning of a performance-management program, and *continually* thereafter. Communication skills can never be perfected. Improvement in rapport building is always possible.

Managers should be involved in choosing their own training. First, they should be asked to describe their performance-management-conference experiences to identify specifically what they need to learn. They should be personally interviewed to determine what they would like to learn.

Second, managers can be asked to review training designs and materials to ensure that their training needs will be addressed. During this process of interview, interaction, and exchange of opinion, managers are helping to shape a training experience in which they will eagerly and profitably participate.

Third, managers should be asked to conduct some of the training sessions, or at least portions of them. Managers who have been through conferences with their employees have a powerful training authority. Unfortunately, many professional trainers simply have not had their managerial baptism of fire, and their words have a hollow ring to them. Some managers will need some train-the-trainer preparation, but that's fine, because they will learn still another skill, and they will build personal confidence.

Fourth, managers should be asked to evaluate the effectiveness of the training program. Were the sessions helpful? Do they feel confident as they face their next performance-management conference? What else might they have learned? Were the practice sessions adequate? Did the instructor explain procedures and techniques thoroughly? Were answers to questions complete and helpful? Did the training improve the outcome of the conferences? Having attempted to apply the communication techniques, what would the managers like to learn to make the next conferences even more successful?

7.3.1 Practicing Responses and Conversations

The best way to learn how to conduct effective conversations is to participate in them. However, people can also learn about conversations by

- Practicing responses to different situations (Figure 7-2 shows a worksheet for doing this)
- Writing the script of a make-believe conversation
- Recreating the script of a past conversation

Teaming with others when writing scripts is particularly helpful, because more opinions will clarify how an actual person might respond. Besides, the variety of potential responses offered by the participants in itself is a lesson.

For a scripted conversation, think of a situation that you expect to occur in the future, but that you are not sure how to handle. Or think of a situation that occurred in the past that you know did not turn out well. Write the other person's expected or actual statement. Quickly, write what you might, or did, say in response. Don't think too much about your response; just write it. Real conversations happen quickly. Then write what the other person would, or did, say. Then write what you would, or did, say. Then what the other person would, or did, say. And so on, until you have a conversation. Team writing, of course, will slow down the process.

Next, check the LIPScale to identify which degrees you and the other person

Figure 7-2. Worksheet for practicing conversational responses using LIPScale.

Think of a statement that you have heard in performance-management conferences. The other person says:

_____

_____

Using each of the eight degrees of the LIPScale, force yourself to respond:

Listening: _____

_____

Agreeing: _____

_____

Asking: _____

_____

Persuading: _____

_____

Giving orders: _____

_____

Comforting: _____

_____

Avoiding: _____

_____

Criticizing: _____

_____

used. What is the outcome of the future conversation? Good, bad, or indifferent? Why? If it was a conversation from the past, why did it not turn out well? What do the degrees used tell you about the success or failure of the conversation, or where it got into trouble?

Then, change the conversation. Use the LIPScale to select more effective responses. Write a new script for an improved conversation. Try out different responses.

7.3.2 Role Playing

Role-playing conversations is also helpful practice. Learning how to participate effectively in conversations requires that you feel the pressure to respond. Nothing, by the way, is a better learning experience than actual conversation.

Background information leading to the conversation must be written for each participant in the role playing, although participants do not know each other's point of view. A role-playing exercise can be videotaped to give trainees an opportunity to observe their performance as often as they wish, privately, and to identify specific opportunities to improve their responses.

There are as many approaches to training people to improve their communication skills as there are people offering suggestions—which tells you something about the complexity of training people how to communicate. Each trainee requires a unique approach, because each person has a unique communication style.

At the same time, people generally need to know the following if they are to improve their communication ability:

1. How people perceive their environment
2. The effect of self-image on what people say and how people respond
3. Why people say what they say and do what they do (motivation)
4. Specific failures when people communicate
5. How words fit together in context and how the choice of words used affects the outcome
6. Nonverbal messages people send that either support or subvert oral communications

People communicate in ways that are comfortable for them. New ways will be uncomfortable, and possibly resisted. People don't change their style easily, mainly because personal change may mean a revolution in values, or a repudiation of the way they have chosen to conduct themselves. Training people to interact in different ways with others is a request for them to change the way they think about themselves and other people—and that is no small request. Go easy. Help them practice new ways.

Project Analyzer (7.3)

Are managers trained to conduct conversations?

_____

_____

What techniques are used in the training sessions?

_____

_____

Is training a continuous process?

_____

_____

Are results of performance-management conferences used to determine training needs?

_____

_____

Are managers interviewed to help them assess their learning requirements?

_____

_____

How successful is training?

_____

_____

Is there follow-up to help managers apply the training?

_____

_____

_____

_____

Are managers required to review their conversation "scripts" before holding a conference with an employee?

_____

_____

Are employees trained to participate in performance-management discussions?

_____

_____

7.4 Strategic Planning

On your first quick walk through the book, record your initial thoughts on policy issues that will have to be decided.

_____

_____

_____

_____

_____

_____

Any notes on tactical procedures?

_____

_____

_____

_____

```
┌─────────────────────────────────┐
│                                 │
│   Chapter 8                     │
│                                 │
│                                 │
│                                 │
│                                 │
│   Getting                       │
│   Performance Up                │
│   to Standard                   │
│                                 │
└─────────────────────────────────┘
```

8.1 Identifying Employee Training and Development Needs

Employees are more apt to perform up to management's expectations when the Performance Standard is made clear to them. The design of the four-dimensional performance-criteria profile helps the manager focus the employee's attention on management's expectations. Still, not each employee is able or willing to perform up to standard.

To begin with, a manager must be certain that the employee is capable of correcting the performance problem. Some managers stop their analysis of employee problems with thinking, "They should *want* to do the job." Performance deficiencies occur for more reasons than just the employee's personal motivation. Deficiencies can occur because of:

- Inadequate recruiting techniques

- Inaccurate performance standards

- Incomplete testing and selection procedures
- Incorrect job qualifications
- Poor job design
- Incomplete or incorrect work procedures

- Incomplete or incorrect job orientation or training
- Inadequate equipment, supplies, or materials
- Poor organization and communications

And, yes, they may also occur because of poor supervision.

A manager must identify not only the true performance problem but also the *cause* of the problem. When managers dig deeply into the situation instead of taking the first-blush answer, they may find causes very different from those they anticipated. More often than not, managers will *not* find a recalcitrant employee.

Furthermore, as managers search thoroughly and realistically to solve a problem, they are likely to trigger a motivation in employees to participate in the search for the cause and the solution. A respectable search avoids triggering a defensive reaction in the employee to being fingered as the sole cause of the problem. The whole notion of gaining employee "buy-in" to the solution of the problem is to have them look objectively at the causes of the problem. Some causes may be beyond their control, but a legitimate search powerfully suggests to them that they should accept the causes that they do contribute.

Once a manager concludes that performance is not meeting expectations, a conversation with the employee is in order—the sooner the better. Some managers mistakenly assume that the employee knows that a problem exists and, furthermore, that the employee will correct the situation without any prodding. Some managers err in the opposite direction when they come down like a ton of bricks on an errant employee.

Performance is easiest to correct when the improvement needed is small. Furthermore, in the case of employee mistakes, correction is easier before the employee's behavior becomes habitual. Performance-improvement conversations will be uncomfortable when employees react angrily that they weren't told sooner about the problem so that they could have corrected their mistakes.

The design of the profile is intended to eliminate the need to appraise an employee's performance as a Problem in a formal, written appraisal. The wording of the profile makes the problem issues clear and obvious so that they can be addressed as soon as they occur.

The major leverage of the profile is that it points to the Performance Standard and suggests: "Perform this way, and we'll all be happy." If a performance gap occurs, the conversation can be directed toward what the employee needs to learn (Improvement) in order to perform up to the Performance Standard, instead of pointing at what's wrong with the employee. (Notice that the Problem statement specifically does not describe employee behavior). Employees are more inclined to participate in a learning experience than in a witch hunt. (After helping employees achieve the Performance Standard, the manager can happily turn to the more rewarding proposition of deciding with an employee whether or not, and how, motivation can be channeled toward the Performance Option.)

8.1.1 Developing Performance by Identifying Learning Needs

Here is a situation of an employee who is not performing up to standard but who is not causing serious problems. The employee needs to improve. The pertinent portion of performance-criteria profile states:

Performance Standard:	Reports are complete and filed on time.
Problem:	Time is wasted when reports are returned and must be corrected.
Improvement:	Needs to review and apply filing procedures; needs to examine the effect of incorrect or late reports.

Let's look at the way a manager can help an employee correct the situation. First, let's assume that the employee is not completing the reports accurately and that the reports are therefore being returned for correction.

The manager writes on the performance-conference form:

Learning Needs, or Comments: Needs to review all possible causes of errors to learn how to prevent them.

Written comments are required on the conference form to prompt dialog between the manager and the employee, to signal to the manager's manager that follow-up will be required, and to document any formal disciplinary action in the future.

A discussion between the manager and the employee can start easily, because the different views of the situation have already been presented in the profile to the employee during orientation and training. The manager need only remind the employee of a previous conversation.

As the conversation develops with the employee, the manager may learn that the employee has not kept up to date with change notices. The questions for the manager and the employee become: 1. How do we recapture all the changes? 2. How do we institute a routine to review new changes?

A performance plan that the manager and the employee fashion might require the employee to read all change notices for the last six months, correlate the applicable change notices with the returned requests for additional information, call the issuing agency to clarify any unclear requirements, and discuss the results of the review effort with the manager at a specified date.

On the other hand, the manager may sense that the employee does not appreciate what problems occur when the reports are not filed on time. The manager might suggest a performance plan requiring the employee to visit with the controlling agency to follow the report through its next steps and to discuss the interruptions with the people who have to deal with late reports. With this experience, the employee will more readily establish a routine to note future changes.

Once learning objectives have been established, a series of performance conferences must be set up at scheduled intervals to monitor compliance with agreed-upon objectives. If performance does not improve as agreed, stricter disciplinary action must begin (actually, disciplinary action technically began the moment the manager informed the employee of a performance deficiency).

8.1.2 Developing Performance With the Written Summary

The Summary section of the Performance-Management-Conference Form identifies how many times each performance level (Performance Standard, Problem, Improvement, and Performance Option) was marked, and closes with a narrative to bring the appraisal to a thoughtful rather than statistical conclusion. A well-written Summary can launch development efforts in the next performance period.

Here is an example. Suzy is one employee in a group of three. She is the best producer, both in quantity and quality, in the group. However, the group is not functioning as a team, and there is tension among the members. Although Suzy is meeting her job results, you sense that she is capable of more and better work. You can count on her to be at work, on time, and to work extra hours if needed. Her appearance is excellent, but her office is in disarray. The manager wonders whether Suzy is a superstar in the eyes of her co-workers, causing some jealousies, and whether Suzy is exercising some informal authority to get the group work accomplished, causing some resentment. Do Suzy's interpersonal skills falter under pressure?

Her manager writes on the conference form:

WRITTEN SUMMARY: Primary job results are being met. Suzy is to be commended for her attendance and punctuality, and willingness to give extra time and effort. Her personal appearance fits the organization's image. We need to look for ways for Suzy's work area to be as appealing—perhaps some more shelves, or another file cabinet.

Because the quantity and quality of work produced is more than that of most others, Suzy may want to consider using more training resources of the organization to learn additional job skills for potential advancement. While Suzy meets deadlines, it seems that meeting them is a source of stress that may be contributing to the interpersonal conflict within her work group.

The Summary points out Suzy's strengths for positive reinforcement, but opens the door to a discussion of potential problems. Using these conversation openers, the manager can move the conversation to explore underlying causes and corrective actions.

8.1.3 Issues of Ability or Willingness

When helping an employee, a manager starts by asking: Is the problem an issue of *ability* or *willingness*? In other words, is the employee unable or unwilling to perform the job? If ability is the issue, the learning needs may be cognitive, affective, or psychomotor. *Cognitive* needs refer to what the employee needs to know in order to perform the job successfully. For example, an employee who aspired to be a supervisor did not understand the concepts of strategic planning or performance management, which was corrected by asking the employee to read relevant information from manuals, texts, periodicals, and the organization's personnel policies.

Affective needs refer to understanding when and how to apply knowledge. For example, an employee who had the requisite knowledge and skills necessary to perform his job had recently been accused by some customers, in separate instances, as having treated them rudely. He corrected his performance by learning to cope, through counseling, with certain emotional problems he had.

Psychomotor needs refer to the physical stamina and dexterity skills required to perform certain job tasks.

Once the learning need is identified, it can be addressed through training, such as on-the-job coaching and practice with the manager or a fellow employee; expert technical advice; formal classroom presentation within the organization or in educational institutions; industry trade shows and seminars; conferences; local or regional workshops; discussion with consultants and specialists; reading or listening to audiocassettes; viewing films or videotapes; or visiting similar work sites.

If the need is not one of an ability that has to be developed, then it's a willingness issue. The employee knows what to do but chooses not to do it. The key to changing the employee's current behavior is to create conditions that make the proposed behavior more rewarding than current performance, or that cause the employee to lose something important, such as pay or opportunity for advancement, if current behavior continues.

8.1.4 Obtaining Learner "Buy-In"

The employee's manager can undoubtedly identify what the employee needs to learn, but the process of obtaining learner "buy-in" to the need is crucial to successful improvement. The employee must "own" the problem before any significant change in behavior can take place. If the employee feels that he or she is working on a problem for the manager's sake only, the employee's change will be superficial.

Managers often think of solving performance problems by sending employees to general training courses instead of helping them acquire *specific* knowledge or skills to correct *specific* deficient job behaviors. For example, a manager may suggest a class on communication, when the specific need is for training in how to give a confrontational message.

When a training director in one organization received a general request for "some classes in communications," he asked to meet in small groups with the employees who would receive the training in order to confirm and specify the training need. He also wanted to reduce potential resistance to training. If the employees did not buy in to the training by having some influence on the topics, the training director reasoned, their resistance would become a block to learning the needed knowledge, skills, and abilities. Thus, by the time the training was presented, the participants had already agreed that they wanted to learn "how to deal with customer complaints."

Additionally, trainees can be asked how they would prefer to have the training conducted (the number of sessions, the length of each session, the structure of the presentation, and so on) to give the trainer some idea about preferred learning styles. Managers who conduct their own training sessions must follow these same buy-in principles.

Pinpointing the deficient behavior allows the manager and the employee to specify performance problems and corrective training solutions. A general accusation by the manager, such as "Does sloppy work," is useless for identifying a corrective training solution. The behavior is pinpointed, for example, when the manager counts the number of errors found in a report submitted by the employee and identifies the nature of the errors.

The next step is to ask the employee to suggest several possible strategies (his or her preferred method of learning) that would achieve the desired behavior change. The manager and the employee should examine the options to determine the one that best meets the needs of the organization and the employee.

Here is a case study to illustrate some of the points about identifying learning needs and solutions. An employee was offending fellow employees. The manager sent the employee to the training department to view some films on getting along with people. After viewing one film, the employee asked a training specialist, "Do you have any other films that I can look at? Maybe if I look at one more, my manager will be satisfied." The training specialist realized that (1) the employee did not "own" the problem and (2) the requested solution was not bringing about the desired change in the employee.

The training specialist made an appointment with the employee to discuss why she thought her manager had asked her to watch the films. The employee gave a vague answer. The training specialist began to pinpoint behavior, attempting to define the performance gap. This moved the focus from the manager's problem to the employee's problem.

Managers can use this same tactic when no training specialist is available to discuss the employee's perception of the problem. Managers must avoid following autocratic instincts to decree the problem and its solution.

As a result of the inquiry, the employee acknowledged that she did not get along with fellow employees. She admitted that she had always dismissed other employees she worked with as less competent and lower-class. This allowed her to rationalize that it was their problem, not hers, that she didn't get along with them. The training specialist and the employee identified some of her personal needs: (1) to be better than other people and (2) not to develop relationships of any depth with other people.

Not until these needs were understood could the manager and the employee bring about the desired change in behavior. Certainly, the generalized request used in the first place would not work. The solution included individual counseling with a professional counselor, journal writing to expose feelings related to the behaviors, and a list of specific tasks the employee would do to develop better working relationships with at least one other employee.

When the needed change involves a relationship between two people, both people can be asked to address the issue. Each person should write down the frustrations in the relationship, identifying behaviors as specifically as possible (see Figure 8-1 for an example). A discussion will determine whether the problem is due to the manager's style, the employee's style, the job function, or some combination. A satisfactory solution that addresses both the employee's and the manager's needs can be formulated.

In one situation, the manager's overall view of the employee was, "He won't do the work," but the employee's view was that the manager "doesn't let me do work the way I want." Discovering these different perceptions helped the manager and the employee each accept a part in the problem, and a part in the solution.

8.1.5 Adults as Learners

Several factors regarding adults as learners, and facts about the learning process, must be considered when planning solutions to identified training needs:

1. Solutions for filling a performance gap should start at a comfortable place for the employee—that is, with what the employee now knows. Training builds on current knowledge, skills, and abilities and points toward how the new learning will help performance.
2. Adults prefer to direct their own learning, and prefer active inquiry. Adult learners want to ask questions and interpret answers in their own language.
3. Adults learn better from real-life tasks and problems. Their own personal experiences are a rich resource for them.
4. Adults are motivated more by their internal needs than by external rewards or punishments.
5. A comfortable and sensitive physical and psychological climate is essential. The psychological climate includes authenticity, mutual respect and trust, collaboration, and openness between the teacher and the learner.

8.1.6 Learning Contracts

A learning contract is a plan developed between a manager and an employee to achieve some new learning. It begins by stating the results to be accomplished (the more specific and measurable, the better). Then, a program is fashioned that allows the employee to choose the best way to learn.

The employee and the manager identify all possible learning resources, including what the manager will do to help the employee learn. Target accom-

Figure 8-1. Sample chart for examining frustrations.

| Frustrations (Employee's View) | FRUSTRATION SOURCE | | | SOLUTION | |
	Supervisor's Style	Employee's Style	Result of Job Function	Supervisor's Need	Employee's Need
1. "Can't make a decision without clearing it with [*supervisor*]."	x	x	x	1. "For employee to trust where I'm coming from; trust my motives."	1. "For supervisor to be more deliberate about clarifying when decision is inappropriate and to let minor, less crucial decisions go as made by employee."

2. "Not sure what's expected of me."	x	x	2. "For employee to ask for clarification when needed."	x	2. "For supervisor to give clarification when asked."
3. "Want to please [*supervisor*] but feel that I can't."	x	x	3. "For employee to take more responsibility for initiating job-related tasks."		3. "For supervisor to give credit and acknowledge when tasks are done well."

plishments and dates are established and agreed to. The employee and the manager enact the plan and meet at the appointed times to check progress and results. Adjustments are made where necessary. Figure 8-2 shows a sample learning contract.

What happens, of course, is that learning, not teaching, becomes the focus of the experience. The onus to "motivate and teach" the employee is off the manager's shoulders. Instead, the manager becomes a participant in the learning process. The responsibility, challenge, opportunity, and reward belong mostly to the employee.

Figure 8-2. A learning contract.

What Must Be Learned? [Be Specific.]	Where Can Helpful Information Be Found?	How Will Information Be Acquired?	By Whom?	When?	When Will Progress Be Reviewed?	Specific Evidence That Learning Has Been Accomplished

Project Analyzer (8.1)

Do managers solve problems or only the symptoms of problems?

_____

_____

Have managers been trained to identify the underlying causes of performance problems?

_____

_____

Do managers distinguish between ability and willingness issues?

_____

_____

When performance problems have occurred, do employees willingly participate in identifying the true cause, or do they just go through the motions of learning in order to satisfy their manager?

_____

_____

What training resources are available to help managers identify performance problems and solutions?

_____

_____

If there is no organizational training department, to whom can managers turn for help?

_____

_____

8.2 Guidelines for the Performance-Improvement Conference

Managers and employees must talk regularly between formal performance-management conferences about progress being made on job expectations and performance plans. Obviously, managers and employees talk daily or weekly as they routinely interact with each other. However, time must be set aside regularly to make a major check on performance—especially when performance is not up to standard.

Here are some guidelines for approaching performance-improvement conferences. They are similar to the conference guidelines presented in Chapter 7, section 7.2, but here the focus is on a perceived problem with performance, and the means to correct it.

1. *Establish rapport.* Prepare for the meeting. Develop a desired outcome and a strategy to accomplish it. Set an appointment. Let the employee know the reason for the meeting. Avoid distracting times. Allow enough time. Start in a friendly, genuine manner. Deal with your own stress. Watch your body language and your tone of voice. Maintain eye contact. Give compliments when appropriate.

2. *Identify the problem.* State the facts as you know them. Use specific examples, not generalities, including:

- The circumstances that preceded the incident
- The setting in which the incident occurred
- Precisely what the employee did that was ineffective
- The consequences of the incident
- The extent to which the consequences were in the control of the employee

Deal with one problem at a time. Don't unload a pile of problems. Ask for the employee's perception of the facts. Clarify information, but don't fight or blame. Probe for the reasons behind actions. Hear what is meant in addition to what is said. Listen for feelings and respond to them. Watch for nonverbal cues. Agree whenever you can. Ask plenty of questions. Talk positively. Assign or accept responsibility.

3. *State the objective.* Get agreement on what needs to happen to correct the behavior. Restate and paraphrase to ensure accurate understanding. Ask for commitment. Explain why achievement of the objective is important.

4. *Consider the options.* Ask for the employee's ideas. Don't just state what you think. Be patient. Don't judge the suggestions. Meet again if necessary. Explore the consequences of each option. Ask: "What do you think would happen if we did that?" Avoid asking leading questions that signal the answer you want to hear. Don't ask for a complete change in personality; ask instead for a small change in behavior.

5. *Prepare a plan*. Work together with the employee to determine what steps will be necessary to accomplish the learning objective. Take notes. State specifically what will be done, when, and by whom. Ask: "What can I do to make sure that we are successful?" Clarify job results and performance standards. Remove obstacles to performance. Identify new sources of help, such as co-workers and experts. Improve methods and organization. Provide facilities and equipment.

Write learning objectives answering these questions:

- What new requirements does the organization have?
- What would the employee like to accomplish?
- What does the employee need to learn in order to perform up to standard?

- What challenging opportunities might motivate the employee to become enthusiastic about the job?
- How can I help?

Then make sure that both you and the employee understand and agree to the objectives.

6. *Plan to check the results*. Establish a follow-up schedule. Change the consequences of performance if they do not encourage good performance or do not discourage poor performance.

8.2.1 Analyzing a Disciplinary Appraisal Conversation with the LIPScale

The LIPScale was introduced and described in Chapter 7, section 7.2. You may want to refer to it for definitions and comments. Here is an example of an ineffective disciplinary appraisal conversation analyzed with the LIPScale (Listening = L; Agreeing = AG; Asking = AS; Persuading = P; Information = P/I; Giving Orders = GO; Comforting = CO; Avoiding = AV; Criticizing = CR):

MANAGER: We received a report that you were rude to a customer. CR [*especially the accusatory word "rude" at the beginning of the conversation*]
EMPLOYEE: I was only enforcing the no-smoking policy. P
MANAGER: I realize that, AG but don't you think you could have handled it better? CR [*notice that the word "but" completely destroyed the agreement*]
EMPLOYEE: I can't change my attitude. P Some people can hide their anger, but I can't. P
MANAGER: I have to tell you that if your attitude doesn't improve, and you're rude to a patient again, you'll be terminated immediately. CR [*especially the words "terminated immediately"*] You know this is the third time this month that you've caused a problem. CR
EMPLOYEE: I can't say that if someone gets on my case I won't jump back. P
MANAGER: If anything happens—*anything*—you just head for the door and contact me. GO If someone else starts the problem, I'll take care of it. P

EMPLOYEE: You will? CR [*this is not* AS, *because of the undercurrent of disbelief*]

MANAGER: Yes. P

EMPLOYEE: O.K., AG I'll try, P but I can't promise anything. AV ["*but" converts the agreement and persuasion*]

MANAGER: Just remember that if you lose your temper, it won't be tolerated. CR

Comment: The supervisor started off on the wrong foot with a critical remark and relied mainly on threats to produce a change in behavior. The anticipated outcome? The supervisor and the employee will have this conversation again, if the employee isn't fired first.

8.2.2 Improved Conversation

Here is the same situation approached differently. Notice the different degrees of the scale used to start the conversation.

MANAGER: Can we talk for a few minutes, Jim? AS [*actually* P *when coming from a manager to an employee*] I received a report of a problem with one of the customers last night. P/I [*a statement of fact*] What happened? AS

EMPLOYEE: Well, this lady was smoking in a no-smoking area, and I told her she couldn't smoke there. P/I

MANAGER: Then what? AS

EMPLOYEE: She gave me some smart remark. P/I

MANAGER: What did she say? AS

EMPLOYEE: I don't remember exactly, something like I didn't have to jump all over her when she didn't know not to smoke there. P/I Same old stuff; they never know they aren't supposed to smoke in restricted areas. P/I

MANAGER: Did you say anything else to her? AS

EMPLOYEE: No, I just told her there was no smoking there and walked away. P/I She got the message the first time. P/I

MANAGER: Did you suggest any other place where she could smoke? AS

EMPLOYEE: No. P/I

MANAGER: From what you just said, it was a short and to-the-point conversation. L

EMPLOYEE: Yeah. AG

MANAGER: The customer complained that you were rude to her. P/I

EMPLOYEE: What else is she going to say? P She was wrong. P/I I was just doing my job. P

MANAGER: Well, partly, anyhow. P Let's face it, GO we don't want people smoking where they shouldn't be, P/I but we also don't want people complaining about us and filing reports, P/I do we? P

EMPLOYEE: No, I guess not. AG

MANAGER: Jim, you know I've talked plenty about helping people rather than just enforcing rules, and how uptight people can be when they come here. P/I You know that already, and we haven't had a problem that we couldn't work out before. P But all of a sudden within the last month, we've had to talk three times about this same kind of thing. P/I Something's bothering you, I can tell. L Why don't you tell me about it? L/P Maybe I can help. P

EMPLOYEE: I guess I have been a little on edge. AG My mother's been sick, and I've been worrying about her. P/I

MANAGER: That would make anybody on edge. L/AG

EMPLOYEE: Yeah, AG and then you think people would know better so you wouldn't have to remind them. P

MANAGER: Reminding people when it's obvious just seems to add to the bother. L

EMPLOYEE: Well, I don't mind if I don't also get some smart remark. P

MANAGER: (Silence) L You know, Jim, I think you were angry L [L *especially since the manager is naming the emotion*] before you got to her, and the way you told her not to smoke there set her off. P You kinda got what you gave her. P

EMPLOYEE: You're right. AG You know, maybe I ought to start off by directing them to a place where they can smoke instead of starting with where they can't. P

MANAGER: I think that would be great. AG I'll bet they'll be more responsive. I think too, Jim, if you find yourself getting upset or in trouble, give me a call. P Maybe we can get things cooled down right away. P Let's talk again in a week. GO

EMPLOYEE: OK. AG Thanks. P

Comment: The manager started off with a statement of fact, without judgment, and immediately asked for more information from the employee. A series of questions obtained more information, but also got the conversation going without any defensive reaction from the employee. Soon, the manager was able to elicit agreement from the employee. Then, with a solid rapport already established, the manager was able to introduce the problem.

A major point in the conversation occurred when the manager gave a Listening response: "Something's bothering you, I can tell." The manager was able to uncover the real issue and offer some helpful suggestions to the employee. The anticipated outcome? A real chance for improvement.

8.2.3 The Performance-Interview Review

After a conversation, a manager should review the event:

1. *Coach on results.* Did I stress job results instead of personal traits? Was criticism job-centered instead of personal?

2. *Get down to cases.* Were the reasons for my opinions specific? Did I refer to specific incidents? Was I candid?
3. *Determine causes.* Did I probe for causes or just stick to the surface facts? Did we get to the real cause?
4. *Make the interview a two-way process.* Was I dominant? Who did most of the talking? Was there good give-and-take discussion? Did I use questions to stimulate thinking?
5. *Set objectives.* Were objectives set? And timetables? Were objectives specific? Were specific on-the-job learning experiences targeted?
6. *Stimulate motivation.* Did I show interest and concern? Was my motivation positive? Will my employee act differently? Are the consequences of no change clear? Do *I* need to change?

8.2.4 Getting Help From Others To Solve Problems

Conflicts between two people may not always be resolved by just the two of them. When an impasse occurs, effective communicators use other means, such as submitting the dispute to a third person who renders a judgment for one side or the other on the basis of the facts presented (arbitration), or asking a third person to intervene in the discussion to help the disputing parties look again at each other's arguments and find new options for a solution (mediation).

8.2.5 Disciplining Employees Whose Performance Does Not Improve or Who Willfully Violate Rules

Usually, the process of identifying problems, setting learning objectives, preparing a performance plan, and following up to ensure results provides enough impetus for an employee to improve. Not always, however. Some employees do not get the message, as the saying goes, or perhaps they choose to ignore it.

Organizations have a right to enforce orderly conduct and compliance with established rules. Disciplining an employee is intended to train employees to perform what management wants, in the way management wants it—within reason, of course. Disciplinary proceedings can turn from training into punishment for continued errant behavior. Punishment is a last resort to make the message perfectly clear.

Disciplinary proceedings should not be viewed as separate and apart from the established philosophy of managing performance. Thought of as only "getting tough" with employees when they do not perform up to standard, disciplinary proceedings are unlikely to motivate employees to improve, and are a likely cause for a rebuke should management's actions be challenged by an employee in a judicial proceeding.

Disciplining to punish an employee cannot begin until the manager knows why a standard of conduct was violated, or why the employee continues to refuse to improve. First, the facts must be investigated, following the guidelines mentioned at the beginning of section 8.2.

Then, the manager must ask: Is discipline necessary in this case? If yes, what kind of discipline? Is the purpose to reinforce performance-improvement measures already taken because somehow the employee did not understand, or to punish because the employee deliberately chose to disregard known standards of conduct?

Next, the manager must decide: What discipline is needed to reinforce previous discussions about lagging performance, to regain order, or to punish the employee?

The basic forms of performance-improvement discipline are *oral* and *written*. The key ingredients of both are (1) an accurate statement of the facts and (2) a clear statement of the consequences if performance does not improve. Performance-improvement disciplinary measures generally proceed from oral to written, depending on the gravity of the situation. The Performance-Management-Conference Form serves as an excellent beginning when formal disciplinary action is required. Only the portions of the form that are used to document deficient performance need be completed.

Employees may be terminated immediately for a deliberate and severe violation of rules. Usually, however, the manager starts the performance-improvement process with an informal conversation, to understand and correct the situation. Next, formal conversations would be held. Notes would be made of the discussion and included in the manager's file on the employee, or possibly the employee's personnel record. Up to this point, as you can see, the process of discussing, reviewing, and recording performance is the same as that already described as performance management.

If the employee fails to heed the manager's direction, however, disciplinary procedures begin with formal letters of reprimand given to the employee by the manager and signed by the employee, with copies given to the employee and placed in the official personnel file. At this point, all previous records from performance-improvement conferences become incorporated into the disciplinary documentation. After formal letters, or sometimes simultaneously with them, employees may be put on probation, meaning that if they do not improve their performance according to a specific improvement plan, they will be subject to harsher discipline, including discharge.

An extreme form of discipline is a suspension from work without pay—a technique used after plenty of discussion and writing have failed. The ultimate punishment, of course, is to discharge an employee for willfully failing to comply with directives.

8.2.6 Taking Disciplinary Action

Here is a decision-making guide to help you understand a situation and take appropriate disciplinary actions. First, ask these questions:

1. What caused the offense?
2. Did management do what was necessary to prevent the offense—that is, inform, warn, train, schedule, supply, instruct?

3. Has management enforced standards consistently and uniformly among all employees?
4. Is any harassment or discrimination issue involved with this employee?
5. How serious is the offense?
6. How does the offense affect the employee's work?
7. What decisions have been made when other employees have committed similar offenses?
8. What is the employee's past record—that is, pattern of performance, related offenses, unrelated offenses, duration of good conduct?
9. What are the prospects for this employee's improvement?
10. Are there any mitigating or extenuating circumstances?
11. Is the disciplinary judgment humane and wise?

After you have answered these questions, you are ready to choose which specific oral or written disciplinary action will be necessary to deal with the situation.

8.2.7 Disciplinary Letters

Taking disciplinary action moves the manager into a legal arena where requirements are quite precise. Any written disciplinary communication should include:

1. The purpose of the document
2. The statement of offense
3. The facts of the offense
4. A restatement of the standard, rule, or policy
5. The opportunity to learn and correct
6. The consequence of continued failure to comply

Figure 8-3 shows a sample letter that contains these ingredients. It also illustrates the use of objective observations instead of subjective conclusions.

What is your reaction to this letter? Do you feel that the description of the employee's position and posture are overly specific and silly? Why not just say that the employee was sleeping? Frankly, sleeping would be an apt description, but years ago, in a contested disciplinary action, an employee claimed that he was not asleep and unattentive to his work, but only resting his eyes because of a headache. Management lost its case.

In many (if not most) judicial reviews, employees get the benefit of the doubt, especially as loss of pay and employment reputation are so important. So, careful wording prevents losing a disciplinary case when jurists want to be overly "fair." Nevertheless, objective instead of subjective wording is good discipline for anyone. Too frequently, we jump to conclusions about events without accurate information or without a clear view from the other person's perspective.

Figure 8-4 shows an example of a written warning for prohibited or unsafe conduct.

Figure 8-3. Sample disciplinary letter with warning.

```
                                                   March 1, 19XX
To: [Employee, SS#]
From: [Manager]


This letter is a written warning because you failed to fulfill the
responsibilities of your job on February 15, 19XX.

On that date, at about 2:50 a.m., you were observed by me sitting with
your back to the machines that you are responsible for operating, at
a window away from your place of work. Your eyes were closed, your
chair was tilted backward, your feet rested on the windowsill, and
you were heard to make heavy and hoarse breathing sounds. Under the
circumstances, you were not alert to the operation of the machines.

With this written warning you are being given an opportunity to
correct your conduct so that you will in the future fulfill all the
responsibilities required of your job. However, should you fail to
correct your performance, you will leave me no choice but to take
additional, and more severe, disciplinary action.


                                   _____
                                   [Manager's signature]


_____
[Employee's signature]
Receipt acknowledged

Date: _____
```

Disciplinary action must become stronger if the employee does not accept the point of orderly conduct and meeting standards. After exhausting all means of oral discussion and written warning, a manager may be forced to suspend an employee from work without pay, with the intent of impressing the employee with the severity of the situation. Figure 8-5 shows an example of a letter of suspension.

8.2.8 Documentation Required To Sustain a Termination

When an employer takes disciplinary action against an employee, the employer should be able to prove that the alleged acts did occur, and that they were sufficiently serious to warrant termination. This means that detailed records must be kept. The employee's conduct must not have been ignored or forgiven. Warning of the consequences of continued violation of job requirements must

Figure 8-4. Sample disciplinary letter about unsafe conduct.

```
                                        August 5, 19XX


To: [Employee, SS#]
From: [Manager]


Last Monday, August 1, 19XX, at about 9:30 a.m., during your regular
scheduled hours of work, you were observed smoking in the passageway
leading from your workplace to the freight elevator. The company's
rules, as you are aware, are: "#13: Smoking is prohibited except in
areas designated for that purpose" and "#17: Violating any safety
rules or practices, or engaging in any conduct that creates a safety
hazard, is prohibited."

The area in which you smoked is not designated for that purpose, and
your action that day created a serious hazard that threatened your
own health and safety, the health and safety of your fellow workers,
and the company's property.

As a result of our discussion, I believe that you now understand the
seriousness of your action and the need to observe all safety rules.
Take this written warning as an opportunity to learn safe work habits
so that no violations occur in the future and so that no other dis-
ciplinary action will be required.


                                   _____
                                   [Manager's signature]



_____
[Employee's signature]
Receipt acknowledged

Date: _____
```

have been given to the employee with reasonable notice and with suggestions for improvement.

Job descriptions, performance-criteria profiles, performance plans, learning contracts, policies, procedures, rules, manager's notes, and disciplinary letters are the documents that support an employer's position. The employer must be able to prove that job expectations and standards of conduct were established and clearly expressed and that a reasonable method existed to determine whether the employee met the standards.

The employee must not have been singled out for punishment. If other em-

Figure 8-5. Sample disciplinary letter announcing temporary suspension.

May 19, 19XX

To: [Employee, SS#]
From: [Manager]

On February 8, 19XX, I gave you a Disciplinary Written Reprimand for your lateness and failure to report regularly for work on time on the dates specified, in accordance with the Company's rules and the duties and responsibilities of your job. I further notified you in that letter of February 8 that if you failed to correct your attendance record and report regularly for work on time in the future, you would subject yourself to further disciplinary action.

On May 12 and 16, 19XX, you were again late for work. The reasons you gave for your lateness were not acceptable. As a result of your failure to correct your attendance record and to meet the requirements of your job, I am suspending you from work without pay, as disciplinary action, for a period of three (3) working days, beginning Tuesday, May 23, 19XX. You must report back for work on Friday, May 26, 19XX, at 8:00 a.m.

If you should fail in the future to cōrrect your attendance record, to report regularly on time, to observe the Company's rules, and to perform all responsibilities of your job, you will subject yourself to further disciplinary action, including the possibility of termination of your employment.

It is my hope that you will accept my action as an opportunity to improve your performance and that you will return to work to participate as a cooperative partner.

_____
[Manager's signature]

_____
[Employee's signature]
Receipt acknowledged

Date: _____

ployees violated the same standards and were not disciplined, one employee cannot be disciplined. The history of the case must show that the employee did not pay attention to the warnings and made no effort to improve. To sustain a termination, the employer must have reason to believe that the misconduct is not temporary but is part of "a consistent and recurring pattern which is unlikely to change in the future."

8.2.9 Training To Conduct Disciplinary Action

Managers can make serious mistakes when they do not understand the legal requirements for taking disciplinary action against employees. Although disciplinary action may be described as *corrective* instead of *punitive*, it is difficult to describe the individuals involved as anything but adversaries.

Training methods to help managers conduct disciplinary procedures correctly are similar to the communication techniques discussed in section 8.3. Discipline is one form of communication. In addition to communicating clearly—getting one's point across as well as listening to another point of view—managers need to learn how to control themselves, and others, when tempers begin to flare.

Employees who are being disciplined are in a crisis. Some employees know the trouble they have caused and are prepared for the consequences. Others know that something went wrong but are unable or unwilling to assume responsibility for their actions. Conversations with these employees can be difficult. Managers need to acquire the skills necessary to help employees cope with the situation in which they find themselves.

Some employees who are being disciplined will not be able to cope with the demands of the situation, and their condition is beyond the talent and responsibility of the typical manager. These employees will need special assistance and professional help. Managers should not be trained to try to help these employees, except to recognize the problem and recommend professional help for the employee.

Group role-playing is a powerful technique to help managers understand the implications of inappropriate disciplinary action. A simulated grievance procedure or arbitration proceeding is an effective technique. Teams can be formed to represent each side in the dispute, as well as to form an independent review board, or to act as an arbitrator. The case is tried with testimony and questioning of witnesses. Background guidelines are required for each group.

8.2.10 Training To Prevent Disciplinary Action

More important than training managers to conduct disciplinary action is training them how to prevent relationships from deteriorating to the point that disciplinary action is necessary. The image of a manager unfortunately still connotes a person who retains authority, makes decisions without concern for the employees involved, and responds only to the organization's requirements. Employees don't like this kind of treatment. Employees want a manager-leader who will look responsibly not only at the goals and needs of the organization but their goals and needs as well.

The challenge of managing and leading is to bridge the conflicting goals and needs of the organization and its employees. People are motivated differently. Human discord is natural. There is no fundamental truth that will show us once and for all how to manage people, especially when they do not agree with our decisions. Such a search for enlightenment, particularly for charismatic leadership, is misguided. The optimum moment of organizational effectiveness, when everybody wants to do the same thing, even for different reasons, is better viewed as a coincidence.

Here is the enigma. Management and leadership are distinctly different, yet one cannot exist without the other. Managers who rely on technical knowledge and ignore the human influence on their position, fail—by all decent standards. Leaders who rely on their relationship with their followers and ignore the need to plan, organize, and control, fail—by all measurable standards. Management without leadership is hollow. Leadership without management is fruitless.

This book's recurring theme of open discussion of job requirements and performance expectations is aimed at helping managers become leaders; yet, at some point, someone has to manage. Effective managers know when to manage and when to lead; they are strong enough to do both, without diminishing either role.

Project Analyzer (8.2)

What is the state of discipline in your organization?

_____

_____

How have disciplinary actions taken affected the general rapport between managers and employees?

_____

_____

Are managers and employees poised for discord between them?

_____

_____

Are harsh discipline and adversarial relationships the current state of affairs?

_____

_____

Is there a backlog of grievances and arbitration cases challenging management's disciplinary actions against employees?

_____

_____

If so, what are the causes of this breakdown in relations?

_____

_____

How well do managers conduct disciplinary actions?

_____

_____

_____

Are managers required to have their actions reviewed before they take them?

_____

_____

Are managers trained to conduct disciplinary procedures?

_____

_____

Are results of disciplinary actions used to determine training needs?

_____

_____

Are managers interviewed to help them assess their learning requirements?

_____

_____

What techniques are used in the training sessions?

_____

_____

_____

Is training a continuous process?

_____

_____

_____

Is there follow-up on training to help managers apply what they learned?

_____

_____

_____

_____

8.3 Strategic Planning

On your first quick walk through the book, record your initial thoughts on policy issues that will have to be decided.

_____

_____

_____

_____

_____

Any notes on tactical procedures?

_____

_____

_____

_____

Chapter 9

Rewarding and Recognizing Performance

9.1 Performance and Pay

Employees are remunerated for their work efforts with wages and salaries (pay), augmented generally by some mixture of noncash benefits and sometimes by incentives and bonuses. Pay and noncash benefits are remuneration for employment, namely, for the performance of routine job content. Incentives and bonuses reward extraordinary performance. Total compensation includes payments from all categories, the blend depending on the needs and desires of the people being compensated, the ability of the organization to fund the various categories, and the motivations that the organization intends to trigger in employees.

One pay policy that an organization must decide on is: Should employees who perform better than other employees be payed more for their better performance? Or should employees receive the same general increases, or increases tied to seniority, on the theory that if they do not perform up to standard, they will be disciplined and possibly terminated? No one system for remunerating employees will work in every kind of organization. Pay programs must be designed specifically to meet the needs and style of each organization and its employees.

The premise of this book is that pay should vary according to individual performance wherever possible. The most fundamental reason for this position is that this notion of reward most closely parallels the tenets of an economic system where survival and reward in the marketplace are most directly linked to the effort of the producer.

Convincing managers and employees that there is an opportunity for greater rewards when pay is tied to performance is not that simple, however. Some objections are:

- Increased rewards do not necessarily induce increased performance.
- Generic and subjective performance criteria impede accurate and equitable appraisals of performance.
- Employees generally have an inflated opinion of their performance.
- Employees have been conditioned to receive general increases and will complain, because they will not be able to plan on certain increases in the future.

Successful programs that tie pay to performance seem to have three ingredients. One, the program fits the human resources style of the organization; in particular, it acknowledges the ability of the organization and the individual to alter work circumstances if they choose. Two, the program includes clearly defined job expectations so that differences in performance can be recognized. Three, clear and continuous communication is an obvious part of the process as the manager and the employee fashion and review a performance plan that is understandable to both. Objections to tying pay to performance wither when these essential ingredients are present.

Fair-minded organizations do not harp on ever-increasing performance. Yes, they take it when they can get it, but more important to them is the basic contract that the employee will perform up to standard. Fulfilling the contract is regarded as respectable performance. Not performing up to standard is very unacceptable. Performing above standard is optional, but welcomed.

Managers need not anguish over determining which employees shall have to buy hamburger and which shall be able to buy filet mignon with the pay they receive. Pay is the consequence of performance. The manager allocates the organization's budget in direct proportion to what each employee earns.

With the performance-criteria profile, employees have a clear picture of what they have to do to earn more money. Performance is their choice, not the manager's. Performance ratings are not the manager's *opinion* of the employee's performance, but are more accurately the conclusions the manager derives about the performance presented by the employee.

Many of the complaints heard in organizations about programs that tie pay to performance come from employees who know that they will receive the smallest rewards. They want the gratification without the effort. Yet, deep down, people understand the notion of greater rewards for greater effort.

Organizations need to be more honest and open about their purpose, objectives, and constraints. Employees have been conditioned to expect more each year, because management has given them more each year, or has made elaborate excuses when pay increases have been reduced. Some managements have been unethical when they have not been candid about the organization's requirements and financial restrictions. Employees can understand a predicament, but only when they are told the circumstances.

When appraising performance, managers compare an employee's performance with job criteria. When paying for performance, managers additionally must compare one employee's performance with the performance of other employees so that pay rewards can be distributed equitably within the organization.

In order to tie performance to pay, performance must be summarized in some manner. Traditional performance-grading scales require managers to translate their assessment of performance into one of several imprecise pay categories. Tying performance to pay with the performance-criteria profile is easier than with vague, generic categories, because the profile states conditions of performance in specific job language. Using job-language criteria, the manager need only observe the employee's performance and identify the proper criterion.

9.1.1 When Job Responsibilities Are Equally Weighted

In order to distribute pay equitably on the basis of performance, management must differentiate job responsibilities according to their individual value to the organization. To demonstrate the difference between equitable and inequitable pay administration, let's look at what can happen when a system is scored without weighting specific job responsibilities. Look at the problem when the performance summaries of two employees are identical. Here each employee is rated as performing at the Performance Option level in five job responsibilities and at the Performance Standard level in 23 job responsibilities.

Employee	Performance Option	Performance Standards Met	Improvement Needed	Problematic
	(In number of items as marked on appraisal form)			
Alice	5	23	—	—
Bill	5	23	—	—

According to pay-distribution systems commonly used in organizations, the pay increases for the two employees would be identical, because most systems only count the number of job responsibilities at each performance level and do not take into account the relative value of the different responsibilities to the organization. In this example, Alice may have performed outstandingly on the "tough" job responsibilities, whereas Bill may have performed outstandingly on "easier-to-achieve" job responsibilities.

Being fair to employees is a problem if job results and performance criteria are not valued separately. In this next example, the performance summaries of four employees are not identical, but the inequitable result is the same:

Employee	Performance Option	Performance Standards Met	Improvement Needed	Problematic
Arlene	8	18	—	—
Bob	5	20	1	—
Cindy	1	19	6	—
Don	8	10	8	—

If points were assigned to the performance summaries as though all job results were valued identically by the organization, then the employees would have accumulated the following points:

Performance Level	Points	Points for Each Employee	
Performance Option	15 points	Arlene	300
Performance Standards Met	10 points	Bob	280
Improvement Needed	5 points	Cindy	235
Problematic	0 points	Don	260

If accumulated points were then tied to pay-increase ranges, the employees would receive these increases:

Points	Pay Increase (in %)	Employees
354 or more	9	
317–353	8	
280–316	7	Arlene, Bob
242–279	6	Don
205–241	5	Cindy
168–204	4	
130–167	3	
129 or less	0	

We will examine how the performance of employees Arlene, Bob, Cindy, and Don can be appraised more accurately and fairly later in this section.

An organization is people coming together to produce together—but with each step in the translation of performance into pay in a statistical system, the mark of the person is diminished. Although pay distribution is a mathematical problem, you must be careful not to ignore the human aspect of the system by directing your attention only to the numbers.

All responsibilities are not of equal value to the organization. Responsibilities should be valued by the manager and the employee when they are planning for performance, so both of them understand which responsibilities are the most important to the organization, and which will have the greater impact on pay during the performance period.

Some performance-management approaches deal with this problem ad nauseum and lose the value of the program in the process. Insidiously, the numbers take on a life of their own. A few misguided efforts have even attempted to measure human performance in tenths of a point!

One problem with precise valuing is that the valuing may change during the performance period. What may be important *today* could be less important *tomorrow* as demands on the organization change. Therefore, when a manager defines the values at the start of the performance period, there is every reason to expect that the values will change during the performance period. Seasoned managers understand this change and thus talk to their employees continually to ensure that each of them is on the same wave length. But you can hear it now, can't you: "With computers we could input the changing values each day and keep a cumulative history so that we know the average mix of values over the performance period so that we can create an index . . ."

Maybe someday we can, but today we must focus our performance and pay systems on individual managers whose "intuitive" computers can do a pretty good job of valuing, appraising, and rewarding performance. Managers have not made effective judgments in the past because they have been required to work with structurally defective systems. When semantic and mathematical incumbrances are not placed between them and their employees, managers can be very effective.

9.1.2 Summarizing Performance for Pay

Let's reexamine the performance of employees Arlene, Bob, Cindy, and Don as a manager would who considers the specific importance of each job responsibility. Summarizing performance is an important step in reaching a final understanding of the employee's performance in the organization, planning performance for the future, and tying pay to performance.

The employee, however, need not be told what the pay summary is. You will remember that the conference form in Chapter 5 (Figure 5-3) shows only the distribution of profile ratings, not the final pay summary. The reasons for not telling employees their pay rating are that this rating (1) is usually only for distributing pay budgets and (2) may detract from the employee's motivation when the employee is being helped to learn and perform up to standard, or when the employee is on the verge of major contributions to the organization.

Employee Arlene

Performance Option	Performance Standards Met	Improvement Needed	Problematic
8	18	—	—

She earned the Performance Option in the following areas:

Job Development (technical plus general knowledge), Quality of Work, Ability to Work with Others, Upward Communication, Punctuality, Attendance, Personal Hygiene, and Confidentiality.

Background:

This employee works on projects for five senior executives. Her appraisals by all five were very similar. Her project work requires the highest level of confidentiality. At times, a project of one executive is unknown to another. Maintaining confidentiality, developing her technical knowledge, producing quality work, and working well with diverse personalities are the most valued job responsibilities, which is where she excelled.

Therefore, her manager summarized her performance as Performance Option for pay purposes.

Employee Bob

Performance Option	Performance Standards Met	Improvement Needed	Problematic
5	20	1	—

He was marked Performance Option in the following areas:

Job Knowledge, Upward Communication, Punctuality, Attendance, and Security.

He was marked Improvement Needed in the following area:

Organizing.

Background:

This manager has more than enough job knowledge, did a fine job on all job results, kept his manager well-informed, and was willing to put in extra hours to get the job done. Unfortunately, some of the extra hours could have been eliminated if he had organized his work better.

Therefore, his manager summarized his performance as Performance Standards Met for pay purposes.

Employee Cindy

Performance Option	Performance Standards Met	Improvement Needed	Problematic
1	19	6	—

She was marked Performance Option in the following area:

Personal Hygiene.

She was marked Improvement Needed in the following areas:

Job Knowledge, Application of Knowledge, Performs According to Job Description, Quality of Work, Results/Volume of Work, and Punctuality.

Background:

This employee is completing the first year of employment. The job qualifications state that one year on-the-job training is required to learn the job. The employee is impeccably groomed but needs improvement in the core elements of the job.

Therefore, her manager summarized her performance as Improvement Needed for pay purposes. If this employee had been with the company for two years and still needed improvement in many of the same areas, then obviously she would not be responding to suggestions to bring performance up to par, and her manager would have to summarize her performance as Problematic.

Employee Don

Performance Option	Performance Standards Met	Improvement Needed	Problematic
8	10	8	—

He was marked Performance Option in the following areas:

Ability to Work with Others, Reaction to Pressure, Punctuality, Attendance, Personal Hygiene, Use of Supplies and Equipment, Work-Area Cleanliness, Safety, and Technical Knowledge.

He was marked Improvement Needed in the following areas:

Application of Knowledge, Performs According to Job Description, Quality of Work, Results/Volume of Work, Communications, Planning, Organizing, and Decision Making.

Background:

This manager was well groomed and kept a spare shirt and tie in his office closet, could be counted on to arrive early for work, stayed late to complete work, maintained a picture-perfect office, looked out for possible safety hazards in the work place, established lasting rapport with a variety of people, was calm in pressure situations, and had technical knowledge far superior to that of his employees.

However, his processing of information was disorganized, details were overlooked, two people or none were scheduled in critical areas when one was required. Though he was willing to work extra hours, assignments were not completed on time; unsupportable assumptions were made when he was communicating with others; notes were left for employees, but understanding was not confirmed. Rapport with subordinates was terrific—he never said no.

When you look at the performance picture painted, you see a highly qualified technical person who is experiencing all the problems of becoming a new manager. He was making every effort but not cutting it as a manager. Will he make it? It's hard to tell.

What pay summary would you select?

The manager selected a summary of Improvement Needed. The proof of the manager's judgment was found in the employee's comments on the planning and appraisal conference form: "Thank you for explaining the areas where I need to improve on my job. Being a new manager has been a great learning experience. Now I know how much I need to learn. I'll give it my best shot."

If performance remained unchanged a year later, the summary would have slipped to Problematic—still a great technician, a good, caring person, but a lousy manager.

The simple ranking of performance by points, as in the example at the beginning of this section, without reference to the value of the individual job responsibilities shows a misunderstanding of the situation. Performance must be valued according to the specific areas in which the employee excelled, performed as expected, or was deficient. Otherwise, comparisons among employees are not fair.

9.1.3 What Is Subjective? What Is Objective?

The search for solid appraisal of nonquantifiable human performance is tenuous. In one sense, it can be argued that the very nature of human opinion is subjective—that is, each of us observes the same performance with a unique value system. Therefore, uniform and consistent opinions among managers about employee performance are impossible.

On the other hand, a substantial majority of managers assembled to observe and rate one employee's performance will come to the same rating conclusion, especially when the criteria they use to rate the performance incorporate specific conditions.

Managers appraise the performance of their employees all the time, sometimes consciously and sometimes unconsciously. They can explain some of their appraisals; others they cannot explain. Years of accumulated life experiences give a manager the intellectual data bank to make judgments, explainable or intuitive, about an employee's performance.

The most perceptive managers organize models in their mind to help them understand their observations. These models identify the possible conditions of employee performance so that the performance can be recognized when they see it. In short, these managers elevate subconscious perceptions to the conscious level, because they recognize what they're looking at. Consequently, being objective instead of subjective means that a manager can recall the specific observations that lead to a summary conclusion about an employee's performance. Objectivity is not a special talent.

In the legalistic society that we have become, the courts want "proof" of managerial opinions that affect employees adversely. Fortunately, the courts are usually impressed with reasonable arguments. Although it may not be possible to describe and defend the nuances of one person's opinion about another, a thoughtful, systematic approach that collects adequate evidence and minimizes errors of evidence is the best defense—as well as fairest to the manager and the employee involved. Managers would be remiss if they did not document their observations and conversations.

9.1.4 Valuing Job Responsibilities

Organizations that attempt to differentiate the "worth" of individual job responsibilities typically do not take the time and effort to finish the job thoroughly, or get so carried away with the numbers that the true meaning of the exercise is lost. *However, weighting complicates the issue considerably.*

Job responsibilities are valued by mathematically weighting each. *The first step* is to determine the value of each job result and universal criteria *before* any numbers are added. The warning here, which we'll demonstrate shortly, is that when numbers become the focus of the system, the values of job responsibilities frequently become distorted.

Let's look at what happens in a manager's mind when he or she weights job responsibilities. A percentage of the job's total worth is assigned to each job result and universal requirement according to the organization's opinion of how valuable each job result is. For example:

		Percentage of Job's Total Worth
Job Result #1	=	15%
Job Result #2	=	20
Job Result #3	=	10
Job Result #4	=	10
Job Result #5	=	10
Universal Criteria #1	=	5
Universal Criteria #2	=	5
Universal Criteria #3	=	10
Universal Criteria #4	=	15
Universal Criteria #5	=	2
Universal Criteria #6	=	5
Universal Criteria #7	=	8
Universal Criteria #8	=	5
Universal Criteria #9	=	5
Total	=	100

Performance-management-conference forms can provide a space to identify a value (weighting) for each job result and universal requirement. For example, Figure 9-1 shows portions of the planning and appraisal form from Figure 5-3 now adjusted to show where valuing (weighting) can be recorded.

Figure 9-1. Performance-management-conference form.

SAMPLE PERFORMANCE MANAGEMENT CONFERENCE

Name: _____   Conference date: _____
Job title: _____   Type of conference: _____
Department: _____   Date of hire: _____
Manager: _____

Section I
Job Description and Related Performance Criteria

Job Description	*Weighted Value of Result*
1. [*Insert specific job description.*]	☐

☐ *Performance Standard* [*Insert related profile*]:

☐ *Problem*:

☐ *Improvement*:

☐ *Performance Option*:

Learning plan or comments: _____

Figure 9-1. (*continued*)

Section II
Universal Performance-Criteria Profiles

Activity	*Weighted Value of Result*
1. Punctuality PS = Work starts on time. P = Other employees' schedules are disrupted. I = Needs to reduce late time. PO = Takes extra precautions to be on time. *Learning Plan, or comments:* _____	☐

[Insert all other categories that are appropriate to include.]

9.1.5 Valuing Performance Levels Within the Performance-Criteria Profile

Performance criteria may also be valued differently according to their relationship within the profile. For example, one profile might be valued this way because the differences in performance between criteria is small:

Performance Standard = 2
Problem   = 0
Improvement   = 1
Performance Option = 3

In another profile, performing at the Performance Option level means that an employee must make a substantial effort. That effort would be recognized with this weighting:

Performance Standard = 2
Problem   = 0
Improvement   = 1
Performance Option = 7

Generally, criteria weighting possibilities within the profile are within this range:

Possible Weighting:		*A*	*B*	*C*	*D*	*E*	*F*	*G*	*H*	*I*
Performance Standard	=	2	2	2	3	3	3	4	4	4
Problem	=	0	0	0	0	0	0	0	0	0
Improvement	=	1	1	1	1	1	1	1	1	1
Performance Option	=	3	4	5	4	5	6	5	6	7

The valuing presented here must be approached with caution and an appreciation of the danger of overkill (such as attempting to "refine" the valuing with weightings of 2.3 or 5.1).

Valuing performance criteria is best thought of as looking deeply into a nuance of the pay system. Such precision dangerously pushes us to the brink of valuing human performance. Remember, managers will do well when appraising their employees' performance without "scientific" techniques if we only give them adequate *basic* tools to work with, such as concrete job descriptions and solid performance-criteria profiles.

You can appreciate that some people who would play with the system for their own advantage can weight the criteria within the profile in order to produce the effect they want. Comparisons of performance between jobs and across department boundaries would be impossible.

The reason this potential for valuing performance criteria is included in this book is because such valuing *does* occur within the minds of managers when they intuitively appraise performance. It is sufficient, and trouble enough, that the major job responsibilities be valued.

Eventually, we will learn to be more precise without valuing the human beings who participate in the system. For now, however, train your managers and let them rely on their *intuition* to sort out the significant differences in performance, and use more finite valuing mechanisms to augment and help, but not replace, that judgment.

If you decide to incorporate numbers into your system to identify the value of individual results and criteria, the valuing must be defined carefully at the start of the performance period, adjusted as needed throughout the performance period (perhaps quarterly), and reaffirmed at the end of the performance period.

The valuing of job results and performance criteria is combined this way. For Job Result #1 above (weighted at 15 percent):

Performance Standard $= 2 \times 1.5$
Problem $\qquad\qquad\quad = 0$
Improvement $\qquad\;\; = 1 \times 1.5$
Performance Option $\;\; = 3 \times 1.5$

For Job Result #2 (weighted at 20 percent), and a different performance profile, the calculation would be:

Performance Standard $= 3 \times 2.0$
Problem $\qquad\qquad\quad = 0$
Improvement $\qquad\;\; = 1 \times 2.0$
Performance Option $\;\; = 5 \times 2.0$

Therefore, if an employee were marked as needing Improvement in Job Result #1, then he or she would receive 1.5 points (1×1.5). If the appraisal for Job Result #2 were Performance Standard, the points would be 6 (3×2.0). Performance ratings would then be totaled for the entire job and used to compare overall performance with the performance summaries of other employees.

Again, make sure that common sense keeps the system reasonable.

Some managers use common sense and avoid the specific nature of valuing results and criteria by simply identifying which job results deserve the most attention during the next performance period.

9.1.6 Tying Pay to Performance

After performance has been summarized, the manager can tie pay to performance. Table 9-1 shows a sample policy guideline. The percentage increases, of course, will vary for each organization.

The pay-increase levels are determined according to the ability of the organization to fund pay increases. In lean times, these percentage increases would be reduced. Additionally, the increase percentages associated with different levels of performance can be varied to emphasize specific levels of performance and different styles of management. Both of these variations will be illustrated in the section 9.3.

Employees being paid at the midpoint or above in the pay range are typically experienced employees who perform all aspects of the job at the Performance Standard or better. Employees being paid below the midpoint pay rate are typically learning their jobs. If an organization believes that the midpoint of a range equals the pay that an employee who performs the job as expected should receive, then employees who perform outstandingly while they are learning the job should move toward that mark at a rate faster than others who do not learn as fast.

Pay guidelines must allow the manager some flexibility to adjust pay to specific performance, yet must produce consistent application of policy among managers. The four major summaries of performance can be further differentiated into nine levels, A through I, for pay purposes:

Performance Option	A
	B
Performance Standards Met	C
	D
	E
Improvement Needed	F
	G
Problematic	H
	I

Following the WXY sample guidelines listed in Table 9-1, more specific pay decisions can be made as follows:

Performance Option:
The employee exercising Performance Options on significant job responsibilities can earn 8 percent or 9 percent.

A. The "superstar" employee does it all, and earns 9 percent
B. The role-model employee earns 8 percent.

Performance Standards Met:
The employee performing at a level where Standards are Met can earn 5 to 7 percent.

C. The employee who meets all or nearly all Performance Standards and exercises some Performance Options earns 7 percent.
D. The employee who meets all or nearly all Performance Standards earns 6 percent.
E. The employee who meets nearly all Performance Standards but needs Improvement in several unessential areas earns 5 percent.

Improvement Needed:
The employee needing Improvement can earn 3 percent or 4 percent.

F. The employee who needs Improvement in several areas that significantly detract from otherwise meeting Performance Standards, and may have exercised some Performance Options, earns 4 percent.
G. The employee who needs Improvement in significant job responsibilities, exercises no significant Performance Options, and is Problematic in one or two unessential areas (who pretty much just passes through the day and the job) earns 3 percent.

Problematic:
The employee performing at the Problematic level in significant job responsibilities earns 0 percent.

H. The employee who is at the Problematic level receives no increase until performance is corrected. If the employee brings his or her performance

Table 9-1. Sample pay guideline, WXY Organization.

Performance Summary	*Pay Increase*	*Timing of Appraisal*
If employee is paid above pay-range midpoint:		
Performance Option	8–9%	12 months
Performance Standards Met	5–7%	12 months
Improvement Needed	3–4%	12 months
Problematic	0–2%	18 months
If employee is paid below pay-range midpoint:		
Performance Option	8–9%	9 months
Performance Standards Met	5–7%	12 months
Improvement Needed	3–4%	12 months
Problematic	0–2%	15 months

level to Improvement Needed (as defined in Improvement Needed–4 percent) by the conclusion of a special review process in three months (for employees below the midpoint) or six months (for employees above the midpoint), then the employee earns 2 percent.

I. If, within the same time frame, the employee improves to Improvement Needed (as defined in Improvement Needed–3 percent), then the employee earns 1 percent.

J. If, within the same time frame, there is no improvement, then the employee still earns 0 percent, and disciplinary action begins.

Following this interpretation, employees Arlene, Bob, Cindy, and Don (see section 9.1.1) would receive these pay increases when management considers the individual value of the job responsibilities:

	Specific Rating	*Pay Increase*	*Employee*
Performance Option	A	9%	Arlene
	B	8%	
	C	7%	
Performance Standards Met	D	6%	Bob
	E	5%	
Improvement Needed	F	4%	Don
	G	3%	Cindy
Problematic	H	2%	
	I	1%	
	J	0%	

Had employee Cindy's performance continued to the next appraisal without significant improvement, her level of performance would have dropped to Problematic, meaning no pay increase. The pay increase would have been delayed three months (to the 15th month after the last increase), with special reviews beginning immediately. If performance improved to Improvement Needed in three months, an increase of one to two percent could be given to her. If performance did not improve thereafter, disciplinary action would have to begin.

Finally, comparing the different pay outcomes of these employees when job responsibilities, and thus summaries of performance, are treated identically (see the pay distribution in section 9.1.1) with the pay when job responsibilities are valued individually, we find:

Employee	*All Results Treated Equally (in %)*	*Each Result Valued Individually (in %)*
Arlene	7	9
Bob	7	6
Cindy	6	3
Don	5	4

Although treating all results equally is more absolute because there is less influence of the manager's judgment in valuing job responsibilities, the approach requiring specific analysis and judgment by the manager is fairer to the employee and, in the long run, more beneficial to the organization.

As a last example, consider the Performance Options taken by these managers:

Manager Arnold: Punctuality, Attendance, Personal Hygiene, Use of Supplies and Equipment, and Work Area Cleanliness

Manager Barbara: Planning, Organizing, Development of Subordinates, Decision Making/Problem Solving, and Budgeting

Manager Barbara is opting to work harder in the more difficult job-result areas, and should receive the larger reward. Pay will not be fair when fairness is forfeited for ease of application and organizational conformity.

9.1.7 The Dangers of Discussing Pay in the Performance-Management Conference

When pay is discussed during the performance-management conference, strange things happen between managers and employees. Suddenly, the entire focus of the conference is on dollars: How many does the manager give? How many does the employee get? Basic job demands and performance plans lose importance. Employees—especially those who need every dollar they can get—sit in near-hysterical deafness until the manager decrees the magic number.

Performance is performance, and pay is pay; they are related issues, but they are not the same issue. Performance should be the topic of one conference, and pay should be the topic of a subsequent conference shortly thereafter—from one to four weeks later.

Managers and employees need a clean shot at being successful with each issue—performance and pay—separately. It is distracting, if not unfair, to put people into the personal pressure-cooker of dealing with pay issues while they are attempting to resolve performance issues.

Furthermore, if the performance-management conference is an opportunity for the manager and the employee to examine performance *together*, then a decision about the employee's pay *before* the conference is hypocritical.

9.1.8 The Final Challenge

The challenge facing organizations is to devise a workable system with which managers and employees can manage performance cooperatively. We know that subjective, vaguely worded performance criteria, coupled with overly precise numerical formulas that do not truly express the organization's values, impair rapport between managers and employees, and inhibit performance toward the organization's mission.

Employees need to know in clear terms what they are expected to accomplish, what they can contribute to the organization's performance, and how they can earn rewards and recognition. Employees and managers need to understand how they can form a partnership to shape and share the future of the organization. Managers need guidance to distribute rewards and recognition fairly among employees. Managers also need flexibility to guide individual performance according to the unique demands of the individual, and to avoid being forced into awkward encounters that they find difficult to explain to employees.

Project Analyzer (9.1)

How is pay tied to performance in your organization now?

___

___

Are managers satisfied with the way pay is tied to performance?

___

___

Are employees satisfied with the way pay is tied to performance?

___

___

Is the organization using its human resources as effectively and efficiently as possible in order to accomplish its purpose?

___

___

Are managers honest when they recommend pay decisions, or are they being forced to "play games" because of the system?

___

___

Do you use a numeric or a generic label to summarize performance?

___

___

___

Are managers consistent among themselves when they make pay recommendations?

___

___

___

Have managers met to build a consensus about the way they tie pay to performance?

_____

_____

_____

9.2 Planning the Pay-Increase Budget

Tying pay to performance begins with an assessment of anticipated pay decisions for *each* employee in the organization. Organizational pay guidelines cannot be established for the organization until a pay-summary mix of all employees has been estimated. This estimate usually occurs during operational planning—generally associated with the beginning of a fiscal year. Figure 9-2 shows a possible format for developing pay estimates for each employee. Figure 9-3 shows the consolidation of individual estimates. A mature organization with seasoned, stable performers must establish a pay-management guideline different from those of a rapidly growing organization in which performance varies significantly among new employees and also different from those of an organization intent on maximizing bonus opportunities.

Figure 9-2. Format for estimating pay-increase budget.

Department: _____ Employee name: Last pay status: Last pay percentage increase: Conference due date: Pay-change due date: [*Transfer the employee names and due dates to a master calendar (see Figure 9-3) so that performance-management conferences and payroll processing can be managed on schedule.*]
Anticipated pay status: Anticipated percentage increase: Anticipated $ increase: Actual annual $ increase:
Variance (budget to actual):

The anticipated pay-summary mix for employees is identified for each operating unit of the organization by the manager of that unit. Financial profit/cost centers typically provide workable focal points for analyzing employee performance. Specifically, each manager must study the performance history of each employee in the unit and estimate what each employee's pay summary will be when a performance-management conference is conducted at the conclusion of individual performance periods.

Estimates of the first-level operating units are collected and combined upward into estimates for major operating units. The control point of performance management within an organization is an operating unit of approximately 200 employees—about as many employees as one manager can reasonably track. These managers are the "consistency controllers" of the organization.

Pay-mix estimates are gathered according to divisions, groups, regions, and so on, paralleling the organizational structure, until information for the entire organization is assembled. "Consistency controllers" must meet with other controllers in order to compare their values and achieve a consensus on the interpretation of performance criteria. Group controllers meet with division controllers, who meet with department controllers, until all controllers understand one another. There is no shortcut if fairness is to be achieved.

Figure 9-3. Sample master pay-change calendar.

Department: _____

Name	Specific Date Due											
	J	F	M	A	M	J	J	A	S	O	N	D
Arlene	13											
Bob	18											
Cindy		2										
Don				14								
Evelyn				23								
Fred					19							
Gerry							1					
Howard									14			
Inez											29	

Only when planning is concluded and a consensus achieved can pay guidelines be structured. Most important, the guidelines must match the unique economic limits of the organization (in the example in this section, up to 9 percent).

Some managements, in an attempt to remain consistent with their competitors, construct guidelines that they cannot afford. They are then forced to take drastic protective actions by freezing pay rates or, worse, laying off employees. In difficult economic times, the spotlight has to shine even more brightly on performance so that small increases are made to mean a lot (and no increase means that you get to keep your job). Additionally, other forms of recognition in lieu of pay rewards must be identified.

And they can be found. The interesting nature of pay and performance is that performance is more valuable than pay. Over the years, studies have pointed out that money is not the top motivator for employees. Although the unique circumstances of the respondents must be considered when analyzing these findings, there is no question that the ability of the employee to apply knowledge and skill to work performance is a powerful motivator, as well as a satisfier. Organizations need only learn how to tap that potential.

Managers can use several techniques to help them assess their situations and plan pay-increase budgets. First, they need to identify the range of performance that exists in their unit. Are all the employees performing at the Performance Option level, or the Improvement level, or in some mix of all levels?

A *forced ranking* of employees places each employee in relation to every other employee in the unit, in order of performance. If there are ten employees in the unit, the manager ranks the employee who is first, the employee who is second, and so on until the tenth-place performer is identified. There is no inference that the tenth employee is not performing acceptably; the ranking merely means that in comparison with nine other employees, this employee is tenth. Once the ranking is determined, the performance of the first and the last is estimated in order to understand the range of performance.

When the number of employees becomes too large to comprehend in a simple ranking, the *paired-comparison technique* can be used. Each employee is compared to every other employee, one at a time. The employee's performance is estimated as better or worse than the other employee's. The employee who most often is estimated as performing better is the top employee in the group; the employee receiving the next fewer marks is second; and so on.

An overlay of a normal mathematical distribution can then be placed on the ranking and the range of performance identified. All things being equal (which they never are), in large populations we can expect 5 percent of employees to be the top performers; the next 10 percent to give a lot of extra effort; and the next 70 percent to do what they are asked to do. Another 10 percent probably shouldn't be working for you, and the final 5 percent probably won't be working for you much longer.

Be careful! The normal distribution should *never* be applied directly to employee populations to determine pay. People just don't fall into such neatly arranged piles. Use the statistical techniques to gain a reasonable estimate, but not as a decision crutch.

9.2.1 Time-of-Year Implications When Planning the Pay Budget

Most organizations prepare a pay-increase budget expressed in annual dollars. What some managers fail to take into account is that the time of year of each pay increase affects the annual percentage differently. If the pay-increase budget is 9 percent, only 9 percent increases awarded at the start of the fiscal year will have a 9 percent impact on the employee's salary and the pay budget in that year.

For example, here are two employees who earn the same percentage increase but whose increases will occur at two different times during the year:

Employee	*Percentage Increase*	*Month Due*	*Percentage Impact on Budget*
Kathy	9	January	9.0
Mike	9	June	4.5

Kathy's increase is in effect for 12 months; Mike's increase is in effect for six months, or 50 percent of the year. Fifty percent of 9 percent equals 4.5 percent.

9.2.2 Compiling the Organization's Total Pay Budget

When all managers have estimated pay statuses for all their employees, on the basis of historical and current indicators, the manager at the next higher organizational level collects the data and determines the total performance dollars to be expended at that level. Data are summarized until one budget is determined for the organization.

Budgets are typically returned to managers in order to shift allocations from one area to another. One manager may request more performance dollars for a large group of high performers, whereas another manager may forgo performance dollars because they are not needed for low performers.

If performance-management conferences are held at one time during the year for all employees, and pay increases are distributed shortly thereafter, then management has an opportunity to review the actual distribution and adjust pay requirements to money available.

Let's look at two departments in an organization: a computer department of three people and an accounting department of seven people.

The computer department consists of a manager, a programmer, and a night operator. The manager is a model manager. The programmer has learned the manager's job in order to keep the department operating smoothly in the manager's absence. The night operator has learned programming so tasks can be completed while nightly reports are run. All three perform at the Performance Option level. With good conscience, their pay increases cannot be distributed on a normal distribution curve, because two of them would be unfairly penalized, since they could not receive increases at the Performance Option level.

The accounting department is another story. Employees perform only what they must. There are no shining stars; two of the employees have received special performance-problem reviews. The normal distribution curve doesn't work in this department either, because some employees would be overrated.

The pay-increase budget is reviewed each time a pay conference is planned; managers must justify to their managers proposed changes to their plans. For example, during the budgeting process, the manager may anticipate that employee Angela will meet Performance Standards. Eight months later, Angela may begin to exercise Performance Options. The manager cannot be influenced only by the last four months of performance, and must be reminded by his or her manager that the performance period is one year. When proper planning and review processes are in place, managers need less reminding.

Senior managers in control of organizational performance can use the performance summaries produced by each manager to review how each manager interprets and applies performance profiles. "Hard" and "soft" raters can be counseled to use the profiles more accurately. Control can also be exercised when one department's performance is out of line with other departments.

Project Analyzer (9.2)

Are pay increases tied to the financial condition of the organization or the "going rate" of increases in other organizations?

_____

_____

Are senior managers the only managers who determine who shall receive how much?

_____

_____

Are managers included in the budget-planning process?

_____

_____

Do managers anticipate pay decisions for their employees?

_____

_____

Is the process formal and attentive or haphazard?

_____

_____

Do senior managers examine pay recommendations as closely as they examine other operational recommendations?

_____

_____

_____

Are senior managers held accountable for pay decisions in their area?

_____

_____

_____

Are pay reviews tied to individual employee anniversary dates or to the date of a general increase?

_____

_____

_____

9.3 Performance-Incentive Rewards

Traditional incentive systems are designed to increase productivity, but they inherently signal to employees that the organization is pleased *only* when they are striving to do more. Managers are subtly driven by the program design to ask employees for more and more performance, and to be disappointed when they do not continually receive extra effort from employees.

From time to time, special incentives, such as incentives to reduce costs, to improve attendance or safety awareness, or to increase productivity, are effective performance motivators, so long as the rewards are meaningful to employees. However, in their eagerness to improve performance in one area, designers of incentives may accidentally hurt performance in another area when the effort to improve in the first area acts as a detriment to performance in the other area. The performance to be rewarded must be studied by management so that it does not subvert other desired performance.

The basic contract of employment between management and employees is remuneration for agreed-upon performance. Management violates that agreement every day when it is not satisfied with performance that matches the expectations expressed at the time of hire. It is not wrong to change the contract and ask for more performance from employees in order for the organization to be all that it can be, but it is a violation of the original employment agreement to put the terms of the contract on a sliding scale and make employees feel that living up to the agreement is not enough effort. Employees should be told that more effort is better for the organization and themselves, but they should not be degraded when they choose not to give more effort.

On the other hand, the pay guideline can be designed to make better performance more attractive by apportioning a significant amount of reward to employees who choose to exercise more Performance Options. For example, compare the pay guidelines of VWX Organization (Table 9-2) with those of WXY Organization (Table 9-1, section 9.1.6). Notice the higher rewards for the Performance Option in Organization VWX.

Other organizations will have different pay goals. Mature, stable organizations in which coordination among jobs and departments is valued more than individual "star" performance can just as easily reduce the emphasis on Performance Options by decreasing the difference in reward between Performance Option and Performance Standards Met. The example in Table 9-3 illustrates this.

Table 9-2. Sample pay guideline, VWX Organization.

Performance Summary	Pay Increase	Timing
If employee is paid above pay-range midpoint:		
Performance Option	11–12%	12 months
Performance Standards Met	5–7%	12 months
Improvement Needed	2–3%	12 months
Problematic	0–1%	18 months
If employee is paid below pay-range midpoint:		
Performance Option	10–12%	9 months
Performance Standards Met	5–7%	12 months
Improvement Needed	2–3%	12 months
Problematic	0–1%	15 months

9.3.1 Performance-Bonus System

The bottom half of the pay range, as it is generally defined from the minimum to the midpoint, guides pay for employees who enter the job and learn it until they are capable of performing the expected requirements. When employees are performing the way management wants them to on the job, they are paid the Performance Standard rate at the pay-range midpoint. The Performance Standard rate is maintained equitably with rates paid in the marketplace for similar jobs.

The top half of the pay range, as it is generally defined from mid-point to maximum, guides pay for employees who perform "meritoriously" for the organization. Unfortunately, "merit" pay increases typically are stacked on top of

Table 9-3. Sample pay guideline, UVW Organization.

Performance Summary	Pay Increase	Timing
If employee is paid above pay-range midpoint:		
Performance Option	5–6%	12 months
Performance Standards Met	3–4%	12 months
Improvement Needed	1–0%	12 months
Problematic	0%	18 months
If employee is paid below pay-range midpoint:		
Performance Option	5–6%	9 months
Performance Standards Met	3–4%	12 months
Improvement Needed	1–2%	12 months
Problematic	0%	15 months

each other year after year, and the employees soon "max out" at the top of the pay range, with no opportunity to earn Performance Option rewards. Worse, employees who have performed meritoriously for two years, but who slack off in the third year, are nevertheless rewarded more, on the whole, for their performance because of their position in the pay range than other employees who have performed better in the third year.

When the reward concept is changed from incentive rewards to Performance Option rewards, the focus shifts to fair rewards for performing the job according to management's expectations, with opportunities for additional rewards for employees who choose to contribute more effort to the organization. There is no need for a pay-range maximum except as an informal guide to the amount of bonus reward. Past rewards are not stacked up year after year. The employee must choose again each year to perform above the Performance Standard.

In other words, the employee will be paid the Performance Standard rate as long as performance meets expectations, and each year the employee is eligible to earn Performance Option rewards. The Performance Standard rate (pay-range midpoint) may change each year according to changes in the marketplace. The Performance Option rewards may change each year according to the financial condition of the organization. Pay is tied to the employee's performance, and to the employee's choice to give more effort to the job. The employee's place in the pay range above the midpoint is immaterial.

Let's look at an illustration of the approach. An employee is hired in year one at the minimum of the pay range. She learns the job following a predetermined orientation program, and at year three has progressed to the midpoint or Performance Standard rate of the range—let's say, $20,000.

Once the employee has attained the Performance Standard rate, the manager and the employee agree to individual work plans, based on the job description, for the upcoming performance period. Let's assume the employee completes the work plan and chooses to do more to earn a bonus reward, and is awarded a bonus of $3,000. The employee is now earning $23,000, except that the $23,000 is composed of the $20,000 base plus the $3,000 bonus, not base pay of $23,000.

The employee may take the $3,000 bonus as a lump sum payment or may have it spread out evenly in the paychecks during the following year. Tax problems must be investigated to assess the implications of each way of taking the bonus payment. Similarly, base pay versus bonus payments may affect benefit programs, especially deferred compensation; these implications must also be examined, and changes in the benefits qualifications may be required.

At the beginning of year four, the manager and the employee again agree to a work plan. Let's suppose that the employee performs very well, and again earns a bonus, even better than last year—this time, $5,000. Now the employee is earning $25,000 (the base pay of $20,000 plus the bonus of $5,000).

The employee is *not* earning $28,000—that is, $23,000 from year three *plus* the new $5,000 bonus. The performance-bonus system is designed to prevent employees from stacking bonuses, or coasting on previous performance. The organization benefits from reduced fixed payroll expense. The Performance Standard rate, or base, of $20,000 may change, of course, as market conditions change, so that the base might be increased to $22,000 and the bonuses added to that. Follow the illustration one more step, and you will see another impact of the system.

In year five, the employee does well again, even better than planned, and again earns a bonus, but not as much as in previous years; this time the bonus is $1,000. In a traditional system where bonus increases accumulate, this employee would earn $29,000 ($20,000 plus previous pay increases of $3,000, $5,000, and $1,000) instead of $21,000 in a performance-bonus system. Other employees might have outperformed this employee, but in a traditional system would not have earned as much unless they, too, had been in the system long enough to accumulate previous bonuses.

Such a system that ties pay rewards directly to effort expended on the job is not new, but such systems are not used to remunerate most employees. Salespeople are the main category of employees paid this way. Presumably, the inability to measure performance in many jobs, and the inability of most employees to influence their environment, has deterred management from instituting performance-bonus systems.

Certainly, vague criteria that inhibit an accurate assessment of performance are a serious impediment to a successful bonus system. Some managers, unions pointed out long ago, will use vagueness as a cover to give rewards to their favorites. However, clearer criteria today open the door to reinvestigate the performance-bonus system.

Managers are more able now to manage equitably, and many employees no longer wish to be lumped into a general-increase package. The notion of fair pay based on the performance each individual chooses to give to the organization is high on the list of most employees.

9.3.2 Group Rewards

Individual rewards are tied to individual contribution; group rewards are tied to the joint contribution of individuals. Different individual contributions to joint efforts should not go unrecognized. It is not fair to reward employees who choose to lead the group effort at the same level as employees who choose to go along with the group. Unfortunately, most group incentive systems do not distinguish among individual contributions within the group.

Having two plans—one to reward individual contribution and another to reward group participation—is an ideal model. Group rewards typically involve sharing in organization profits, value-added performance, productivity gains, and cost saving.

Group reward systems require a management approach different from that used for individual reward systems. The group must be managed as a team to prevent or minimize disgruntlements among the group members. Whereas individuals can decide for themselves whether to work for an incentive to win rewards, in order for the group to win rewards, the total effort of all individuals in the group must produce the desired objective. Each member of the group must decide to participate, or else some members must carry a bigger share of the effort.

The requirement for individual employees to participate in the group effort usually means that management must participate by supplying more information so that employees can make informed decisions. Such participation is not a system that can be installed without regard to the surrounding culture. Participative management differs sharply from other styles such as the autocratic style.

9.3.3 Reward System Considerations

Here are some issues you should consider when installing individual or group reward systems:

1. *Design system objectives to meet specific needs in your organization.* Do not pick a system off the shelf just because everyone else is using it. Gain a commitment among managers, before the program is implemented, to reward objectives. Study the implications and what-ifs of the program to preclude disasters and disgruntlements with reward payments. Many rewards look good until they are analyzed for their faults.

2. *Clarify who can receive what rewards.* Principally, be sure that employees can influence the factors that will earn them rewards. Make sure that the rewards are tied to all aspects of an employee's job, the profitable and the unprofitable, and all responsibilities of the job, the favorable and the unfavorable, so that employees share in all dimensions of performance.

3. *Make sure reward criteria fit with the organization's objectives, so you avoid contradictory motivations.* If long-term growth of the organization is needed, short-term rewards will impair the long-term objective. New organizations cannot be hampered by high salaries as a fixed expense; these organizations should offer greater incentive rewards to employees for meeting growth objectives. Growth in mature organizations is usually more stable, so that there is less opportunity for substantial rewards for few employees and more opportunity for rewards among many employees.

4. *Match rewards criteria with operational cycles and time them to coincide with revenues.* For example, if revenues are high in only one quarter of the year, rewards should be tied to a yearly cycle instead of a quarterly cycle so that employees not only receive the benefit of the good quarter but also share equally in the difficult times of the other three quarters.

5. *Discuss expectations before effort is expended in the pursuit and management of reward objectives.* Generally speaking, the more measurable and predictable the reward criteria, the easier it will be for manager and employee to avoid complaints and dissatisfaction. However, the pursuit of measurability and predictability can be dangerous, for sometimes the more measurable and predictable we try to make a system, the more we kill its motivational value.

Many times, "subjective" criteria can be made measurable with only a little effort when manager and employee discuss their perceptions of success. The notion of identifying and discussing job results and performance criteria as expressed in this book is not intended to reduce the manager–employee relation to certainty (for that is impossible) but to point the manager and employee together toward the important issues they must discuss.

Not all important organizational values are quantifiable in the measurable sense of how many dollars were saved or how many more tickets were processed. Particularly in the area of human rapport and service, measurements are elusive. The components of *courtesy and tact*, for example, and how to teach our ideals to someone else, are not certain. Yet, we cannot drop these values from our organizations just because they are difficult to measure. In fact, customers *know* when they have been treated *discourteously and tactlessly*. At least in discussion, criteria can be clarified sufficiently so that employees can perform up to the organization's expectations.

6. *Focus rewards on those gains that are most desirable for the organization, the individual, or the group.* Reward payments may be immediate or deferred, cash or something else of value, mandatory or voluntary, and various combinations of these. Tax considerations are essential when the organization is planning requirements and options in the system.

7. *Match reward payments to the difficulty of attaining the objective.* Three different conditions of difficulty and reward may exist: (1) The next objective is just as difficult to achieve as the previous one, and therefore the reward payment is the same for each new objective attained; (2) the next objective is *more* difficult to achieve than the previous one, and therefore the reward payment is larger for each new objective attained; or (3) the next objective is *less* difficult to achieve than the previous one, and therefore the reward payment is smaller for each new objective attained.

8. *Consider the scheduling of reward payments.* Reward payments can be scheduled to begin only after certain conditions are met—e.g., no reward, or a limited reward paid until a certain amount of revenue is received. Reward payments might be paid only if the employee were still employed when the reward was earned.

Project Analyzer (9.3)

Does your organization use incentive systems?

_____

_____

Have the incentive systems increased the organization's performance?

_____

_____

Have they increased employee satisfaction?

_____

_____

Are incentives worth the investment?

_____

_____

Do employees play "beat the system"?

_____

_____

Can the system be beaten?

_____

_____

_____

9.4 Recognizing Performance

People work for many reasons beside pay. Some observers of organizationland tell us that these other reasons are more important to employees than pay itself. There is no universal answer to the question of whether pay or other motivators are more important.

Similarly, there is no universal guide for determining when employees should be rewarded with pay for their work contribution and when they should be recognized personally with symbols, gestures, and payments-in-kind. The most effective mix of pay rewards and personal recognition for an individual depends on the needs and desires of that individual.

Recognition may be anything that the employee considers meaningful, such as:

Professional Recognition

- A trip to a trade show
- Membership on a task force
- A new job title
- Attendance at a seminar
- Exclusive training
- A conference with a consultant
- The performer-of-the-year (day, week, month, quarter) award
- A suggestion award
- A certificate
- Publication of research findings
- A professional announcement
- A plaque inscribed for outstanding achievement
- A picture in the organization or local newspaper
- An introduction before assembled peers

Esteem Recognition

- A stripe on uniform
- A patch
- A hat
- An embroidered shirt or blouse
- A pin
- A name tag with descriptive title
- Selection privileges for office furniture or equipment
- Distinctive accessories
- A larger office
- An office with a window
- A more convenient or comfortable work location
- A private parking space
- Use of a special automobile for the month
- An extended break
- Flexible work schedule
- Time off
- A credit card
- Carpeting
- Privacy
- A uniform
- Limousine service

Social Recognition

- A letter of congratulations
- A personal visit from the chief executive officer
- A photograph of the winning team
- A visit by famous personalities
- A celebrity autograph
- A birthday or anniversary card
- A flower
- A gift for the spouse
- A thank-you note
- A visit by the manager to off-shifts
- Lunch with an executive
- A party

In-Kind-Value Recognition

- A fishing trip to the company lodge
- A ticket for children's events
- A purchase discount
- A loan

- A food basket
- A ticket to a sporting event
- A prize
- A lottery
- A vacation
- A lunch

Some forms of recognition are more subtle. For example:

- *Communication* recognizes employees as capable participants in organizational efforts.
- *Managing participatively* recognizes employees' creativity and dignity.

- *Promotion from within* recognizes the value of diligence and loyalty.
- *Allowing professionals to develop new programs or products* recognizes their knowledge as a direct contribution to the organization.

Intrapreneuring, the darling concept of the 1980s, attempts to tap the spirit of individualism in people, to induce them to strike out from the bureaucracy and restriction of the organization, to find a sense of themselves by performing and failing (we hope not, however) according to their own resources. Organizations are searching desperately for ways to tap the value of the "different" employee—the person who wants more than the status quo, the person who questions the system in order to make it better.

Ironically, this potential contribution has always been within our organizations. People with unlimited energy come to work every day. Unfortunately, by the end of the day, their energy has been effectively sapped and squelched by scientific method, conformity, or the psychological inadequacy of their managers.

When people are treated as machines—remunerated for each output, or restricted because someone is emotionally unable or unwilling to recognize the value of their contribution to the organization—they give up and respond according to the dictates of the system. They perceive no value in performance, and thus perform perfunctorily to maintain compliance. The promise of performance is lost.

Recognition is an important force that must be integrated into the total compensation program along with pay, benefits, and performance options. Without personal recognition, compensation programs bring out the worst mercenary motivations of people—to extract the most coins out of the organization. The organization becomes nothing more than a cash drawer, which sooner or later becomes empty.

Pay reward and personal recognition reinforce performance most powerfully when they are given, or communicated (as in the case of long-term, deferred benefits), shortly after they are earned. When a manager waits too long to reward or recognize an employee's performance, the value of the reward or recognition is diminished, or may even turn into an insult if the employee believes that the manager forgot or, worse, had to be reminded to express the appreciation.

On the other hand, when rewards and recognitions are "administered" immediately after every special performance, the appreciation becomes a conditioned reflex of the organization, fully anticipated by the employee, with no benefit derived by the employee or the organization.

Project Analyzer (9.4)

How important is pay to employees in your organization?

_____

_____

How important are other forms of recognition?

_____

_____

What is the basis of your opinion?

_____

_____

_____

What is your organization's experience with using other forms of recognition? (List the forms your organization has used and the results of using each.)

_____

_____

_____

Have you used special awards?

_____

_____

_____

Have you used the subtle "goodwill" forms of recognition, such as better communication programs?

_____

_____

_____

9.5 Strategic Planning

On your first quick walk through the book, record your initial thoughts on policy issues that will have to be decided.

_____

_____

_____

_____

_____

Any notes on tactical procedures?

_____

_____

_____

_____

Chapter 10

Installing the Program

10.1 Committing to Performance Management

It is foolish and dangerous to begin a performance-management program without a commitment from management to have it succeed. Commitment comes from an agreement that the program is needed and will give new satisfactions, achieve new objectives, and solve old problems. The easiest programs to install are those where the CEO says—and means—it shall be so. Go for the bell at the top of the pole, because when this bell rings, all hear.

10.1.1 Present a Complete Proposal

Start with a complete proposal so that everybody concerned understands thoroughly what is involved in the program. Go easy. Lay out the entire pitch, but be ready to take what you can get and run. The psychology here is important: People will make something work if they believe in it. Be ready to give in here and there; many issues are not that big a deal, or can be dealt with later.

Top managers want to know that you have thought through the opportunities, options, and obstacles of installing the program. They want good staff work; they do not want more work than when they started. They usually do not want to examine all your planning details, but they want to know that the details were examined by *someone*.

Some managers will want to know it all. Assess the managerial style of your top manager and respond accordingly. If you do not interact with the top manager, think beyond any intermediary manager to the ultimate approval authority. Whatever you can do to help others sell your program will come home to help you.

In large organizations, specific support from the top is not essential, though tacit approval is always required. Get formal approval from one management level higher than the highest manager whose employees are affected by the project. Resolve project priority conflicts up front.

10.1.2 Sell Fundamental Benefits

Sell management on the strategic implications of the performance-management program: increased productivity, improved performance, and greater job satisfaction, all resulting from the clarification of the results required and the agreement on performance criteria between managers and employees. Identify specific goals as benefits.

10.1.3 Get Tangible Support

Push for visible support from top management. Nothing sells harder than unabashed support. On the other hand, keep a low profile if the true support is mere acceptance instead of enthusiasm. Stay on the side of reality and work with the cards that you are dealt.

Focus on acceptance of your program from the very start; take every opportunity to help others believe in its merits. Sell, sell, sell. Many good programs have whithered for lack of attention and interest, and excellent benefits have been lost to both the organization and its employees.

Solicit support for your program, but also obtain commitment. People can support a program by not saying anything negative about it. Commitment arises out of appreciation for the merits of a performance-management program and the belief that the benefits will be helpful to the organization. Commitment means advocacy.

People do not inherently resist change. People resist change when they do not understand it or don't agree with it. Resistance is not always permanent; you will sometimes hear, "I'll support the change, but not at this time."

10.1.4 Dealing With "Busy" Managers

Some managers are always busy with their regular (that is, technical) work; human resources projects are secondary issues. Mature managers understand that they do not accomplish work as managers except through other people. Sometimes it takes a disaster to capture a manager's attention. If you are starting from a disaster, make the most of this motivational advantage. If you do not have one handy, describe what can happen to the organization when it is defenseless without a reasonable and legal performance-management program.

10.1.5 Dealing With Protective Managers

It should come as no surprise to you that the managers who protest the loudest against programs intended to help them manage are the very managers who need the most help. You undoubtedly suspect that these managers know how much help they need.

Most of these managers have a problem with their authority; they're afraid of losing it, or don't know how to use it. Some managers mistakenly believe that they can accomplish work through others because authority has been delegated to them. They do not accept that employees may choose to ignore directives, or respond less than enthusiastically. These managers want to protect what has been granted to them, and any program that appears to usurp their authority will be resisted and/or attacked.

10.1.6 Help, Don't Hurt

Fighting back is not a team tactic. You will lose it all if you counterattack when you are rebuffed. Managers who attack will continue to fight as long as you are willing to scrap, and they will probably win, because they have had more practice. Every once in a while you may win a fight, but since you have now shamed your opponent, you must be aware of a new game called getting even. The whole thing adds up to a lot of wasted energy.

Don't resist in a confrontation. Let an argument go past without a challenge, but as it passes, examine it. Look not only for its weaknesses but also for its strengths. Acknowledge the strengths, for they are fact; nothing dispels anger better than agreement.

Be patient. You must win your managers' acceptance from the start. Go to them, in person, and work for their support. Be willing to explain, and reexplain. Don't catch them out on a limb. Don't give them a final solution. Remember that they are being held accountable for what happens, or fails to happen, in their area of responsibility. How do they know that a performance-management program will help them if they do not understand it?

10.1.7 Offer Information

Most managers simply want to know what is going on, how a program will affect them, how they can influence requirements about to be imposed on them, and how they can make adjustments for the demands of their own situation.

Give them information where they lack it or where they misunderstand. Lack of information is easily corrected; uncovering misunderstandings is much more difficult. Be patient. Let them talk; let them ask questions. Be helpful. Accept that people do what seems sensible to them, no matter whether it is right or wrong. Managers fight because it is the only sensible thing for them to do at the moment. With other information and other options, they most likely would choose to do something else.

Managers respond according to their experiences, and you have to know up front that there are far too many inadequate performance-management programs out there in organizationland. Consequently, you can expect a negative reaction from many managers, because experience tells them that this program is just more trouble. Although information can eliminate some objections, only positive experiences can change some minds.

10.1.8 Acceptance vs. Agreement

If you can obtain agreement for your program, get it, but settle for acceptance that the program should be done if that is all you can get. Pay attention to this subtle, but important, distinction. If you cannot have positive support, at least stop the fighting.

Why can you afford to wait calmly while recalcitrant managers dissipate their frustrations? Because you know that you are going to win them over in the end. Your program is going to work; it will make their job easier, and more satisfying, and thus more productive. Yes, you will have your moments of indecision and anxiety, but that's O.K. Your confidence will build as you begin to experience the application of your work. Your program will solve problems in your organization and take advantage of opportunities. What could be more welcome?

Managers might be forced to participate in the program, or they might willingly participate; you will witness many postures, and you will have to use different tactics to encounter each of your managers. Forcing managers to participate is the least desirable tactic, because they will give lip service at best to the project, and their lack of enthusiasm and support will influence employees and other managers.

10.1.9 Engineering Agreement

Opinion molders are useful people to help win acceptance; they are respected for their thinking, not for their style. They are already vocal, but not loud. Occasionally, of course, mob psychology comes into play, and a person stumbles into favor and that person, supposedly, speaks for the group.

Opinion molders are informal leaders whose decision to agree or disagree with a program sways other people. If you can get these influential people to *support* your program, you will achieve your goals; with their *commitment*, you will alter the course of your organization's success.

10.1.10 Talking to Employees

Employees, like managers, want to know what is going on and how the performance-management program will affect them. Employees, we know, have plenty of opinions about their jobs and performance criteria, and how jobs and performance ought to be managed. Some employees are not particularly interested in discussing these issues and would prefer that you decide; others would like to discuss the issue but figure, what's the use, management will do what it wants to do anyway.

More and more, however, employees are expressing themselves about issues that affect them, and in some instances, they are expecting an invitation to participate in planning discussions. Occasionally, employees want to control the process—unions certainly want a strong voice—but more often than not, employees only want to know that you heard and considered their opinion.

Successful performance-management programs are built on accurate information and blend the organization's needs with the needs of people, both managers and employees. Successful project managers go to the people who have information and opinion. They ask, and they listen. They cooperate and coordinate. They build credibility for their project and themselves, not only on the technical merits of the work, but also on the rapport they establish.

10.1.11 The Participative Approach

Let us agree up front that any management style will work so long as the participants agree to it. However, in the long run, some styles are not as effective as others.

Autocracy does not build independence, and in our Western culture, at this time, employees highly value freedom to act without continual direction.

Democracy—giving ultimate governing power to employees—is nearly unworkable at this stage of our society's interactive skills. Treating management and employees as equals also conflicts with the rights of investors. Investors who have risked economically are entitled to exert some control over the business through management, which is accountable to them.

Participatory management seems to give us the most help in achieving the organization's objectives. We know that autocracy is more efficient than democracy. We know that democracy gives rights to employees who invest, not money, but themselves in the enterprise. Participation purports to marry these two values.

In short, under a participatory style, ideas for the management of the enterprise can come from either managers or employees; they should be considered by both, and consensus should be achieved where feasible. Failing consensus, management is accountable for moving forward, and employees must trust in that movement. If we look at such a style from a practical angle, the key to success seems to rest in the opportunity (perhaps even the right) for everyone to speak to the issue and to be considered, but not in the right of refusal.

10.1.12 Authority Retained

Participatory management does not necessarily mean giving up decision-making authority, although this was the impression when the style was first discussed in the literature. Participation can be as minimal as presenting a decision and asking for comments, or it can include discussions about options available to solve a problem, or it can even include free-form discussion to identify the problem.

Participatory management is not a universal style to be applied in all situations. You may choose to participate with employees on some issues of your program but not on others.

Undoubtedly, the performance-management program you now have in your organization has been there for a while. Getting everyone to change to a new system will take some time; acceptance cannot be decreed. Employees need time to get used to a new idea and to understand it; letting them participate along the way does just that.

10.1.13 Management's Basic Beliefs

How managers choose to interact with their employees is a matter of their choice, which stems from the assumptions they hold about the capability and behavior of employees. No steps can be taken in the design of a performance-management program until management's style is clearly understood.

If you were, for example, to design and introduce a program based on so-called modern prescripts of organizational behavior to a group of managers who regard participation as an affront to their position authority and who think that employees are not able to function effectively and efficiently without direction and control, you would be in for a lot of trouble.

Each organization determines its values in its own manner, be it by decree from the top autocrat or by never-ending debates of laissez-faire committees. The important learning point here is that you must understand and accept what your organization believes now before you can consider moving it along in a different direction.

You will not be able to determine management's beliefs about performance management until the principals sit down and examine options and outcomes. They don't necessarily have to do this in a group, mind you, as some groups would undoubtedly end up in a fistfight if they ever tried to reason together. You don't need more schisms. In such a situation, one person would need to make the rounds of the organization and, in private conversation, elicit ideas about the way management should conduct itself. This person would then distill the divergent opinions into an acceptable draft, which would then be negotiated with the original respondents.

Where managers can sit together and debate a policy, they should. Naturally, this process requires someone to manage the discussion in order to achieve fruitful results, but the unification of opinion achieved by this direct approach will be strong.

10.1.14 The Educational Value of Participation

Announcing and conducting a typical training session in management styles, employee behavior, motivation, and the like usually produces yawns. But if you ask managers to gather to express their considered judgment on the important facets of the proposed performance-management program, they just might be willing to do it. And what will they discuss? Management styles, employee behavior, motivation, and the like—but you won't tell.

Gently point out the inevitable success or failure of various suggestions. Bring in new information. Let them talk out the differences. Let them test and try. Let them come to an agreement.

Agreement is easiest at global levels. Get your management group to work on the purpose of your performance-management program first. Why do they want this program? Then ease into the discussion of program details, and how they want to implement the program.

Use the materials in this book to guide your discussions. Generally, groups work better when you give them some straw work to tear apart rather than asking them to start with a blank piece of paper. Offer the ideas of this book as sacrificial lambs; better they focus their editorial wrath on these ideas than on you.

Again: take your organization where it's at in management style, even if it does not conform to modern theory. It's all you have. Set goals for new ways to act, if change is required. Sometimes, you will want to talk out these new directions; in other cases, you will simply start acting that way and let everyone learn from your model.

Project Analyzer (10.1)

Who is the top manager from whom you must obtain support and commitment?

_____

_____

What is the typical posture of the top manager toward human resources programs?

_____

_____

What preconceived notions exist in the organization about performance-management programs?

_____

_____

What are the prospects for support for this program?

_____

_____

What commitment and support do you want?

_____

_____

How will you publish that commitment and support to the organization?

_____

_____

Is change typically welcomed or resisted?

_____

_____

Who are your most effective change agents?

_____

_____

How are human resources programs typically received?

_____

_____

What tactics have generally helped managers understand and accept human resources programs?

_____

_____

Who are your opponents?

_____

_____

What are their strengths?

_____

_____

What are their weaknesses?

_____

_____

How autocratic and bureaucratic, versus democratic and open, is the management style?

_____

_____

Does management share goal setting and problem solving with employees?

_____

_____

What is the prospect for cooperation between management and employees?

_____

_____

How could it begin?

_____

_____

How urgently is a performance-management program needed?

_____

_____

When can you begin the program?

_____

_____

When are busy times for the organization?

_____

_____

When are slow times?

_____

_____

What other responsibilities do you have?

_____

_____

What kind of help will be available to you?

_____

_____

Is a planning task force a viable idea?

_____

_____

_____

Who might be on such a task force?

_____

_____

How will you proceed?

_____

_____

_____

_____

10.2 Communication Plans and Programs

Employees want to know what's going on, especially when it will affect their job security and, ultimately, their pocketbook. We typically wait too long before telling employees anything—generally, we say something after all the decisions have been made. In most cases, that is too late. Obviously, if you intend to have employees participate with you to write or review job descriptions and performance-criteria profiles, you will be communicating with them as you go along.

As you work through this book, you will want to consider what you want to tell employees and what you do not. Experience demonstrates that we say less when we are not confident of what we are saying. Adhering to the steps described in this book will give you confidence in what you do. Still, you may choose to tell this and not tell that.

Some design features of a performance-management program may be difficult to explain, but none is impossible to understand. The onus is on us to find the words and devise the ways to make ourselves understood.

10.2.1 Focusing on Acceptance

Keep in mind that you are working toward acceptance of the program when it is announced. Do more than keep acceptance in your mind; _focus_ on it. If your program is not "bought" by managers and employees when it is announced, you are in deep trouble. You could lose it all.

You will take much time to deliberate whether to build your program this way or that; your employees similarly will need time to accept this instead of that. If you wait to unload the entire program at once, employees will be overloaded. Build acceptance each step of the way.

10.2.2 Starting With a Proper Explanation

Start with explaining how the performance-management program fits together and why each of the elements is necessary. Intellectual organization demands that we understand the overview of what we are trying to comprehend so that we can assemble the pieces accordingly in our mind. Otherwise, the pieces that we are fed make no sense until we can discern their interrelatedness. Do not make the mistake of believing that the ultimate value of the program will unfold through its self-evident, logical design. Deal with inquisitiveness: Why are we doing this? What will we get out of it?

10.2.3 Choosing an Effective Communication Style and Technique

Each organization communicates in its own manner, habitually using the same technique and form. Understand your channels of communications and use them, for they are expected, but do not be restricted by them. Be innovative. Be sharp. Be thorough. If the medium is the message, demonstrate to your managers and employees that you mean business, that you are thorough, and that you are doing state-of-the-art work.

Here are some of the approaches you may use:

- Written announcements from the chief executive officer
- Speeches by top management to large groups
- Department meetings
- Small-group discussions with human resources specialists
- Private conversations with informal leaders
- Articles in the organization newspaper
- Special letters to employees and families
- Payroll inserts
- Films, audiotapes, slide shows, videotapes
- Teleconferences
- Training sessions by consultants
- Procedural instruction sessions
- Impromptu hallway discussions

You might even use contests and awards. Tailor the approach to the topic at hand. Get help from trainers, public-relations and advertising specialists, writers and artists.

10.2.4 Anticipating the Reception of the Program by Employees

Employees have a perception of management, which enhances or taints their perception of management's programs. Where communication has been poor in the past, the design and development of a performance-management program offer fruitful opportunities to open some doors. While some of the program elements are sensitive and confidential, others, as you can see in this book, are straightforward and lend themselves to safe discussion.

Remind yourself that where employees have been systematically excluded from information and participation, they may be wary of sudden overtures to share intimacies. Employees may be more than guarded: they may be suspicious and feel threatened. Easy does it. A fairly reliable truism of work motivation is that employees want to know what management is doing to them, even if it is only to protect what they have.

10.2.5 Do We Have To Tell?

Major strategies need to be decided up front: What are we going to tell, and when? One of the principal reasons managements shy away from projects to install performance and pay programs is the impending discovery of pay inequities. Little wonder, for all the sacred cows that exist in organizations. So, your communication plan will derive from the strategic positions management takes.

If management is unwilling to take the heat, you may decide to tell little or nothing. If management is willing to face the music, you will need a strong theme that right will be right in the end. Although it may not be feasible in every organization, in the best programs, management eventually puts all the cards on the table.

Experience has demonstrated that when management holds its cards close to its chest, employees are forced to guess what management is about; they begin to wonder whether they should continue to play the game or bluff. Management will need to think through a lot of what-if's before it embarks on any strategy.

Communication gives life to the project. How much to communicate, and in what style, is what management must decide.

10.2.6 Introducing the Program to Managers and Employees

Because the performance-criteria profile approach involves job-specific information, the new program is best explained in the logical work groups or departments that make up the job structure of the organization. The presentations of the program should be made to small groups to allow adequate opportunity for questions and discussion.

Managers should play a key role in the introduction, since they will administer the program. Obviously, managers need to receive ample training before they begin to explain the program to their employees.

Instead of presenting the job descriptions and the performance-criteria profiles to employees as finished products, the documents can be offered as working drafts for the manager and employees to review for clarification and accuracy. Dry-run conferences afford both managers and employees an opportunity to work with the system and to correct any problems before the program goes live.

Project Analyzer (10.2)

What is the communication atmosphere in your organization now?

_____

_____

Does management communicate openly with employees?

_____

_____

What kind of a communication posture would management like to have with employees?

_____

_____

What do employees *like* to hear?

_____

_____

What do employees *need* to hear?

_____

_____

Will employees listen?

_____

_____

What communication techniques are used now?

_____

_____

Are people with communication-arts background available to work on this project?

_____

_____

What audiovisual equipment is available?

How will the impact of the communication be measured?

10.3 Policies and Procedures

Policies and procedures guide action. They are the lifestyle of the organization, the way in which it operates differently from other organizations. Policies and procedures define the organization's uniqueness.

This book is not a reference on the many ways in which performance-management policy and procedure can be defined. Such books already exist. Other organizations are excellent resources; ask them how they deal with performance and pay issues. Then fashion guides to meet your organization's goals, needs, and preferences.

Here are the areas that need definition:

Performance Management

- Purpose
- When performance-management conference are conducted
- Performance plans
- Performance criteria
- Employee participation
- Tying pay to performance
- Recognition
- Disciplinary procedures
- Review
- Approval

Job Analysis

- Purpose
- When it is required
- Who conducts it
- Who approves it
- How it is processed

Job Descriptions

- Purpose
- Who prepares them
- Preparation instructions
- Format
- Revisions
- Review
- Approval
- New jobs

Project Analyzer (10.3)

Are guides on performance-management policy and procedure available to management?

_____

_____

Which policies and procedures are written?

_____

_____

Which need to be written?

_____

_____

Are managers trained to understand and use policies and procedures?

_____

_____

How are revisions considered and circulated?

_____

_____

10.4 Protecting Your Investment in the Program

If you do not maintain your performance-management program once it has been established, you will lose more than just time, effort, and opportunity costs. You can lose the goodwill of both management and employees. A deteriorated program sends a message that the value of the effort expended is not as important as it once was.

Control only appears to be the answer. Yes, establish procedural work-flow checkpoints involving changes in job descriptions, performance criteria, and pay to remind people that the mechanical elements of the program must be reviewed at designated times in order to ensure that details are not forgotten and that the desired results will be produced.

However, more than procedural attention to duty is required; managers must recognize the value of remaining current and of applying performance standards consistently. When managers understand the value of a human resources program, they process information properly and maintain the system without reminder. Why wouldn't they? They reap the benefits.

10.4.1 Planning To Meet the Predictable—and the Not So Predictable

Successful human resource management means anticipation of predictable events, preparedness to meet the unexpected, and innovation to match new realities. Human resource management is much more than the administration of the status quo; it is the development of a strategy, blended with all other strategies of the organization, for getting the performance and productivity necessary to accomplish organizational goals and objectives.

Organizations that do not plan with accurate models find themselves in an economic crunch. And people always seem to suffer first—through hiring and pay freezes or reductions, layoffs, terminations, and other cost controls. It conveys a poor message.

Organization goals and structures are not defined or implemented apart from people. People *are* the enterprise, and their performance, or lack of it, determines the success or failure of the organization. Performance is the relationship between the organization and its members. Once you have clarified this relationship, do your best to maintain it.

10.4.2 Plaudits and Grievances

Listen to the participants in the system. Although no program will satisfy all of the people all of the time—not anywhere close—and there may be times when unpopular decisions will have to be made, encourage people to express their likes and dislikes about performance management, in the comments section of the performance planning and appraisal conference form as well as in informal ways.

Take the performance-management program out from under the shroud of secrecy. Let the fresh air of observation and discussion invigorate the system so that it produces up to expectations. When legitimate concerns are voiced, study them. If the program is wrong, correct the error; otherwise bask in your glory.

10.4.3 Don't Let Them Get You Down

Building a performance-management program is a tough road, but a rewarding one. Try as you might, some managers and some employees just will not like the program and will get more of a kick out of picking the thing apart or trying to outmaneuver the guidelines. Don't cave in. Hang in there and look for new ways to educate people who seem uninterested in participating. Help them understand the benefits of a thoughtful program.

10.4.4 Maintenance and Audits

Analyzing jobs and writing job descriptions and performance-criteria profiles are projects that most folks prefer to do only once in life. The work is demanding, tedious, and time-consuming.

So, keep the system up to date. On a daily basis, as changes in job descriptions and performance-criteria profiles occur, maintain your records. When a job is vacated and is to be advertised or posted, verify the job results and performance criteria with the manager and record the audit or the change on the master copy of the job description and the performance-criteria profile. New jobs are evaluated as they are proposed in order to determine base pay. Descriptions for new jobs are usually treated as tentative in order to accommodate necessary changes to make the job fit into the organizational scheme.

Once a year, review all job descriptions that have not surfaced for audit to determine whether changes have been made but not recorded. A simple checkpoint is the question on the annual performance planning and appraisal form: Are the job descriptions and performance criteria current?

Examine the impact of jobs and appraisals on career progression, turnover, affirmative action, pay equality, and the other major indicators of human resource management. Look for negative trends, and make appropriate adjustments.

10.4.5 Maintenance During the Project

Months will pass between job analysis, job-description and performance-criteria writing, and the use of the system in actual practice—enough time for jobs to have changed. Inform managers that these changes should be incorporated into the project as they occur, not saved until the conclusion of the project when job changes may look like a deluge.

Generally, changes during the project are not numerous, since managers assemble proposed changes during job analysis and incorporate them into the project at that time. Good planning on your part, with plenty of advance notice to managers, will reduce mid-project adjustments. However cumbersome mid-project adjustments may be, demonstrating flexibility to deal with change is an excellent message to send to managers and employees about your organization's program.

Project Analyzer (10.4)

How much job change do you experience in your organization?

_____

_____

Can managers be relied upon to incorporate job changes into the official record?

_____

_____

Where can checkpoints be established to ensure attention to procedure?

_____

_____

What mechanisms are in place to obtain positive and negative comments about the program?

_____

_____

What mechanisms need to be instituted?

_____

_____

How often should major audits be conducted?

_____

_____

How can the maintenance and audit procedures be incorporated into other planning and review processes?

_____

_____

_____

10.5 Strategic Planning

On your first quick walk through the book, record your initial thoughts on policy issues that will have to be decided.

_____

_____

_____

_____

_____

_____

Any notes on tactical procedures?

_____

_____

_____

_____

Chapter 11

Adhering to Legal Guidelines

11.1 Employers' and Employees' Rights

Managing employee performance legally begins with an understanding of the rights of an employer to manage organization resources. Without a written contract, an employee serves at the will of an employer and may be discharged at any time. For what reason? For good reason, for bad reason, or for no reason at all. This is the concept of at-will employment.

Some states accept this notion; others do not. Some jurists believe in the concept; others do not. Many countries in the world have limited the authority of an employer to discharge an employee without good cause.

Please keep in mind that the comments in this chapter are based on a general view of the law, and of management practices, and do not take into account the differences among the laws of different states. Check with a lawyer familiar with the laws in the states with which you are concerned.

The principal argument in favor of at-will rights for the employer is that the *employee* may end the employment relationship at any time, for any reason at all, whether or not the reason makes sense for the employer. So, why shouldn't the employer have the same right? Ostensibly, legislatures attempt to protect the employee against the overwhelming economic position of the employer. The employer can continue in business without the employee, whereas the employee out of a job is out of income. Your organization's position on this matter is entirely up to it, except if your organization is within the province of a state that does not recognize the at-will concept.

Whether an employee can sue an organization for what he or she considers a wrongful discharge hinges on whether the discharge is injurious to the common welfare—that is, whether it is a matter of public policy rather than just a private dispute between the employer and the employee. The guidelines for this determination are, unfortunately, vague and subject to jurists' personal interpretation of what constitutes "reasonable human welfare." Obviously, the interpretation may change with each examination.

Performance management may lead to the employee's dismissal. By examining performance-management systems that the courts have decided are unreasonable, unfair, and indefensible, we can construct guidelines that will minimize challenges to a system. Furthermore, performance-management programs designed with these guidelines in mind go a long way toward preventing the kinds of abuses by managers that give merit to employee challenges in the first place. The guidelines in this book will keep your organization as safe from challenge as any system can guarantee.

Do not be misled. No system can make managers act morally and ethically, and no system can prevent them from treating employees disgracefully if they choose to do so. However, a solid system can surely make it difficult for managers to act this way. On the positive side, a solid system points managers in the proper direction of equitable employee relations and reminds them from time to time about the proper procedures.

Most legal challenges to performance-management programs arise from criteria that are not job-related, or from ratings that are biased. Occasionally, management's inconsistent application of policy is challenged. The best defense against a challenge is a thorough, thoughtful approach, which this book is designed to give you.

One lesson has surely been learned from challenges that have been tried in a court of law: Employers that do not have a formal program are hard pressed to defend their actions against employees, and they are typically found liable. Judges have no choice, without specific policy and procedure to the contrary, but to infer what they can from established norms within the organization—not always the norms employers want paraded before them.

11.1.1 Essential Ingredients of an Effective and Legally Sound Performance-Management Program

Here are guidelines, distilled from court cases, that you can use to design your performance planning and appraisal program. In their opinions, the courts have directly or indirectly suggested that you:

1. Identify and validate job requirements and performance criteria through job analysis.

2. Provide employees with written job descriptions and performance criteria.
3. Train managers to observe and appraise performance.
4. Require that the manager's manager review the content of the appraisal before it is presented to the employee, and approve the outcome of the conference—including performance plans and employee comments—after it is conducted.
5. Design a performance-management form that includes
   a. Instructions on how to use the form
   b. A space for the employee to comment on the appraisal or plan
   c. A signature space for the employee to acknowledge receiving a copy of the form.
6. Tell employees how their performance compares with job requirements and performance criteria.
7. Provide a procedure for employees to appeal performance plans and appraisals that appear unjust to them.
8. Monitor the way managers operate within the system.
9. Audit the program to assess its effectiveness, and conduct statistical checks to identify any adverse impact on minorities and other protected groups of employees.
10. Ensure the confidentiality of personal performance-management papers.

Here is some help for you with each of these legal guidelines.

Guideline #1:

Identify and validate job requirements and performance criteria through job analysis.

Following the outline of Chapter 3 will satisfy this guideline. Make no mistake—management has the right to decide what jobs will be performed, how, and how well. Management, however, cannot make changes in jobs without some modicum of warning to employees. Management is likely to get into trouble when changes appear to give employees little opportunity to comply with new requirements. Management is asking for trouble when it deliberately changes job requirements in order to put a particular employee in an awkward position.

In short, follow a time-honored system to identify what work you expect your employees to accomplish:

1. Clearly state the purpose of your organization.
2. Define objectives to accomplish the purpose.
3. Determine what type of organizational structure will best accomplish the objectives.
4. Define specific job expectations within the structure that will enact the objectives.
5. Define how well the objectives must be accomplished.

Guideline #2:

Provide employees with written job descriptions and performance criteria.

Using the techniques presented in Chapters 4 and 5 will help you satisfy this requirement. Surely, you have had ineffective experiences with oral communications. "Is that what you meant?" "I don't remember." Some managements have not dealt honorably with employees and have claimed that information was provided to employees when it had not been.

New employees can easily be informed of job requirements and performance-criteria profiles when they are given their orientation to the organization. Besides, telling employees what's expected of them makes all the sense in the world if management wants employees to perform to the best of their ability. Be prepared, however, to have to *prove* some day that your employees were informed of job requirements and performance criteria.

Include the dissemination of this information as part of your orientation package for new employees. Have employees sign to indicate their receipt of the information. Have a similar orientation package for newly promoted employees, and place a checkoff reminder on job-processing forms, such as on requests for job reevaluations, to ensure that job changes are always communicated to employees. A question on the Performance-Management-Conference Form to determine that the job description and the performance-criteria profiles are current—as shown in the model form (Figure 5-3) in Chapter 5—will serve as a periodic audit.

Should different formats for job descriptions and performance-management approaches be used for exempt and nonexempt employees? No, different systems are unnecessary. All employees, regardless of their Fair Labor Standards Act status, should have, and be informed of, their job descriptions and performance-criteria profiles.

Guideline #3:

Train managers to observe and appraise performance.

Specific help with this was detailed in Chapters 6 and 7. In most situations, managers are able to interact personally with their employees and thus observe their performance in order to appraise it. Some managers, however, are on different shifts or may be located in different geographical areas.

The operative word is *observe*. When performance criteria describe how employees are to behave (that is, when they express criteria in *behavioral* terms), managers must *actually observe* the employee behaving in order to make a legitimate appraisal of performance. However, when criteria are expressed in results-oriented terms, as was demonstrated in Chapter 5, only the *results* of behavior need to be examined.

This is an important shift in thinking about performance criteria. Many guides will advise you to "express performance criteria in behavioral terms." Behavioral terms are certainly more appropriate than naming or describing the personal *traits* that an employee must display in order to perform effectively. However, the way an employee behaves focuses attention on what the employee *does*, not what the employee *accomplishes*. We eliminate many of the employee challenges to our performance-management programs when we communicate with employees in terms of the results they must accomplish.

Nonetheless, because it's the employee's behavior that produces (or fails to produce) results, employees who do not produce the results required need to change their behavior. Thus, a manager will ultimately need to observe behavior directly in order to offer helpful guidance to the employee.

Using group leaders to help with performance appraisals. Managers may designate employees as group leaders to coach other employees. Group leaders may even recommend disciplinary action for an employee. Guideline #3 means that group leaders should be trained to observe and appraise performance. However, even if group leaders offer their opinions about employees' performance, the managers remain ultimately accountable.

Using peer opinions. Should peers be asked to appraise each other's performance? Usually not. Employees do have opinions about each other's performance, but it is not their responsibility to offer these formally as appraisals in the place of management.

Legally, you could conjecture that a judge might not put much weight on a peer's appraisal, because the peer's appraisal carries no organizational authority. The manager, on the other hand, is the legal agent of the organization. If peers were asked to render their appraisal, then they would need to be trained to participate in appraisals.

Ill feelings are easily created within a group when peers appraise each other's performance in a formal way. Most groups deal better with such opinions informally. Frankly, it's a good bet that any manager who asks employees to conduct appraisals on one another does not want to conduct appraisals. Exchange of opinion among peers is a reasonable tactic only when the employees relate closely with each other as a team of highly interdependent members.

Asking for peer opinions, though not appraisals, is a reasonable tactic for a manager to collect different points of view about an employee's performance. Similarly, opinions about performance should be collected from other managers and individuals with whom the employee comes in contact, and from "customers" within and outside the organization who are served by the employee. Immediately, the potentially biased judgment of one manager is reduced.

Lastly, do not place the onus of conduct appraisals only on the manager's back. The more employees are made to participate in the performance-management process, the less they can sit back and complain when the process does not meet their preconceived notion of how they should be treated. Managers have put themselves in the position of making all the decisions, leaving themselves open for attack for the results of their decisions in all quarters. While the ultimate accountability may not be avoided by the manager, absolving employees from their responsibility to participate thoughtfully and responsibly is foolish. Employees should be invited to complete a self-appraisal of their performance and bring it with them to the planning and appraisal conference for discussion.

(*text continues*)

Project Analyzer for Legal Guideline #3

	Yes	No
Are managers able to observe the performance of their employees?	☐	☐
Is there follow-up to training to ensure that what was taught to managers was learned and applied by them?	☐	☐
Are managers counseled when they make errors in the appraisal process?	☐	☐
Are managers appraised on their ability to appraise employees?	☐	☐
If group leaders are involved in conducting performance-management conferences, how are their comments made part of the process?	☐	☐
Do other employees understand the group leader's authority?	☐	☐
Are peer opinions and the opinions of others who work with an employee obtained for the employee's appraisal?	☐	☐
Are employees asked to complete a self-evaluation?	☐	☐

Guideline #4:

Require that the manager's manager review the content of the appraisal before it is presented to the employee, and approve the outcome of the conference—including performance plans and employee comments—after it is conducted.

The manager's manager, and possibly even one manager higher, should review the appraisal documentation before the conference, but only to ensure that the opening dialog is clear.

There is a danger here. The conference is a discussion of past, present, and future performance. Before the conference, the manager and the employee prepare a *draft* of an appraisal. Perceptions may change during the discussion. For example, the manager may be mistaken about some facts of the employee's past performance or personal ambition. Open dialog will clarify the situation. If, however, the review with a higher-level manager becomes a commitment to a conclusion, the open nature of the conference will be lost. The purpose of the review is to uncover faulty thinking before it leads to emotional clashes and an appeal by the employee.

Some managers are uncomfortable with bringing a poor rating on one of their employees to their boss, because the boss might be the intolerant type who wonders why problems weren't solved before they occur. No system can stop a narrowminded attitude. However, an objective system helps people through thoughtful and reasonable conversations.

After the conference, the final outcome should also be approved by the manager's manager.

Project Analyzer for Legal Guideline #4

What is management's attitude toward reviewing documentation and plans before the conference?

_____

_____

Who is involved in the review process?

_____

_____

When does the review occur?

_____

_____

What kinds of changes typically have been made during the review process?

_____

_____

Is the review viewed as a helping or a controlling process?

_____

_____

What needs to happen to improve the review process?

_____

_____

_____

Have reviewers been trained to counsel their subordinate managers?

_____

_____

_____

Guideline #5:

Design a performance-management form that includes (1) instructions on how to use the form, (2) a space for the employee to comment on the appraisal or plan, (3) a signature space for the employee to acknowledge receiving a copy of the form.

Figure 5-3 in Chapter 5, section 5.3 shows a model conference form that includes appropriate instructions on the use of the form.

Whether or not an employee's performance is up to par, an employee should be required to acknowledge in writing that he or she received the manager's comments about performance and, where appropriate, the plan for improving performance. In the worst of all scenarios, an employee might deny having received proper notification of impending disciplinary action if there is no signature to the contrary. If an employee refuses to sign the form, the refusal should be witnessed.

The signature line should not require the employee to *agree* with the content of the conference, but only ask to acknowledge receipt of the words, or a copy of the form. Again, Figure 5-3 illustrates a proper approach.

Employees should have space on the conference form to write a reaction to the conference if they choose to do so, but they should not be required to write anything if they do not want to. Most employees, because they are treated more fairly in a system based on job-language criteria, will comment that the appraisal and the plan are fair, even though they may not agree with each of the manager's perceptions.

Employees should be encouraged to write remarks in disagreement with any of their manager's observations. This not only protects their rights but also gives the manager and the organization a chance to take another thoughtful look at the disagreement.

Most organizations file a copy of performance plans and appraisals in the employee's personnel record to prove that conferences were held, and to make the record available when follow-up is needed. Most managers are encouraged to keep a copy to guide employee performance, but, unfortunately, most employees do not receive a copy for self-guidance. Oddly, management sets time aside to talk to employees about performance and planned improvement, yet does not allow employees a copy of the plan itself as a convenient reminder. Both participants in the conference should have a record of the conversation and agreement or at least have easy access to a copy.

Project Analyzer for Legal Guideline #5

Are complete instructions included on the Performance-Management-Conference Form?

_____

_____

Are additional instructions regarding policy and procedure available for managers?

_____

_____

Do employees have access to and understand policy and procedure?

_____

_____

Is space available for employees to comment?

_____

_____

Do employees use the Comments sections?

_____

_____

What kinds of reactions do employees have to the appraisals?

_____

_____

_____

Have changes in the process been made as a result of employee comments?

_____

_____

Do employees show a reluctance to sign the form?

_____

_____

What problems have arisen in connection with required signatures?

_____

_____

Guideline #6:

Tell employees how their performance compares with job requirements and performance criteria.

No law requires organizations to have a performance-management program. However, perhaps there *should* be a law that requires organizations to tell employees how well they are performing their jobs. The guidelines in this chapter, derived from court decisions, talk around the issue. The guidelines address aspects of the system, but not the fundamental issue that if an organization tells employees what to do, then it ought to tell them how well they're doing. No courts have ever ordered it, either.

Management may lose a legal challenge because it has made mistakes. But except for cases employees win because of a legal technicality, management almost always wins when it designs a reasonable program and follows its own guidelines for fair treatment.

Timing of performance-management conferences. Performance-management conferences should be held at times that make sense in the cycle of work being performed. A reasonable guide is that performance ought to be reviewed at least once a year in a formal way. Informally, performance is reviewed each working day, as managers make routine observations. If performance begins to fall apart, a conversation should be held immediately, even with just a few words. Similarly, reinforcement of outstanding performance is most valuable at the time it is earned.

Timing by employee anniversary date vs. operational cycle. Many organizations tie performance-management conferences to the employee's anniversary date. This timing subtly emphasizes the personal cycle of the employee tenure instead of more properly on the operational cycle of the organization. Conferences are traditionally scheduled on personal anniversary dates in order to spread the time consumed over the whole year in consideration of the manager's schedule instead of concentrating the conferences in a short period.

However, conferences are most effective when they are held immediately following regular operational cycles so that they can reinforce excellent performance as it occurs or shore up performance that is sagging. Cycles may be shorter than a year or longer—up to two or three years. During long cycles, performance can be examined at project milestones to keep performance on track. When performance is unsatisfactory, conferences are required at shorter intervals in order to clarify performance targets and correct the way they are being pursued.

Timing of conferences for new employees. Most organizations do not hold conferences with employees after they are hired or promoted until the third month or later, depending on the orientation cycle of the job. Most new employees should receive complete appraisals of their initial performance after 30, 60, and 90 days, and then again after six months, not for a legal reason so much as to establish rapport and orient the employee to the performance-management philosophy.

Yes, more time is involved in managing performance when conferences are held that frequently, but the payoff comes for managers when they need not spend their time chasing problems. Instead, they can spend their time exploring opportunities. The simple question for managers is: How do you want to spend your time?

Frequent reviews pick up on problems quickly and demonstrate management's interest in helping employees succeed. Employees get used to the system and understand what performance means to the organization. The beginning of employment is a fresh start for managers and employees alike. They are more open to discuss what is important to them before personality issues set in to detract from the relationship.

Conferences after transfers or promotions. Upon transfer or promotion of an employee, a conference with the current manager to "close the books" is in order. When an employee's work is the responsibility of more than one manager, such as in project work, each manager should confer with the employee to agree on what is to be accomplished and then, at the close of the project, meet again to discuss how well the work accomplished the results required. One manager would take the lead in consolidating the individual appraisals.

(*text continues*)

Project Analyzer for Legal Guideline #6

When are conferences held with new employees?

_____

_____

When are regular performance-management conferences held? At employee anniversary date? All at the same time? Some other cycle?

_____

_____

Have managers or employees expressed any problems with the timing of conferences?

_____

_____

What work cycles exist in your organization?

_____

_____

Can conferences be tied to work cycles instead of employee anniversary dates?

_____

_____

Will managers tolerate conducting conferences on an as-earned basis?

_____

Guideline #7:

Provide a procedure for employees to appeal performance plans and appraisals that appear unjust to them.

An appeal is a basic right in our legal system. Thus, employees should have the same right within their work organization.

Left unresolved, conflict festers and contaminates relationships. Appeals are a healthy process to bring misunderstanding out into the open. Though some conflict will never be resolved, it's better for the manager to know its implacability than to assume that it is a minor grievance that will eventually disappear.

The appeal process need not be complicated or fraught with hostility. When the conference takes place, the manager and the employee will learn that they disagree. If the error is of simple fact, it can be cleared up at that moment, or shortly thereafter. If the facts are not so simple, an appeal in writing will help the employee think through the situation and present an organized argument. If anger is involved in the disagreement, the act of writing serves to vent feelings.

The manager, receiving a reasoned argument, has an opportunity to consider the appeal in quiet contemplation. The process insulates the manager and reduces the possibility of an emotional backlash at the employee.

The manager and the employee who continue to disagree may need help from a third party to mediate or arbitrate the dispute. The human resources department might play a conciliatory role to help the two parties explore opposite views. A senior manager can do the same thing. In extreme situations, a person outside the organization might help. However, sooner or later, someone will have to decide which perception will prevail.

How many appeals the employee may have is management's discretion. To allow several appeals up the management hierarchy is not too many. Look at the situation this way: If management does not give a disagreement the time and place to air within its organization, there are outside agencies that will force the time to be allotted—and management probably won't like the experience.

(text continues)

Project Analyzer for Legal Guideline #7

Is an appeal policy and procedure available to guide managers?

Do employees have access to, and understand, the appeal policy and procedure?

Do employees use the appeal process?

For what reasons do employees make appeals?

Have changes in the process been made as a result of employee appeals?

Guideline #8:

Monitor the way managers operate within the system.

Usually, a human resources professional participates in the development of the performance-management policy and program and trains managers to manage performance accordingly. Professionals should be available to (1) advise managers on how to proceed in ticklish situations and (2) counsel employees who are not coping well with a manager's suggestions on how to improve performance.

Once the program is in place, the human resources department keeps track of when conferences are due and makes sure that they are properly recorded and that documentation is filed. The human resources department helps ensure consistency among the managers' decisions once the program is established.

The opinions that managers state when appraising employee performance can come back to haunt them if employees believe that their reputation has been defamed and that they have been injured in some way, such as being rejected for other jobs because of negative comments about their performance in your organization.

Employers generally have a legal privilege to appraise performance, and this privilege gives them a defense in such challenges. Still, fairness—and the need for a solid legal defense—dictates that managers be informed of, and be required to follow, the specific procedures for discussing an employee's performance, with the employee as well as with others. In particular, managers cannot make off-the-cuff derogatory remarks. Any derogatory remarks must be based on factual evidence.

Courts of law are asking managers to be more precise in their judgments. More to the point, the courts are warning managers not to rely on their unique view of the world but instead to examine and compare their internal criteria openly in order to minimize errors of ignorance or incompleteness. The fact of life for organizations and jurists is that human beings cannot be unequivocably precise when explaining their opinions about the qualitative aspects of human performance. We must learn not to try to make human beings do something beyond their capabilities. It is the open examination of our internal thought processes that is the key to more accurate and complete appraisals of performance.

Using computers to process, retrieve, and analyze appraisals. With a computer, you can quickly retrieve performance-management forms and analyses, including the job description and the performance-criteria profiles; a history of all prior appraisals of the employee; a comparison of ratings with other individuals performing similar work; a summary and average of several opinions; and an index of the manager's rating history.

Appraisals written by people on computers, however, will not be any more objective than those written with a quill pen. Don't be dazzled by computerized systems that move bad structures and judgments around quickly. In particular, be wary of the definitions of criteria imbedded in the software, such as what a programmer might define "initiative" to be. Where computers offer a useful and natural addition to your system, use them.

(text continues)

Project Analyzer for Legal Guideline #8

How are human resources professionals involved in monitoring the way managers operate within the program?

___

___

Do managers respect the participation of human resources professionals?

___

___

Who else is involved in the reviewing managers' performance?

___

___

Are any external observers used to monitor managers' effectiveness?

___

___

Guideline #9:

Audit the program to assess its effectiveness, and conduct statistical checks to identify any adverse impact on minorities and other protected groups of employees.

Do the policies and procedures of your program have any adverse effect on minorities and other protected groups of employees? Race, creed, national origin, sex, age, handicap, and veteran status are the factors to consider as you answer that question. For example, do minority employees receive a percentage of low ratings that is disproportionate to their percentage in the total population? Do women typically receive lower performance ratings than men? An audit should be conducted to examine the ratings of minorities and other protected groups under the program, as well as the use of the data in personnel decisions such as pay increases and promotions.

Employers are responsible for validating employment and testing procedures, such as a performance-management program. Yet, one validation expert allegedly said, "I know of no studies to measure the validity of performance-management procedures in an operational context." To validate means to substantiate, typically by statistical methods. However, it is difficult to validate a performance-management program with quantifiable measures. Instead, because we know that judges are conditioned to think in terms of what is "reasonable," a better way to think of the validation requirement is to think of it as a requirement to be reasonable.

The performance-management program should be reviewed continually as managers and employees use the system and comment on it. A formal audit of program effectiveness is best accomplished as part of the usual organizational audit of operations. In most organizations, this audit occurs annually.

Set up the performance-management program in parallel with operational and financial planning and control systems. Managers who are responsible for functional and financial management in their area should also be responsible for performance management in their area.

If a task force was set up to establish or redefine the performance-management program, have the task force assess the outcome of its work yearly.

Auditing pay increases. If pay increases are tied to performance, the increases given to employees should correlate with the performance appraisals they received. That is, higher performance ratings should merit larger pay increases. The same relationship should exist if promotions, or any other forms of reward and recognition, are tied to performance appraisals. The warning is more obvious in the obverse. Disciplinary actions, especially terminations, when based on job performance, should correlate with poor performance appraisals.

Don't go overboard. Beware. Some performance-management systems purport to reduce "rater error," that is, the tendency of the rater to be unjustly harsh on some employees or excessively lenient on others. Other systems supposedly demonstrate a rater's decisiveness or consistency when rating employees. Most of these systems require some sort of consensus judgment and forced distribution against which individual managers' ratings can be compared. A few systems use algebraic equations to calculate an index.

The problem with these systems is that more often than not they only provoke the rater to concentrate on ways to beat the system. Furthermore, these systems almost universally involve a behavioral rather than results-oriented scale.

No system can obviate a manager's prejudices, biases, or weaknesses. Feelings about race, color, creed, sex, and age—or just plain dislike—are, unfortunately, in the fabric of human relationships. Systems that allow a manager to "mark" people on personal criteria will fail when managers have a field day with their get-evens. Systems that focus on results will not prevent managers from twisting the system, but surely transgressions are more difficult when objective criteria are the focus.

(*text continues*)

Project Analyzer for Legal Guideline #9

Where are operational and financial control points in your organization?

Who are your principal controllers?

Where do you anticipate control problems?

How can you prevent them?

In what ways are human resources professionals involved in auditing program effectiveness now?

What is the best way for human resources professionals to audit program effectiveness?

Who else is involved in reviewing program effectiveness?

Are external resources used to monitor program effectiveness?

_____

_____

_____

Guideline #10:

Ensure the confidentiality of performance-management papers.

The information contained in performance-management conference forms and disciplinary action documents is, obviously, highly personal and, in some cases, very sensitive. Just as obviously, employees are more concerned with keeping negative comments private than they are with having positive comments publicized. Performance-management papers must be protected, and access to them limited. Careless release of information by some organizations has led to charges of libel and slander by employees.

Some employers are legally required by state law to manage information carefully and to make it available to the person whom it might affect. Where there is no legal requirement, to what degree management wishes to comply voluntarily with such a notion is up to it. However, we can expect that all employers will eventually need to comply with some sort of information-management law.

Here are some information-management guidelines:

1. Formal policies defining the proper collection, use, and dissemination of employee information should be written and communicated to managers and employees.
2. Employee information should be collected, used, and disseminated openly, not in secrecy, so that the process can be scrutinized.
3. Employees should be permitted to inspect information that directly affects their employment status, except for those documents that have been specifically excluded.
4. Employees should have a formal means to correct information errors in their records.
5. Releases of personal information within and outside the organization should be controlled by written procedures. Only people with a legitimate reason should have access to such classified information. Releases beyond the organization (except where required by state law) should have the employee's consent.
6. Managers should be instructed that unauthorized dissemination of personal information is a breech of policy.
7. Only relevant information should be used in decisions affecting an employee's employment status.

Project Analyzer for Legal Guideline #10

Is access to personal information limited?

_____

_____

Is release of personal information controlled?

_____

_____

Are there written policies to manage information?

_____

_____

Is only relevant information maintained on employees?

_____

_____

11.1.2 In Conclusion

What is reasonable and what is not differs with each observer. The decisions of some court cases beg a new interpretation, as they seem to fly in the face of reason. Still, they were so decided. There can be no absolute protection against the whims of jurists, especially when fundamental guidelines are not available to them as they make their decisions. They bring their biases and prejudices along with them to the bench. However, so does management when it manages employee performance.

So, organizations are best counseled to follow *traditional, tested wisdom,* as embodied in the guidelines in this chapter. Giving each employee due process invokes the very nature of the laws of our land, if not of civilized conduct. In this way, the employee learns of problems to be corrected, and managers have an opportunity to review their decisions before they are enacted. Judgments can be tested for reasonableness. Along the way, records are kept so that the process may be reviewed by a neutral party if a dispute arises. Thus, there is a good chance that reasonableness will be the final outcome.

Finally, for a brief, thorough, and readable background to the legal issues involved in performance appraisal and related employment law, consult *Employment at Will and Employer Liability* by Daniel Murnane Mackey (New York: AMA Membership Publications Division, 1986).

(text continues)

Project Analyzer (11.1)

What legal challenges have been brought against your organization regarding unfair appraisal decisions and practices?

_____

_____

What did you learn from these challenges about improvements needed in your program?

_____

_____

What challenges do you worry about, but so far have been lucky enough to avoid?

_____

_____

What needs to happen for you to "get legal"?

_____

_____

Does management support a legally sound program?

_____

_____

Is management willing to enforce a legally sound program?

_____

_____

Are individual managers, rather than the entire management team, the only violators?

_____

_____

What can be done to teach these managers the bad effects of continued violations?

_____

_____

_____

11.2 Strategic Planning

On your first quick walk through the book, record your initial thoughts on policy issues that will have to be decided.

_____

_____

_____

_____

_____

_____

Any notes on tactical procedures?

_____

_____

_____

_____

Appendix A

Examples of Job-Specific Performance-Criteria Profiles

Here are some examples of job results and four-dimensional performance-criteria profiles written in the language of the job results to which they are tied.

JOB TITLE: CAFETERIA MANAGER

Job Result:	Manages company cafeteria by using an outside vendor.
Performance Standard:	Vendor is reviewed on a regular basis to ensure proper service and food quality; problems are corrected immediately.
Problem:	Employees complain about food or service; budget overruns are out of hand; employees stop using the cafeteria.
Improvement:	Needs to interview employees to ascertain attitudes and reactions; needs to meet with vendor to discuss service; needs to learn and apply accounting procedures.
Performance Option:	Perceives problems before employees complain, or before budget overruns cannot be corrected.

JOB TITLE: WORD PROCESSOR OPERATOR

Job Result: Produces prescribed quantity of documents by operating a word processor.
Performance Standard: Produces 800 lines of data per day.
Problem: Produces 600 lines of data per day.
Improvement: Produces 700 lines of data per day.
Performance Option: Produces 900 lines of data per day.

JOB TITLE: EEO COMPLIANCE OFFICER

Job Result: Complies with federal and state regulations by keeping abreast of changes and advising management.
Performance Standard: Managers are aware of all requirements.
Problem: Fines are imposed; goodwill is lost; litigation is likely.
Improvement: Needs to read applicable laws and develop methods to monitor compliance.
Performance Option: Recognizes trends in miscompliance and recommends policies/procedures to assure compliance.

JOB TITLE: SALARY ADMINISTRATOR

Job Result: Recommends competitive salaries by conducting surveys.
Performance Standard: Labor market surveys are assembled and analyzed correctly and are ready when needed.
Problem: Employees are not attracted to the organization, or are not retained, due to low pay; employee goodwill is lost; labor costs are too high.
Improvement: Needs to identify other organizations where employees might work; needs to establish job comparisons; needs to organize time and set priorities; needs to learn necessary statistical methods; needs to accumulate sufficient information to make analyses.
Performance Option: Provides supplemental information to reflect changing trends.

JOB TITLE: TELLER TRAINER

Job Result: Maintains teller training program by revising instructional materials, including identifying and implementing new training methods.
Performance Standard: Teller training program is evaluated, updated, and state of the art.

Problem: Work performance of tellers does not meet their Performance Standards; procedures are violated; tellers become frustrated with work procedures; customers do not receive correct service.

Improvement: Needs to analyze teller performance and test scores; needs to maintain contact with vendors of instructional materials; needs to read professional journals and attend banking conferences.

Performance Option: Creates new training designs and methods.

JOB TITLE: RESPIRATORY THERAPIST

Job Result: Provides patient therapy by following physician's orders.

Performance Standard: Patient receives prescribed therapy.

Problem: Patient suffers serious injury; physician is dissatisfied.

Improvement: Needs to check that written or standing orders are available prior to therapy or immediately following administration of emergency care; needs to verify inaccurate or questionable orders.

Performance Option: Contacts physician to renew orders and to avoid interruption of therapy; advises physician on alternative therapy.

JOB TITLE: ACCOUNTANT

Job Result: Keeps the President, Board of Directors, and designated funding sources informed of financial condition by communicating all budgets, cost analyses, internal audits, tax preparation, and new formats.

Performance Standard: People who use financial documents understand them and are prepared to act.

Problem: Complaints are voiced regarding lack of information or misinformation.

Improvement: Needs to analyze data and develop effective methods to communicate the financial condition of the agency.

Performance Option: Anticipates difficult-to-understand situations and goes out of his/her way to clarify meaning of financial conditions.

JOB TITLE: PHYSICAL THERAPY SECRETARY

Job Result: Provides historical references by establishing and maintaining recordkeeping system, and by filing and retrieving department information.

Performance Standard: References are available when needed.

Problem: Department information is lost, possibly resulting in legal action.

Improvement:	Needs to study documents and records to be filed; needs to review and apply procedures for retrieving information.
Performance Option:	Develops new systems to ensure accuracy of filing and recordkeeping. Develops a comprehensive retrieval system of all records.

JOB TITLE: EMPLOYEE RELATIONS SPECIALIST

Job Result:	Helps employees with their personal problems by counseling and advising them when requested.
Performance Standard:	Employees receive the necessary help to ameliorate or eliminate their problems.
Problem:	Employees express a concern that the company is not interested in their welfare.
Improvement:	Needs to apply counseling skills/techniques that will assist the employees; needs to attend professional counseling courses to sharpen skills.
Performance Option:	Recognizes solutions to employee problems before such problems develop into crises.

JOB TITLE: REGISTERED NURSE

Job Result:	Prevents patients from receiving infection by following aseptic procedures.
Performance Standard:	Maintains aseptic techniques.
Problem:	Infections occur due to failure to recognize when, where, how, and why sterile items have become contaminated.
Improvement:	Needs to review and apply aseptic technique procedures; needs to recognize breaks in technique.
Performance Option:	Recognizes potential risks to asepsis and takes steps to prevent contamination.

JOB TITLE: PURCHASING COORDINATOR

Job Result:	Maintains inventory mix and quantity by anticipating and understanding store needs.
Performance Standard:	93 percent of items requisitioned by stores are available for issue.
Problem:	Shortages delay production.
Improvement:	Needs to verify incoming-item numbers with supply description and numbers to ensure that correct items are ordered.
Performance Option:	Anticipates seasonal demand and is able to maintain a 98 percent fill rate on stores' requisitions.

Job Title: MONITOR TECHNICIAN

Job Result: Monitors cardiac patients by observing them and operating equipment.

Performance Standard: Cardiac patients are monitored accurately.

Problem: Cardiac arhythmias are not detected; rhythms cannot be observed on oscilloscope.

Improvement: Needs to study cardiac rhythms; needs to review and apply procedures to adjust telemetry equipment.

Performance Option: Teaches other technicians how to use equipment.

Job Title: MEDICAL TRANSCRIPTIONIST

Job Result: Completes radiology reports by transcribing dictation.

Performance Standard: Radiology reports are transcribed according to radiologists' dictation; reports are ready for review when needed.

Problem: Patient services are delayed; radiologists complain.

Improvement: Needs to review medical terminology; needs to discuss editing options.

Performance Option: Corrects and edits reports so that no more than 2 percent are returned by the radiologists for correction.

Job Title: ACCOUNTS PAYABLE CLERK

Job Result: Takes advantage of available discounts by processing approved invoices for payment.

Performance Standard: Approved invoices are paid within seven days of receipt.

Problem: Vendor relations are damaged; discounts are lost; administrative costs increase.

Improvement: Needs to review how vendor discounting is timed in order to take advantage of available discounts.

Performance Option: Establishes procedures and develops systems to ensure timely payment in his/her absence.

Job Title: STOREROOM CLERK/TRANSPORTER

Job Result: Keeps food preparation on schedule by issuing food stuffs and supplies.

Performance Standard: Food stuffs and supplies are available and usable to complete menus according to production sheets; meals are ready on time.

Problem: Production is interrupted, and tray-line personnel waste time hunting for articles or substitutes; food items that should be thawed are frozen, causing substitutions or delays in schedules.

Improvement:	Needs to learn how long it takes for different foods to thaw and how to determine the supply needs of the department.
Performance Option:	Avoids all shortages of food or supplies due to improper handling or issuing.

Job Title: SANDER

Job Result:	Prepares parts for sanding by inspecting surfaces.
Performance Standard:	Required sanding operations are identified.
Problem:	Time is wasted; parts-per-hour efficiencies are reduced; parts do not meet quality standards.
Improvement:	Needs to review and apply inspection procedures; needs to learn to recognize recurring defects and/or parts that require minimal preparation.
Performance Option:	Identifies defects that are not obvious.

Job Title: MAILROOM ATTENDANT

Job Result:	Gets information to the addressee by distributing mail.
Performance Standard:	Incoming mail is opened and distributed on schedule to the appropriate individual.
Problem:	Deadlines are missed; additional expenses are incurred.
Improvement:	Needs to arrange work schedule to meet distribution schedules.
Performance Option:	Categorizes and establishes mail priority; attaches appropriate files when necessary.

Job Title: HEAD COOK

Job Result:	Supervises food preparation by observing and training cooks.
Performance Standard:	Cooks consistently produce the same product, regardless of the person filling the position; cooks are observed studying recipes and production sheets while preparing meals.
Problem:	One person's macaroni and cheese is rich, creamy, and tastes great; the other's is dry and tasteless. One day the cream of chicken soup has three pounds of meat; the next day it has four ounces. The head cook does most of the cooking.
Improvement:	Needs to teach and motivate (includes disciplining) employees to use quality control tools; needs to learn methods of instilling a spirit of cooperation among cooks.
Performance Option:	Gets cooks to pull together as a team to accomplish tasks.

JOB TITLE: MATERIALS HANDLER

Job Result: Organizes inventory by arranging merchandise in primary and secondary locations; by assigning locations to inventory and labeling that location; by keeping merchandise in order; and by updating computer records on locations.

Performance Standard: Materials are stored in correct location; safe and proper storage place is established and identified; stored items are free of damage and risk.

Problem: Personnel cannot find products, which means wasted time for others.

Improvement: Needs to store materials in a way that keeps them safe from elements; needs to put bin labels on locations of materials; needs to place materials to maximize use of space; needs to learn locations of materials.

Performance Option: Identifies ways to store materials that drastically and permanently saves money and space.

Appendix B

Examples of Universal Performance-Criteria Profiles

Not all performance requirements will be tied directly to specific job results. Some requirements apply to a wide range of jobs. Management expects, for example, that all employees will be at work on time, will use supplies carefully, and will work safely. Similarly, managers are required to perform certain basic functions, such as planning and cost control, regardless of their specific job assignment. These universal criteria must be stated for employees, in addition to job-specific criteria.

Here are some profiles* that may be used on an appraisal form:

Punctuality
- PS = Work starts on time.
- P = Work flow is interrupted; other employees' schedules are disrupted.
- I = Needs to reduce late time.
- PO = Takes extra precaution to be on time.

---

* Abbreviations used throughout the examples are: Performance Standard = PS; Problem = P; Improvement = I; Performance Option = PO.

Attendance
    PS = Work continues without interruption.
    P = Other employees' schedules are disrupted.
    I = Needs to reduce absences.
    PO = Takes extra precautions to be present.

Personal Appearance
    PS = Personal appearance matches the organization's image.
    P = Work or service is interrupted as clients, visitors, and/or fellow work-
         ers are distracted by unusual appearance.
    I = Needs to develop habits that maintain personal appearance.
    PO = Takes extra precautions to maintain appearance.

Supplies and Equipment
    PS = Supplies and equipment are used with care, and no more are used
         than is necessary.
    P = Costs and downtime exceed acceptable levels.
    I = Needs to learn about the cost and proper use of supplies and
         equipment.
    PO = Finds new ways to economize and prevent misuse of equipment; offers
         suggestions to other employees.

Work-Area Cleanliness
    PS = Work area is clean and orderly.
    P = Work is lost or damaged or must be redone.
    I = Needs to study the impact of unclean and disorderly work area on
         others; needs to schedule time to clean up or maintain order.
    PO = Helps others clean up.

Patient/Employee/Visitor Safety
    PS = No one is hurt.
    P = People suffer; time is wasted; costs increase.
    I = Needs to study and apply safety procedures, and to eliminate actions
         that could cause injury to others or endanger their safety.
    PO = Influences others to follow safe procedures.

Confidentiality
    PS = Sensitive information is kept confidential.
    P = Organization is subject to lawsuit or embarrassment or loses com-
         petitive advantage.
    I = Needs to take caution to prevent disclosure of sensitive information.
    PO = Cautions others when information security might be violated.

Security
    PS = Facilities are secured and protected.
    P = Items are stolen or misused.

I = Needs to study security measures and identify potential breaches; needs to ask the supervisor when uncertain about security requirements.

PO = Goes beyond routine measures to maintain security; investigates suspicious circumstances.

Planning

PS = Plans accomplish desired results.

P = Problems are not anticipated; opportunities are lost.

I = Needs to gather information; needs to examine options and evaluate options.

PO = Considers issues not presented in the original requirements.

Organizing

PS = Plans are implemented on schedule.

P = Resources are not in the right time, place, or quantity to achieve desired results.

I = Needs to find ways to assemble resources according to plan.

PO = Assembles and uses resources in productive and imaginative ways.

Decision Making/Problem Solving

PS = Problems are recognized and solved.

P = Solutions do not identify the essential nature of the problem and do not eliminate the problem.

I = Needs to analyze data to identify the true problem and study the implications of all available options.

PO = Uses judgment not only to solve the present problem but to prevent recurrence.

Downward Communications

PS = Essential information is brought to subordinates' attention.

P = Subordinates are incorrectly informed or complain about being "left out."

I = Needs to establish employee information programs.

PO = Ensures that subordinates are prepared in advance with information.

Development of Subordinates

PS = Subordinates are able to accept new and more challenging assignments.

P = Subordinates are stagnating, or leave the organization, or transfer due to inability to accept new opportunities.

I = Needs to coach subordinates to help them improve performance.

PO = Helps subordinates find new and creative ways to use their talents.

Performance Management

PS = Subordinates accomplish organizational and personal performance objectives as identified in the performance-criteria profiles for their jobs.

P = Subordinates impede achievement of organizational objectives by causing Problems and needing Improvement.

I = Needs to conduct performance-management conferences regularly or as required; needs to conduct conversations in a manner that helps subordinates achieve agreed-upon objectives; needs to take disciplinary action when required.

PO = Subordinates choose to make significant improvements and contributions to organizational performance beyond management's expectations.

Cost Control/Budgeting

PS = Costs are within budget.

P = Controllable expenses exceed budget.

I = Needs to enforce existing containment efforts, or develop new ones.

PO = Expenses are lower than budget because of judicious management.

Ability To Work With Others

PS = Individual work schedule is adjusted to meet team responsibilities.

P = Projects requiring joint effort are not accomplished.

I = Needs to participate with others to accomplish group responsibilities.

PO = Goes out of his/her way to help others.

Initiative

PS = Additional assignments are assumed willingly.

P = Extra work and special projects are not finished on time.

I = Needs to review the organizational need for additional temporary assignments.

PO = Seeks out additional assignments without being asked.

Reaction to Deadlines

PS = Work is accomplished despite deadlines and difficulties.

P = Quality and/or volume of work is reduced or disrupted.

I = Needs to find ways to prevent stress from interfering with work efficiency and quality.

PO = Offers a model of stability to other employees by remaining calm under deadlines.

Communications: Written and Oral

PS = Communications are clear and concise and recorded.

P = Work is not accomplished because messages are lost, misinterpreted, or conveyed inaccurately.

I = Needs to develop habits that prevent errors and ensure clarity in messages.

PO = Goes out of his/her way to clarify the meaning of messages.

Upward Communications

PS = Essential information is brought to the supervisor's attention on time.

P = Work is delayed or missed.

I = Needs to identify information that is essential for the supervisor to have.

PO = Prepares supervisor with advance information.

Job Knowledge

PS = Job knowledge is sufficient to accomplish job responsibilities.

P = Job requirements are unaccomplished or incomplete.

I = Needs to identify job methods that are needed to fulfill all job responsibilities.

PO = Seeks ways to expand job knowledge through formal education or informal learning.

Application of Job Knowledge

PS = Job knowledge is applied to the accomplishment of job responsibilities.

P = Organizational objectives are not achieved.

I = Needs to recognize ways to apply job knowledge.

PO = Helps others recognize and apply their knowledge to job requirements.

Quality of Work

PS = Work is performed within accepted quality standards.

P = Work is interrupted or must be redone, resulting in delays and excessive costs.

I = Needs to study quality standards and to develop consistent work habits so that frequent supervision is not required in order to prevent errors.

PO = Takes extra precaution to prevent errors from occurring.

Quantity of Work

PS = Agreed-upon workload is produced.

P = Work is bottlenecked or unfinished.

I = Needs to develop efficient work habits.

PO = Invents new work methods.

The universal performance-criteria profiles just presented should be rewritten to meet organization standards. New profiles can be written for other organizational requirements, such as flexibility, creativity, teamwork, public relations, or institutional development; they need only follow the writing instructions presented earlier. Value-laden as some criteria may be, they can be expressed in objective terms if you follow the writing instructions discussed throughout the book.

Here's one example from an organization whose mission involves helping individuals learn about other cultures:

PS = Project results are accomplished with respect for individual differences and with a commitment to achieve mutual understanding of personal values.

P = Individuals express feelings of alienation or being disconnected from the organization; opportunities to learn from others are missed.

I = Needs to listen to others, consider their point of view, and adjust action where feasible.

PO = Helps others increase awareness and understanding of different cultural perspectives.

Index

About the Authors

Roger J. Plachy has more than 20 years' experience as a consultant in performance planning and appraisal, pay administration, compensation structures, management-skills training, employee communications, and other aspects of human resources management. Formerly, he held positions with several industrial and health care organizations.

Mr. Plachy has been a course leader for the American Management Association since 1971, conducting seminars in job evaluation and pay administration and in performance planning and appraisal. He is the author of *When I Lead, Why Don't They Follow?* (rev. ed., Bonus Books, 1986) and *Building a Fair Pay Program: A Step-by-Step Guide* (AMACOM, 1986).

Sandra J. Plachy is a consultant specializing in performance management systems, strategic planning, management and leadership skill development, and customer service program development and training. She has held various executive positions in the health care industry and has been a course leader for the American Management Association since 1976.